Disclaimer

The information provided in this book is designed to provide helpful information. This book is not meant to be used, nor should it be used, to diagnose or treat any medical condition. For diagnosis or treatment of any medical problem, consult your own physician. The publisher and author are not responsible for any specific health or allergy needs that may require medical supervision and are not liable for any damages or negative consequences from any treatment, action, application or preparation to any person reading or following the information in this book. References are provided for informational purposes only and do not constitute endorsement of any websites or other sources.

Written by
Eduardo Duran

Edited by
Rebecca Nichols
Kimberly Wilson

Special thanks to
Christina Hill, Athella, Inge Bardor, Drunvalo Melchizedek, Elisa Medhus, Erik Medhus, Josef, and all friends from Sirius.

Introduction

While traveling the world for several years, carrying only a backpack, I met many people who told me stories. These stories were not the stories we grow up with. In many parts of the world, the stories are similar. Sometimes, even the description of the characters in the stories are similar. After noticing all this, I started to realize that something is connecting every part of the world. I realized that the history of the world might not be as we were told. I started to doubt if what I learned in school was accurate. Many of these stories were related to the history of the world, ancient civilizations, religions and science. This made me wonder if anything I knew was accurate. As an engineer and someone who is passionate about physics, I started to wonder if all the science I knew was correct.

The history of the world and most of the science I knew made no sense to me anymore. I decided to find out if anyone else noticed these abnormalities but when I asked, friends started to think that I had mental problems. I started to spend more time alone. I spent most of my time traveling alone and researching. I got to know many cultures around the world and their stories. Then, after an extraordinary spiritual experience, I realized that everything I experienced was supposed to be that way. I was about to start an amazing journey and I would find people who understood me. Some of them would not be human.

I wrote this book in order to document everything I have experienced in the last years, and to put all my thoughts together. After sharing a few parts with some friends, they convinced me to share it as a book. Thank you for all your support.

What I will share with you here is a combination of what I have seen while visiting almost every country in the world, stories I have heard from local people, interesting information about cultures around the world, some information about science, and my personal experience with non-humans. Those experiences helped me develop a better understanding of the world, history and the human body. They helped me understand something I always thought was impossible to know - who we are and why we are here. This information is not something motivational, philosophical or religious. Everything I will share with you is real and my personal experience.

My intention is not to convince you of anything. I didn't believe in any of this but I experienced it directly. I lived it, I saw it, I felt it, and now nothing can take it away from me. My intention is not to cause controversy or any kind of fear; this book is intended to help you to remember who you are. It's intended to make you feel loved and nothing else.

If you are already aware of this information please share it, with love, in your own way.

If you already remember why you came here please don't forget about the contract you made before you were born. You probably came here to help. It hasn't been easy but that is why we are here.

If this information is new for you, enjoy it with love.

This information is very important and every human has the right to know it. Unfortunately, not every person is ready to receive this information. That is fine. Not everyone needs the information. Each person will get it in their own way and at the right time. If you feel uncomfortable while reading this book, I recommend that you stop and come back later if you want.

My goal is to share my insights with you as simply as possible.

"I'm so very grateful for the opportunity to be part of this book. I'm an avid reader and bibliophile, and have always wanted to edit a book. When Eduardo asked for a native English speaker to help make his book more readable in English, I offered. Here was the opportunity I've been waiting for!

The information contained in this book is amazing. I've loved learning about Eduardo's journey and the things he learned along the way. His guides, Athella, and other sources of information have given him beautiful insights. They're consistent with other sources I read about our ascension into the 4th and 5th dimensions. Eduardo has managed to convey it all without fear, and with love. Reading his work is like talking to a good friend. He's insightful and caring, but doesn't come across as too intellectual.

Thank you, Eduardo, for allowing me to be part of this amazing project!"

— **Kimberly Wilson**
Editor from the United States

"This book is a must read for anyone that wants to know more about our past and possible future. The insightful information gathered by Eduardo is incredible and the way in which he writes is simple yet engaging and enthralling. I'm amazed by his courage and determination to follow his passion and go on a journey throughout the world discovering himself and the world in which we are all a part of. If you want to be lead on a magical path of adventure and knowledge, then this is the book for you. The author lived it and tells it, so there's a real feeling of authenticity when you read this book. I recommend you do yourself a favour by reading it and taking yourself along on Eduardo's ride of a lifetime."

— **Tim Morgan**
Teacher from England

"Eduardo uses a simple language that is easy to understand, which is unusual as many spiritual concepts can be hard to comprehend for the layman. His travels were interesting but I enjoyed mostly his spiritual journey. Which was really a quest to find his true self and his place in the Universe. It is a quest we will all undertake at some stage. No matter where we are on our personal journey we can learn something from Eduardo's path. The story is like a catalogue of experiences that we all may come across at some stage in our lives. There were also some things in the book that challenged my beliefs and that is a good thing if we wish to continue to evolve."

— John Wills
Business contractor from Australia

"One of the most eye-opening books in recent years! Eduardo wrote it, in the style of 'talking to a friend' which makes it entertaining, but also accessible. You will feel like you were on a trip around the world with him. However, the eye-opening part is in the second half of the book. The information and insights he received from high dimensional beings are exciting. Although channeling and remote viewing may be difficult concepts for many people to accept. Overall, I enjoyed the book and recommend it to anyone who wants to know the true history of mankind."

— Jeerawat Kulsapudom
Top corporate business executive from Thailand

"In a fascinating story of many discoveries while travelling around the world, Eduardo bravely shares what he has learned and encourages us to become better people. If all the stories in this book ever feel overwhelming, just remember the most beautiful message brought by Eduardo's guides: Focus on love!"

— **Thereza Howling**
   Yoga/Mindfulness teacher & Reiki Master from Brazil

"This dazzling story is thought-provoking and full of inspiring wisdom. What started out as Eduardo's goal to visit 100 countries around the world, turns into a discovery of treasures found within himself and the Universe.

Eduardo's story is a testament to the transforming power of traveling and the highest vibration, Love."

— **Agnieszka Helm**
   Realtor, spiritual healer, & Reiki Master from the United States/Poland

"I was searching for the meaning of life, I wanted to know myself better. I was looking for an inward journey. Then, I was blessed to find this eye-opening book by Eduardo. He believed and followed his inner guidance to put this awesome book together. I felt that I wasn't alone. It resonated with my inner knowing. I digested it one day at the time. Awesome, inspiring and riveting."

— **Hesthings Aribeb**
   Nuclear energy engineer from Namibia

"I could not stop myself to keep reading all the super mind-blowing informations contained in this book, based on Eduardo's own personal experiences.

I had to admit this book really opening and changing my mind completely in seeing our human world with different eyes and understanding. Intuitively I knew that what he shared with us here through this book were all true and, despite its quite shocking but awesome knowledges, it would help many other people worldwide who had felt lost and confused in experiencing the similar ones in their lives to get more encouraged in continuing their special paths with no confusion, fear and doubt anymore.

Eduardo is definitely brave and clearly straight-forward in sharing these informative and profound messages with us. Our human world would need more people like him for better improvement and upgraded realization as well as consciousness."

— **Anitta Suhn**
Designer from Indonesia

"If you have lots of information or you are just trying to make sense of who we are as humans in the bigger picture of us as spiritual beings in this journey, this book will clarify and explain as you follow Eduardo's path of questioning and discovering. The beauty of it, is that you get to discover all of it with him, through his pure heart and the innocence of his eyes, with no prejudices, judgement or fear.

I've found this to be inspiring at so many levels, but mostly, the freedom that Playing with Forms show us of what it's possible: knowing exactly what it's happening in the world, today and historically, and the power we have once we understand how creation happens. It's available to all of us. I am grateful to Eduardo and all his/our guides for the dedication, love and wisdom in continuously supporting us into becoming the empowered sovereign beings that we are."

— **Maria Serrano**
Life coach, healer, & crystals expert from Argentina

"I am so grateful to Eduardo for having this opportunity to get to know and witness his unique and extraordinary experience and knowledge, and especially for the love conducted through each word and sentence in the book! I believe it will set a spark of curiosity and ignite the flame of unconditional love in everyone!"

— **Asel Kojokulova**
Diplomatic service officer from Kyrgyzstan

"Focus on love. Eduardo Duran's tale is not just a story, but that of an epic journey of his (not so) ordinary life experiences which have naturally taken him from everyday, you and me, material layman to spiritual master. I presume the humble Eduardo would not accept this title nonetheless, of this there is an impression on my mind too strong to admit of doubt. A learned and inspired individual I am grateful to have had the opportunity to read this book for I can undeniably confirm I have learned (or remembered) the unimaginable beauty and synchronistic flow of the universe and how, even in the midst of our hectic lives, we are all a part of. As Mr. Duran advises - return to nature, turn off your brain sometimes and live through your heart. Let's keep creating, and let's keep playing."

— **James Bartlett**
Businessman, personal trainer, journalist, & musician from England

"One of the best spiritual books I've ever read! If you are in the path of awakening, ascension or if you are just an open-minded individual who wants to hear big chunks of truth about us and the universe, you must not miss the opportunity to read this book."

— **Keesha Katrina**
Spiritual teacher from the Philippines

"This book is written about the travels of a young man finding his way from the academic world, to the opening up of new spiritual experiences which challenge his former concepts of what he learnt and held as truth. The author takes us thru various places he visits and uncovers knowledge of many places that are hidden. With simple to read facts as well as pictures to outline what he has gained along the way it was such a joy to read. What was most interesting is how learning each countries language gave a richer insight into how certain behaviors were tolerated. The profound knowledge of this book is heart stopping as it uncovers and delves into ancient history and artifacts. The sensing of energy in places is an added bonus for any empaths who wish to experience a place of heightened awareness."

— **Tania Hopkins**

Therapist & Metaphysical researcher from New Zealand

"It was a true pleasure reading this book. It is a beautiful blend of real life adventure and spiritual endeavors. It is fun and eye opening to ride along with Eduardo as he travels. From his humble beginnings in Mexico to Europe and beyond; from his remote viewing journeys and channeling experiences, this book is truly a gem. Eduardo does an excellent job of observing the 3D world and connecting many dots in a simplistic manner, while at the same time uncovering higher dimensional perspectives and insights. In my opinion, a must read for those on the spiritual path."

— **Kevin Wickart**

Soccer Coach from the United States

"If you are looking for something to challenge your deepest beliefs, spark new thoughts and open your eyes to new horizons that is easy to understand, then look no further. If you are starting your spiritual journey and you feel completely and utterly lost, then here is a perfect tool to help your quest."

— **Melissa Browne**
Business owner from Australia

"Eduardo's journey to find the truth that exists beyond our day to day reality was so interesting to read. His story is one of an inner and outer journey. In his travels around the world he made many important realizations of some of the world's mysteries including symbolism, ancient structures, important land masses, energy vortexes, etc. Along the way he learns how to connect with his guides and receive insights not available through our regular senses. In this way, much of what he writes about is unique and from a higher perspective, and not just information learned from reading or from others. He includes much important information regarding our ongoing ascension into the 4th, and eventually 5th dimension that I had not heard elsewhere. His work with Athella, channeled through Christina Hill, is fascinating and enlightening as well. If you would like to learn how to create an authentic connection with your higher self and your guides there is much you can learn from Eduardo's life and story"

— **Mechele Tison**
Holy Fire III Reiki Practitioner from the United States

"I am very grateful that Eduardo shared his amazing story with us. It has given me hope, direction, and bolstered my belief in the magic and mystery of the universe. His life has been truly extraordinary, and he pens it simply, beautifully. He truly is proof positive that remarkable things happen to real people."

— Jamie Roberts

Realtor, yoga teacher, & Reiki Master from the United States

"In this inspiring and enlightening book, Eduardo recounts his experiences as he ventures across many different parts of the world, including very sacred destinations. His journey always leads him to new spiritual encounters, where he always seemed to be in the right place at the right time.

It really took a lot for me to be able to put this book down once I picked it up. If you're in the awakening phase of your life, or just looking for an adventurous and eye-opening story, this is the one to start with. It helps to unlock the many mysteries of humankind and this place we call Mother Earth."

— Liz Sonexaythiketh

Business professional from the United States

"Reading this book was intensely personal. It resonated in many ways and it was a challenge to continue reading at times but I finished it because I was going to. I'm grateful to come across Eduardo and his book. It is not for the faint of heart and will definitely lead you to many questions but also show you answers to questions you have had before. If you are reading this book, then you are ready for it. Happy reading."

— Shaila Alam

Marketing professional from Bangladesh

Table of Contents

Chapter 1 – The Numbers 16

Chapter 2 – The Invisible 31

Chapter 3 – The Plasma 34

Chapter 4 – The Sound 40

Chapter 5 – The Backpack 46

Chapter 6 – The Symbols 53

Chapter 7 – The Atoms 66

Chapter 8 – The Desert 70

Chapter 9 – The Geometry 79

Chapter 10 – The Circles 92

Chapter 11 – The Dragons 101

Chapter 12 – The Cells 118

Chapter 13 – The Download 124

Chapter 14 – The Lights 131

Chapter 15 – The Skin 148

Chapter 16 – The Words 157

Chapter 17 – The Upgrade 190

Chapter 18 – The Forms 208

Chapter 19 – The Movements 218

Chapter 20 – The Money 244

Chapter 21 – The Decision 258

Chapter 22 – The Channel 266

Chapter 23 – The Predictions 288

Chapter 24 – The Smoke 306

Chapter 25 – The Past 314
Chapter 26 – The Modern 358
Chapter 27 – The Pyramids 379
Bibliography 399

Chapter 1 – The Numbers

I was 19 years old and in my first year studying engineering at the university. I got a phone call from my mathematics teacher from high school. I had a good relationship with him but it was the first time he called me. It was very unusual. The teacher said that he had to leave the city immediately and he needed a replacement at the high school for his classes.

I didn't understand why he was telling me this. After a few minutes talking to him, I realized that he was asking me to be his replacement. I thought it was not possible for me to do that since I was still a student at the university. I didn't have a diploma yet. My teacher insisted. I decided to go to the high school and ask if they really wanted me to become the mathematics teacher.

When I arrived at the high school, I met with the principal of the school. I told him that I was there to ask for more information about why they wanted me to be the mathematics teacher. The principal was very busy and wasn't really paying attention to what I said. He just took me to the classroom and introduced me to the students. He didn't even know my name. He told the students that I was their new teacher and left me alone with them. I didn't know why this was happening. I was in front of many students and they were waiting for me to say something. I obviously wasn't prepared for the class but it felt very natural. I started to remember all the topics I learned in high school so I talked about them. I felt very confident.

After the class, I went to see the principal. I tried to explain to him that I was still a student and didn't have a diploma. He told me that I had been recommended by several teachers and it was okay. He said that he had good feedback about me from the students and he wanted me to be the new mathematics teacher for the rest of the semester. I was not sure if that was ethical or even legal but I accepted. I ended up teaching mathematics for four years.

In the mornings, I was a mathematics teacher, and in the evenings, I attended the university. During my free time I programmed applications just for fun. Everything I did was about numbers.

After a few weeks of teaching at the high school, I realized that my attitude could have a big impact on the students. I could make their day a little bit harder or a little bit easier just by my behavior toward them. I saw how much influence I could have on their daily life. I wanted them to have a good time and at the same time I wanted to be a good teacher. I felt like it was a big responsibility for me and wanted to do my best.

This made me wonder about leaders and people in mass media. They had a lot of responsibility. They affect people's lives with their information.

I was very aware that I was affecting students' lives with my behavior. I learned how to be patient with them. I learned how teach them properly while having a good time. I wanted to keep them motivated. Many students were not motivated about mathematics or numbers in general. I decided to research interesting facts about numbers - things they would find interesting and engage them in class activities.

After some research, I found ways to teach mathematics in interesting ways. I found information about numbers that the students would be familiar with and could apply to their daily lives. I found out about the Fibonacci sequence. It fascinated me. I started studying these numbers. I will explain the sequence as simply as I can.

1,1,2,3,5,8,13,21,34,55,89,144,233,377...

1+1=2	13+21=34
1+2=3	21+34=55
2+3=5	34+55=89
3+5=8	55+89=144
5+8=13	89+144=233
8+13=21	144+233=377

You start with 1+1=2. The next number in the sequence can be found by adding the previous two values - in this case, 1+2=3. Then add the result (in this case 3) and the last number (in this case 2) and you have 2+3=5. Continue the pattern until you get to the desired number.

The sequence isn't just a funny, mathematical way to play with numbers. It is found in the human body, animals, art, nature and even in the location of pyramids around the world. I found it amazing that these numbers could be found in trees, flowers, animals and nature in general. For example, the branches of some trees split into Fibonacci numbers. Shells also grow following this pattern.

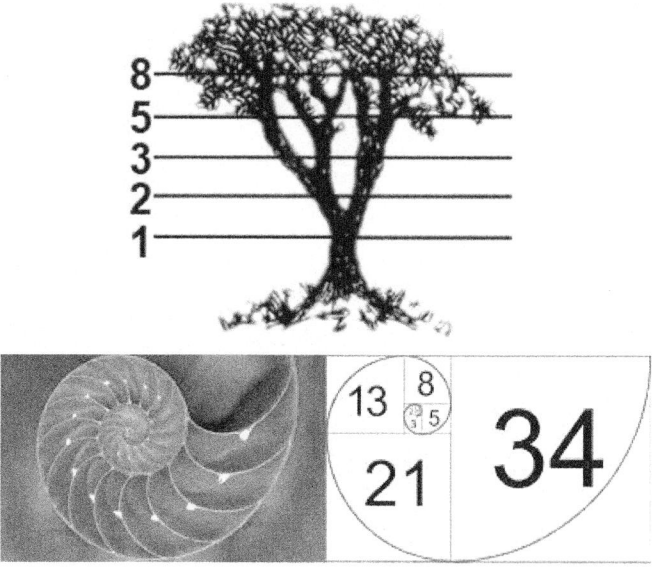

I was fascinated with the numbers in the Fibonacci sequence. The Fibonacci sequence contains the numbers 5, 8, 13 and 21. Most flowers have these numbers of petals. I had previously thought it was a random coincidence. Flowers with more than 21 petals usually have 34, which is also a Fibonacci number.

Another number that fascinated me was phi, 1.618 - also called the golden ratio. It can be found by dividing the numbers in the Fibonacci sequence.

2/1	2.00000
3/2	1.50000
5/3	1.66667
8/5	1.60000
13/8	1.62500
21/13	1.61538
34/21	1.61905
55/34	1.61765
89/55	1.61818

First, 2/1=2. Next, take the sum of these numbers (2 and 1, which equals 3) and divide 3 by the last number (which is 2), so 3/2=1.5. Continue doing this until you get approximately 1.618. You can continue the pattern with bigger numbers, but it will remain 1.618.

The golden ratio and the Fibonacci numbers are not the same but both patterns will get the number 1.618. Taking the distance of one part the human body and multiplying it by 1.618 will result in the distance for the next part of the body.

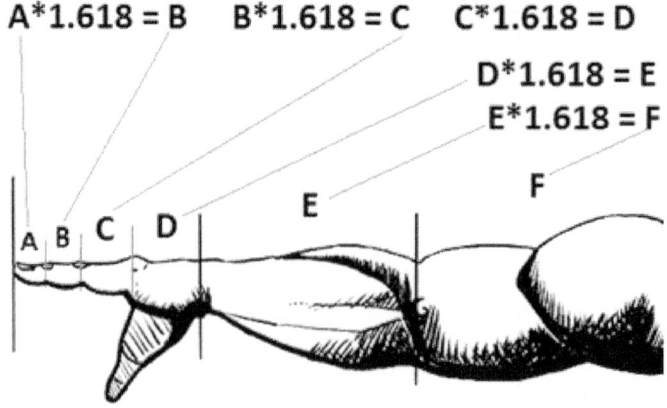

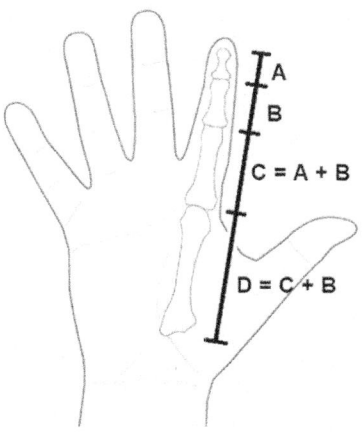

Another interesting fact about the golden ratio is that it is found in the Vitruvian Man, a drawing by Leonardo da Vinci. This picture contains many relationships using the number 1.618.

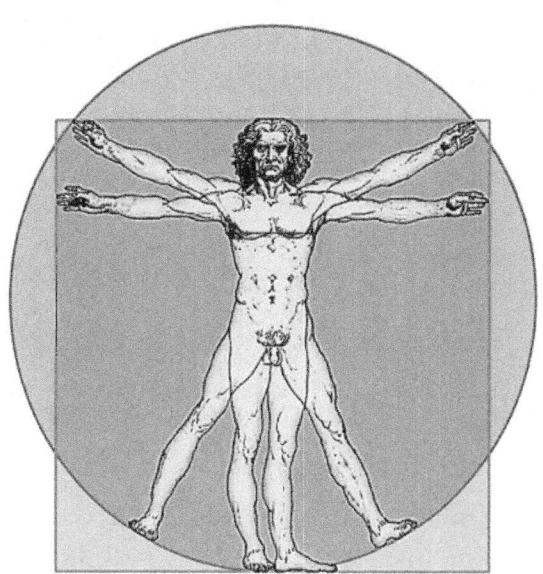

The Vitruvian Man also contains a relationship between the size of the Earth and Moon. It can be found by creating an additional circle between the top of the square and circle. The big circle would be the size of the Earth. The small circle is proportionate to the size of the Moon.

It seems that in the past, many people knew about these proportions. This number is found in many sculptures from ancient Greece.

At this point I was curious about these numbers so I researched them deeply. As a joke, I thought that if the Fibonacci sequence contained the number five, maybe it represented the number of fingers that humans have on their hands. Maybe aliens with seven fingers have different

Fibonacci sequences on their planets. I found out about that much later.

During the time I taught at the high school, I also had the chance to teach physics. I felt like I should know everything about physics so I would be prepared for unexpected questions. I wanted to look serious and professional. I started studying physics deeply during my free time.

I needed to focus on the behavior of objects. I studied the physics of physical objects as much as possible but I was not aware of the physics of non-physical objects. The human body can see only what is inside the visible light spectrum. The rest is invisible to the human eyes but it's there and affects our physical world, or what we understand as reality.

I found some interesting facts about light. Scientists say that the speed of light in a vacuum is around 300,000,000 meters per second (186,282 miles per second), which means that if you could imagine that there is a person 300,000,000 meters away from you, and this person jumps.

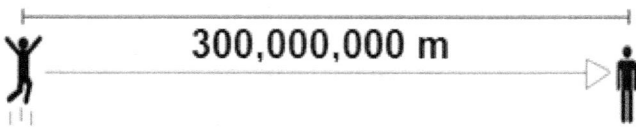

It will take one second for you to see this person jump because the light of the other person will take one second to arrive to you.

Another example would be the Sun. The Sun is far from Earth and the light from the Sun is traveling at the speed of light. This light takes around 8 minutes to reach Earth. This means that when we are looking at the Sun, we are actually looking at the Sun 8 minutes ago. The same happens with the stars in the sky. They are so far away that we are actually seeing the past of the star. This made me wonder a lot of things about the understanding of time and space. I studied as much as possible about this topic to be prepared for unexpected questions from the students.

After a few months of teaching, I was able to answer all the questions from the students. I felt like an expert on mathematics and physics. My ego grew big. One day, I was walking around the school and I heard some students having a discussion about electronic devices. When they saw me they said, "Let's ask the teacher. He knows everything." My ego grew even more inflated. I felt like a physics guru, but I was not prepared for what they asked.

The students looked at me. They felt very confident that they would get an answer from me. They asked, "Is it possible to create infinite energy?" I really didn't know. I didn't want to give them an answer about something I was not sure of, and I had a reputation as a physics guru. I just said, "It is hard to explain. I will explain it tomorrow."

After researching for a few hours, I found information about Nikola Tesla. He talked about free energy and a different type of electricity. Since I thought that I was an expert on physics, I felt like I was supposed to know that. I wanted to know everything about Nikola Tesla.

Nikola Tesla was an inventor. He knew that there was a way of getting electricity without the need for cables. He created a coil that was able to generate electricity from the air - free and clean energy. The coil he created required a lot of volts, which cannot be done with traditional electricity. He wanted to create free energy for everyone on the planet. He was receiving money from banks to work on his project, but when the bankers realized what he wanted to do they cut all the funds for his project. They also convinced other business people to avoid funding his project. They didn't like the idea of having free energy because companies would not be able to charge people. The project and the information related to free energy was confiscated after Nikola Tesla died.

Nikola Tesla believed strongly in aliens, and he also believed that he was in contact with them. I found this funny and interesting at the same time. I didn't believe in aliens. For me, only science was acceptable.

Nikola Tesla said two things that I didn't understand when I read it for the first time. It took me 9 years to understand what he meant. He said, "If you want to find the secrets of the universe think in terms of energy, frequency, and vibration." Also, "The day science begins to study non-physical phenomena, it will make more progress in one decade than in all the previous centuries of its existence".

While studying Nikola Tesla's work I found, by coincidence, information about a person who claimed to know the answers for free energy. He created a coil based on pure mathematics that works. It is clean and free energy. The coil had a shape of a donut, it was all related to mathematics, and it was simple. I read everything about it. The name of that person was Marko Rodin. This is a very quick explanation of Marko Rodin's mathematical pattern. You don't really have to pay attention to this part. I am just explaining it because it helped me to realize many things later.

If we double numbers and add them, we will have a pattern. For example:

1+1=**2**

2+2=**4**

4+4=**8**

8+8=**16**

Then we separate the numbers from the result, 1 and 6. We add them, so 1+6 =**7**.

You keep doing this, every time you get two digits as result.

16+16=32 (3+2=**5**)

32+32=64 (6+4=10, then we add 1+0=**1**)

64+64=128 (1+2+8=11, then we add 1+1=**2**)

128+128=256 (2+5+6=13, then we add 1+3=**4**)

As you can see, the result has a pattern - 1, 2, 4, 8, 7, 5 - can go on forever.

As you can see, the numbers 3, 6 and 9 are never in the pattern. But if we double the number 3 we will have a different pattern.

3+3=**6**

6+6=12 (1+2=**3**)

12+12=24 (2+4=**6**)

24+24=48 (4+8=12, then we add 1+2=**3**)

In this pattern we get always 3 and 6, but we never get the number 9.

But if we double 9, we will get always 9.

9+9=18 (8+1=**9**)

18+18=36 (3+6=**9**)

36+36=72 (7+2=**9**)

72+72=144 (1+4+4=**9**)

All the numbers in the previous patterns can be visualized in the following picture. You don't really have to understand it. But all the previous patterns are in this figure.

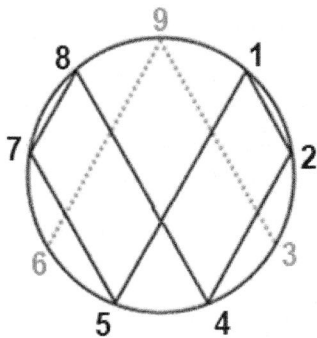

When I saw this symbol, it reminded me of another symbol I was familiar with.

This symbol is from a group of people called Masons. When I was a boy, I used to spend time in El Paso, Texas, USA. I saw this symbol a few times there but I never paid attention. I thought it was a religion, and the letter G represented "God". After some research I realized that the

27

G represented "geometry". The Masons is not a religious group, they are more like a secret society. They accept people from all religions, with the condition that every member has to believe in one God, but during their meetings they don't discuss information about their Gods.

I didn't know why geometry was so important for them and why they had to hide the information. I thought that they could just go to the TV station and present the information to the public.

My mother told me that my grandfather was a member of a secret society in Mexico, and he was meeting people every week in a secret place. My mother's family didn't know anything about it. My mother realized what was happening because she followed him one day. My grandfather told them about the secret meetings a few days before he died, but he didn't say anything about what was happening in the meetings.

I was a boy when my mother told me this, so I didn't care at that time, but it made me feel more curious about geometry and numbers.

If there are numbers to explain the behavior of energy, there are probably numbers to explain the behavior of other things. You can play with the numbers in the previous patterns and you will always find the same behavior. The pattern is related to the numbers 3, 6 and 9. This would help me to understand so many things about our reality. Marko Rodin's coil follows this pattern in 3D, and it forms an amazing shape. Just try to remember this shape of Marko Rodin's coil.

The same patterns can be found in geometry. For example, in the 360 degrees of the circles (3+6+0=9), 90 degrees (9+0=9), 45 degrees (4+5=9), 22.5 degrees (2+2+5=9), and so on. I also found out about sacred geometry, something that the philosopher Plato from Ancient Greece talked about. I will talk about it later.

Marko Rodin believed that numbers are related to our daily life. It's called numerology, and ancient cultures used it in their religions. These numbers can also be found in nature, ancient texts, even in stars and black holes. But for me it was just a beautiful coincidence. I didn't believe in any religion, spirituality or numerology.

At this point is not important to talk more about Marko Rodin's work. What is important for now is to remember the shape of this coil that can generate free energy. This information would help me very much in the future.

The next day, I went to the high school ready to answer the question about free energy. I wanted to say that free energy is possible, but it seemed that not many people knew about it. It seemed that there were no projects working on that. I noticed that the students were not as excited as I was.

I tried to explain as simply as possible everything I found the day before, but they were not as interested in the topic anymore.

Another topic that I found interesting was visible light. When we see something the eyes send a signal to the brain, and the brain decodes the information. The colors we decode with our brain are what we understand as visible light. Every color we see has a frequency, but there are other frequencies that our brains are not capable of decoding, therefore they are invisible to us.

We can decode colors from red to violet and any color in between, but any higher or lower frequency is invisible to us. Longer frequencies are infrared, microwaves and radio waves. Shorter frequencies are ultraviolet, x-rays and gamma rays.

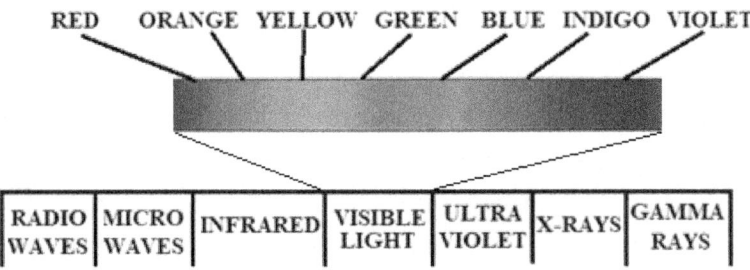

These colors are the same colors we see in a rainbow, or when light is passing through some crystals. In Hinduism and Buddhism, the same colors appear in some points of the human body called chakras. I didn't believe in chakras or anything related to that, but for sure it was interesting.

Chapter 2 – The Invisible

"Teacher, how can you explain spirits?" This question popped up out of nowhere from a student during a conversation about video games, specifically *Zelda*. "Science has not proven the existence of such things, so they are not real." I steered the conversation back to *Zelda*.

The next morning, when I arrived at the high school, and many students were visibly shaken, and some were crying. I heard a student saying, "I knew he would do it someday, he was planning this a long time ago." The students told me that one student in the class, the same student I was talking to the day before, committed suicide.

I felt guilty. I blamed myself for a few minutes, I started to analyze everything we talked about the day before. Nothing was unusual, and he didn't look sad, depressed or likely to do anything crazy. I was thinking about all the conversations we had, especially about his question related to spirits. I was trying to see if my answer had an impact on him. Maybe he was trying to tell me something and I didn't understand. I was thinking about a better answer to his question related to spirits, but I couldn't find a better answer. I started to think deeply about spirits, but I didn't believe in them.

After talking to several students, I learned that the student was planning this a long time ago. From that moment, I started to be more careful with everything I said because it could have an impact on every person. That is why I am careful with the information I am sharing here in this book. I want to share only accurate and useful information.

Suddenly, some memories started to come to my mind. I started to remember things that happened to me when I was a child, but had never spoken about.

When I was a child, around 10 years old, I was very angry with my mother, but I don't remember why. I left my house one morning during summer. I decided to leave the house and never come back. I went away from my house and walked for several hours. Then, at some point, I decided to take a rest. I was alone on a hill. There was nothing around me, not even trees, only sand and a little creek. After few minutes sitting there I started to hear a voice talking to me. The voice was telling me beautiful things. I was not scared. It was very natural for me in that moment. It felt like talking to a friend.

The voice was coming from somewhere in the sand. I could hear it clearly. I asked, "Are you the sand?" The voice answered, "I am the sand, I am you, I am everything." The voice kept saying beautiful things to me. I remember the voice saying, "You are loved, and you are never alone." After few seconds talking to this voice, I started to wonder if I was crazy. I said to the voice, "Wait a second, am I really talking to someone or it is just my imagination?" and the voice just said, "We will talk again in the future." After this conversation with the voice, I decided to go back home. My mother never knew that I was going to run away that day. I always thought that it was my imagination until 18 years later when I talked to the voice again.

Another memory came to my mind. I remember when I was around 13 years old, I used to rent movies at a video rental store not so far from my house. One day, I came home from playing football (soccer) with my neighbors. My parents were not at home. I had to return the movies before they closed the store and I had only a few minutes left. I had to pay for the movie rentals when I returned them, but I didn't have money. I couldn't ask my parents for money because they were not at home. That would mean that I would have to pay an extra fee the next day for not returning the movies on time.

I remember I was sitting alone in a corner of the kitchen, thinking about what to do. I needed 48 Mexican pesos and my parents were not at home. Suddenly. A peacefulness came over me and something was starting to appear in the middle of the kitchen. Out of nowhere, 50 Mexican pesos were laying on the kitchen floor. I took the money and went to the store to return the movie. I remember that day clearly because I told the people in the store to keep the change because it was very special money. I never wondered why this happened. I accepted it like something special, but I never told anyone.

The experiences of the voice talking to me in the sand, and the money appearing out of nowhere were the only things I could say were extraordinary events. It took me a while to accept that a person died a few hours after having a conversation with me, but I moved on.

I was 19 years old. Most of my friends at that age were drinking alcohol every weekend. For some reason I never did. I didn't know why. Some people made fun of me, but I never cared. I just knew that I was doing the right thing. I was an extrovert. I never had problems talking to people, but I was not like my friends. I was going to parties and doing what most people do at that age, but I never drank alcohol, I never smoked, and I never tried any drugs. It took me a few years to realize why it had to be like this.

Chapter 3 – The Plasma

During the 5 years that I was attending the university, I didn't have much time to socialize. Most of the time I was busy. The only people I interacted with were the students in the high school and some friends at the university, but most of the time I was alone.

I was born in the north of Mexico. The region is a desert, and it is not a typical tourist destination. For some reason I was not interested in traveling; I don't know why. I traveled to few places in northern Mexico and the southern United States, but I never went far away from home.

One day, I was having a good conversation with a friend at the university. We were talking about personal things and she confessed to me something very unusual. When she was younger, she used to have an unusual, but very beautiful, feeling around her body. After having this feeling, she became unconscious and she was not aware of what was happening. People around her could see what was happening, and they told her what happened once she became conscious again. They told her that during the time she was unconscious, she started to speak, but with a different voice. The voice was like that of a man.

The words coming out of her mouth were things she would not usually say. Most of the things were related to energy, love, and people doing beautiful things for humanity.

I didn't believe my friend. I asked her if she could do it in front of me. She said that she didn't know how to make it happen, and that it was not happening anymore.

A few months before I graduated from the university, I was walking around the parking lot trying to find my car. I couldn't find it. Then I met a friend in the parking lot. She seemed to be in a rush. I asked her where she was going. She said that she was a volunteer in an organization and she was recruiting new people. I asked her about the organization and she explained it to me. She was volunteering in an organization called AIESEC.

AIESEC (*Association internationale des étudiants en sciences économiques et commerciales*) is an international organization for students who want to develop their leadership skills and attend motivational conferences with other members around the world. I was not interested in that, but then she said something very interesting. She said that the organization also has a program of internships and I could go to another country. She said that she could send me directly for an interview and apply to be a member and that I needed to go with her at that very moment, otherwise it would be too late. I didn't know exactly what it was all about, but I did it and I went for the interview.

I arrived at the interview and there was a guy from Greece and he started speaking English. My native language is Spanish and I didn't speak English. I was not sure what was happening, and I was not sure if I could have a conversation in English, but I tried. I don't know how it happened, but I started to speak fluent English. The interview went well and I became a member of the organization.

After I became a member of AIESEC, I started to meet people from different countries. They were foreigners doing internships in my city. I attended several conferences in other cities in Mexico, and for the first time ever I started to travel.

Some of my new foreign friends were organizing a trip around all Mexico. They had one empty space in their car so I joined them. One morning during this trip, I woke up earlier than usual and before all my friends. We were staying in a hostel somewhere close to the beach. I went to the reception desk to ask for information about the places to see in the area. The receptionist was younger than me. I asked for information about the area, but she said that she didn't know because it was her first day in the region. I was very surprised by her answer. I asked her where she was from, and she said she was "from many places". I thought she was making fun of me, but then she explained to me why she said that.

What she told me inspired me so much, I still remember everything she said. She was abandoned by her biological parents, then she was adopted when she was still a little girl. She never felt comfortable with her new family, and eventually she left her house when she was a teenager. Since she didn't have a house, she was moving from one place to another, working and moving to the next place. Once she was able to get a passport, she went abroad. She said that she went to South America for a while, then she took a boat to Africa where she learned English and French. She had problems with visas in Africa, so she went to Europe. She worked in many places in Europe, where she learned many more languages. Then she returned to Mexico. She was getting used to the Mexican culture again.

I didn't believe her, so I asked her specific questions about the places she said she visited. She answered everything very confidently about these places, the languages and even funny facts about the different cultures. At that time, I was learning German and Portuguese by myself on the internet. I tried to speak to her in German and Portuguese just to test her, and she was way more fluent than me, correcting me many times. I don't know if her story was real or not but it motivated me. I never met this girl again. A few years after this, I met someone with a similar past. But instead of trips around the world this person would travel to other types of places. I will talk more about it later.

During that trip, we stopped at the pyramids in Teotihuacan, close to Mexico City. We arrived very early so we could see the pyramids before all the tourists arrived. I went to the top of the biggest pyramid (the Pyramid of the Sun) as fast as possible. I wanted to be the first one at the top. When I arrived at the top of the pyramid, I was very tired so I stopped for a while. I needed to breathe better so I opened my arms. This is a technique I learned while playing football. I opened my arms to take more oxygen in my lungs, and then something happened. For the first time ever, I felt something unusual. It was a weird but a beautiful feeling running through my body. I was not able to explain it, but I could not deny it.

Since I couldn't explain it, I just ignored it. Later that morning I noticed that the Sun was very strong and shining bright. The Sun was facing one side of the pyramid as if the pyramid was made to point exactly to the Sun that day. I noticed a lot of people climbing the pyramid - many people completely dressed in white clothes. I wanted to ask them about the white clothes so I waited for them to reach the top.

I asked them, "Why so many people and why the white clothes?" They said that it was the winter solstice, the shortest day of the year. The white clothes were because it was a very special day for spiritual people. I didn't understand anything spiritual. I never liked anything related to that. I just ignored them, but I was not able to ignore the feeling I had when I was on the top of the pyramid alone.

One of my friends took this picture after we came down from the top of the pyramid. You can see the people with white clothes going up to the top of the pyramid.

After the pyramids, my friends and I visited other places in Mexico. I saw how beautiful the country was, and decided to travel more.

On the way back to the northern part of Mexico, I saw several lights in the sky. My first thought was that it could be UFOs. I had never seen anything like that before. The only ideas I had about UFOs were the ones I saw on TV - the typical metallic objects levitating in the sky. The lights I saw were different. They were pure light. Sometimes they looked orange and at other times white.

I didn't want to say anything to my friends about the lights. I was afraid they would think I was crazy. But eventually I decided to tell them. I pointed at the area where I saw the lights, but they couldn't see them. They ignored me and maybe they thought that I was just making fun of them.

The lights had a beautiful shape and orange color, and they didn't look completely solid. They looked like people levitating in the sky with some sort of electromagnetic field around them. At some point they got a little bit closer. It seemed to me as if they wanted to be seen, and were even trying to say something. A few years after seeing these lights, I found out that these lights are real beings, and the shape is formed by the light coming out of their bodies. They live underground in caves, usually in caves with crystals. Some people in Mexico know about them. Some people have interacted with them. They describe them as humanoid beings, but very advanced, peaceful and loving beings. Some people call them plasma beings.

Chapter 4 – The Sound

After I graduated from university, I decided to go for an internship abroad. I sent applications to several companies all over the world. I applied also for a software company where I was accepted. The company was in Slovakia. I didn't know so much about this country, but I decided to go.

It was my first time abroad. I arrived in a region with many apartments. All of the buildings looked very similar.

Everyone had white skin. I was not used to that. My skin is darker, and so for some reason I started to believe that they didn't like people with darker skin. I felt very uncomfortable with this. But after few hours I started to wonder if they really were thinking that. Maybe it was just me having all these ideas in my mind. Maybe I was making myself feel bad with my own thoughts. I tried to talk to people but then I discovered that it was not the same as in Mexico. People usually don't talk to strangers on the street. Again, I started to have the same thoughts - I started to think that they didn't like me for having darker skin.

In Mexico, most people had brown skin. But people with white skin were in almost all of the advertisements. Because people on TV had white skin and people with brown skin were seen as less beautiful, I grew up thinking that people with white skin were better. I knew that my mind was programmed to believe things that I saw on TV during my childhood.

I grew up thinking that having brown skin meant ugly. I had these thoughts for many years. One day in Slovakia, I realized that actually some people considered me exotic.

There were not many people with dark skin in the region where I was living. Some people told me that they would love to have my skin color. This was a shock for me. These people were actually having nice thoughts about me, but in my mind, I was thinking the opposite. I was just hurting myself with my own thoughts.

There are some people with dark skin in Slovakia, known as *Gypsies* or *Roma*. They are originally from India, but they have been living in Europe for many years. They have their language and culture, but they also speak the Slovak language. In Slovakia, some of them are known for being problematic. I was fascinated with these people. I had never heard about them before. For me it was amazing that they are so different compared to the white people who live in the same place. There must have been something different, not only the skin color. Whatever it was, I wanted to know everything about it. I learned the Slovak language. I communicated with them several times. I wanted to understand how they see their world.

Gypsies, or Roma, have a very similar skin as mine. I started to have destructive thoughts again. I thought that some people in Slovakia would think that I could be one of them, and therefore they would think that I am a problematic person. But I wore different clothes and behaved differently. People could see immediately that I was not a Gypsy. I became more aware of the destructive thoughts. I knew that I was hurting myself with my own thoughts. I was able to stop thinking about that just by being aware of my own thoughts.

I wanted to know why Gypsies had similar skin as mine. These people, in general, tend to show their emotions more than white Europeans. People in Latin America are also known for being emotional. So if Gypsies have origins in India, there had to be something connecting India with Latin America. According to science, all Homo sapiens (modern humans) originated in Africa millions of years ago, then humans migrated all over the world.

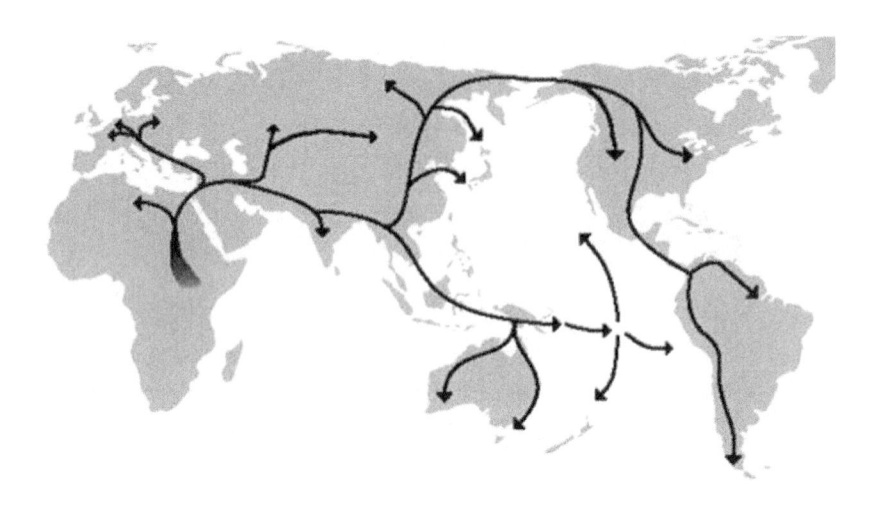

I thought that it was not possible to have any connection between India and Latin America because humans arrived in India first, then much later in Latin America. I believed in science, so if science said it, then it was true. A few years later, I realized that this theory of human history was not correct, and the real one was very different. I will talk more about it later.

When I was learning the Slovak language, I noticed that the Slovak alphabet had more letters than the ones I knew, and every letter had a different sound. I was not familiar with many of these sounds so my brain was not able to recognize them.

That meant that if I had to learn the language properly, I would have to learn around 19 new sounds. And some words in the Slovak language don't have vowels (a, e, i, o, u). I really wanted to learn these new sounds. I was excited about it, and I was amazed that my brain was not able to recognize some of these sounds. For example, in the Slovak language you have the letters C, S, and Z. In the Spanish language (except in some parts of Spain), they are pronounced the same way. But in the Slovak language, every letter has a different sound. If you don't pronounce it properly people might not understand you. This happens with many letters in the Slovak language. My brain didn't hear it initially, therefore I was not able to recognize it.

I was aware that sounds are waves recognized by the cells in the ears. These cells send the decoded information to the brain. My brain was not used to decoding the information sent by the cells, so it was decoding it as the closest thing my brain was capable of decoding. I had to train my brain to get used to these waves until it recognized them.

It took me a few months of practice, but I did it. After I got used to the letters and I was able to pronounce them, I was surprised that my brain was not able to recognize them before. Now when I say these words in the Slovak language to someone who doesn't have these sounds in their alphabet, they cannot recognize it. Something similar happens with Chinese people when they try to pronounce the letter "L". Since they don't have it in their alphabet, they pronounce it as "R". And this happens with many other languages in the world. This made me wonder if something similar happens with other things outside of languages.

I heard several stories that I found interesting. I don't know if these stories are real or not, but I definitely understand the point.

One story says that when the Spanish people were coming to America for the first time, the native people from America were not able to see the ships coming. Their brains were not used to seeing something like that.

Ferdinand Magellan, a Portuguese explorer who explored some parts of Asia, knew that he would not be able to see something unless he had an idea of what it may look like. In other words, he knew that you cannot see something that your brain is not familiar with even if it's close to you. This is because your brain doesn't have an idea of it, and it may ignore it.

Another story I heard was about monkeys. It says the following: Some scientists put a group of 5 monkeys in a room. In the middle of the room they put bananas on the top of a ladder. Every time a monkey went up the ladder trying to get the bananas, the scientist soaked the rest of the monkeys with cold water. After a while, every time a monkey went up the ladder trying to get the bananas, the other monkeys beat up the monkey on the ladder (so nobody would throw water on them). After some time, the monkey didn't dare to go up the ladder regardless of the temptation. Scientists then decided to substitute one of the monkeys. The first thing this new monkey did was to go up the ladder. Immediately the other monkeys beat him up. After several beatings, the new member learned not to climb the ladder even though he never knew why. Then a second monkey was substituted, and the same occurred. The new monkey tried to go up the ladder and the others beat him up. A third was substituted and the same happened. The same happened until the cage had only new monkeys that were not part of the first group. These 5 monkeys were never soaked with cold water, but they were beating up every monkey who tried to go up the ladder. If we could ask the monkeys why they would beat up all those who attempted to go up the ladder, they would probably say "I don't know, it is how things are done here." I wondered if humans do something similar. I wondered if humans do things without knowing the reason. At that time, I was not aware of many things I am aware of now. Yet even without knowing, I was going in the right direction.

After learning the Slovak language, I became fascinated with the human brain. I did a lot of research. I started to study psychology online, and I had many hours of discussions with friends who are psychologists.

I found an interesting fact. According to scientists, before we are born, when the male sperm fertilizes a female egg, the cells start to divide until eventually it creates an embryo. Then, the first organ that appears is the heart. After the heart is formed, all the other organs start to be created from the heart. The tongue is the second organ created. It is physically connected to the heart. I always thought that the brain was the most important organ in the human body. But I wondered why the brain was the most important organ if the heart was created first. When we are babies, basically we are the heart, and for a while we live without a brain. It was also interesting that Buddhists believe that the soul of a person comes to the body at 6 weeks of pregnancy. This is exactly the time when doctors can detect that a heart starts to function.

Chapter 5 – The Backpack

During the first months living in Slovakia, I met a lot of people, most of them foreigners. I didn't like to be alone. I wanted to be surrounded by people all the time, or anything to entertain myself. I was not able to be quiet. I had to have music or any other sound around me. Anything that could keep my mind busy.

Since almost all my friends were foreigners, I noticed that in many cases we were having misunderstandings. Because of cultural differences, for some people, certain things are more important than others. For example, in Latin America, when you talk about your family, it's like something that's a fundamental part of you for your entire life. In Latin America people often say "family is family", meaning that there is nothing more important in the whole world than that. Some parts of Europe are different. People are more independent from their families. So the meaning of the word family might not mean the same for these two different cultures. In Europe, when people say that they will come at a specific time, they really mean it. In Latin America, people tend to arrive later than the time established. Also, in Latin America, people tend to express their emotions more openly. In Europe they are more conservative. These are just some examples.

So, every time we talked about family, we were putting a different meaning to the word. In other words, every time I say something, I assign my own interpretation to the words, and these words might not be received with the same interpretation I intended. This is because every person understands the words according to the interpretation they assign to that word. Since every person has an interpretation for every word, when I was trying to send a message, it was received and decoded according to the other person's understanding of the message. So people with the same culture are more likely to understand each other better because they decode words in a similar way.

So whatever you say, your message will be decoded according to the other person's belief system. I wondered - if I were born in a different part of the world, I would probably learn and behave according to what I learned in that culture.

After noticing all this, I was thinking that we never communicate properly using words. I wondered if there was a better way of communicating. I also wonder what we really are. We could be the thoughts in the brain. But the thoughts are created and can be different according to the place where we are born. Then, what makes us be ourselves? I thought that I would never know. And I thought that nobody knew, so I stopped asking myself these questions.

In the north of Mexico, not far from where I was born, there is a group of indigenous people living in the mountains. They moved to the mountains when the Spanish people came to Mexico. They are known as *Tarahumara* or *Raramuri*. These people are known for being able to run long distances and for a long period of time, much more than any average person. They don't work out, stretch or use special clothes for running, and some of them don't wear shoes. These people are incredible runners. Sometimes they participate in marathons and they get the first places. I have personally asked them how they do it and they said that they just believe they can do it. Therefore, they do it. I always wondered that if I had grown up with them, I would probably be able to run the way they do. I thought that they had different DNA in their blood, therefore they were able to do it.

I remember when I was a child, I used to play with my friends and try to find out who was the fastest. We knew that if we ran without shoes, we would be able to run faster. This was not influenced by the *Tarahumara* people. Unfortunately, we don't learn so much about them in school even though they live in the same area. When the running competitions with my friends were getting serious, we removed our shoes. We knew that it was getting serious once we were barefoot. I don't know when and why we stopped doing it.

Also, in the north of Mexico, there is a group of people called Mennonites. There is a similar group of people in the United States called Amish. They are people from Germany who moved to Canada and eventually they migrated to Mexico. They were escaping from persecution in Europe. They are very easy to recognize in Mexico not only because of their white skin and blue eyes, but also because they keep old traditions and they avoid any technology from the modern world. They believe that many things in the modern world are not good for people. This was very interesting for me. When I heard about the Mennonites, for the first time ever I wondered if there is something wrong with the modern world.

Something that was very interesting for me was that many indigenous people around the world talk about the importance of connecting with nature. I wondered if that was the reason why they were always without shoes. Maybe this way they could connect their skin with nature. In Mexico, in school, we learned that indigenous people were not very smart, especially because they don't know how to live like most people do in this modern world. We learned that the Mayans knew many mysterious things about the universe. There are still Mayan people living in Mexico, and some of them still follow old Mayan traditions. But they are not taken seriously by most people. In Europe, a few people asked me about the pyramids, but not so much about the Mayans. This was great for me because I was not good with history. I didn't find the history of Mexico interesting, especially the history of ancient civilizations.

In Slovakia, I started traveling with friends. We started traveling around countries surrounding Slovakia. We went to Austria, the Czech Republic, Hungary, and Germany. There were big cultural differences in these countries compared to Slovakia even though they were very close to each other. Something that I also noticed was the difference between my friends and me. We enjoyed different things and didn't share the same perspectives. I was focused on the history of the places, the cultural differences, the language, the way people live and what makes them different from countries just a few kilometers away from them.

Some of my friends were focused more on the food, the drinks, nightlife and events in the places. For some reason, I was not interested in that. When I asked my friends about their opinion of certain places we saw, they said that they didn't even notice what I was talking about. That made me wonder if we were actually seeing the same things, or maybe I was just focused on boring things for them. I started to remember the story about the native people in America who were not able to see the Spanish ships. I wondered if there was something that my friends could see, and I could not.

During my free time, I researched information about the brain. I was becoming more and more fascinated with that. I wanted to know why the brain is capable of ignoring objects, even if they are in front of us. One example is the nose. Our eyes are capable of seeing our nose at any time, but the brain somehow decides to ignore it. At this point, I started to doubt if my eyes were actually seeing everything in our reality. If the brain can ignore some things, then I may not be seeing everything that exists around me. Since I was not able to trust my own eyes, I wondered, "Then, what is reality?"

I really didn't know where to find information. I tried to find answers in science, more precisely in physics, understanding String theory. I studied String theory as much as I could. But I ended up with more questions than answers so I gave up.

Ever since I taught physics in high school, there was something that I never stopped thinking about. "We see with our brain, not with our eyes." I knew that the eyes send signals to the brain, then the brain decodes that information. Sometimes I thought about animals. Many animals don't have eyes. One example is worms. They don't have eyes but they have light receptors. Some other animals use vibrations to locate objects around them, and this is how they move. Some animals use vibration to communicate. These animals experience reality in a totally different way. I wondered if we could use other organs of the human body to send signals to the brain. In other words, I wanted to know if we could see with organs other than the eyes. At that time, I thought that it was impossible, until a few years later when I met someone who could do it.

After traveling in few countries in Europe with my friends, I decided to try traveling alone. My internship was for one year, and I had a few months left. I really wanted to travel as much as possible while living in Europe. I didn't have much money, so I had to find a way to save money and travel cheap. I started by changing the way I was eating. I decided to stop eating meat because it was more expensive than other food. I was concerned about risking my health, but I decided to do it anyway. Also, I stopped buying clothes and other things I really didn't need. I was changing my lifestyle. I didn't care, I just wanted to travel.

Two months later, I could see that my life was already different. I felt very good and healthy. I donated all the things I was not using often, and I kept only basic things. I was cooking at home every day and I was not going to restaurants. During my free time, I was researching how to travel cheap. Many of my friends knew what I was doing, but they didn't like it. They thought that I was limiting myself too much. I felt great, and I was saving enough money to travel.

I started to prepare for many trips in Europe. My first trip was to Rome, Italy. I told some friends about it and one of my friends gave me one of the best recommendations I've had in my life. My friend said, "Try Couchsurfing." I didn't understand what it was so I researched it on the internet. Couchsurfing is a community on the internet where travelers can request to sleep in houses of other members and spend time with them. They could sleep on a sofa or any available place in the house. At the same time, you could host people visiting your city. This could be a good opportunity to get to know people, and everything is for free. I couldn't believe that something like that could work. I was curious, so I tried.

I created a profile on Couchsurfing, but since I was a new member, I didn't have any experience hosting or being hosted. Therefore, I didn't have any references on my profile. Members usually trust only people with references. I sent messages to many people in Rome, but the most common answer I got was, "You don't have references, I am not sure if I can trust you." Then, after many negative answers, a person replied, "Yes, you can stay in my house. I have a sofa where you can sleep. This is my address and my phone..." I still wasn't sure if that was really working.

I prepared my backpack and went to Rome. I went to the address this person gave me and I called him. He was there. He was a very friendly Italian guy named Angelo. He opened the door of his house and showed me the sofa where I could sleep. His roommate named Emiliano was also there. They showed me around the city, and they even insisted on cooking Italian food for me. I couldn't believe what was happening. I was making new friends - nice and open-minded people. I had a great time. I will always be very thankful to Angelo and Emiliano for this beautiful experience.

After one week in Rome, I went back to Slovakia. I had new friends in Rome and nice stories to tell. Also, since I didn't have to pay for a place to stay, I could save more money and travel more. When I was unpacking at home, I realized that almost everything I own was inside the backpack. For some reason, when I realized this it gave me a huge sense of freedom. I could be anywhere and have everything I need with me in my backpack. I got inspired. I wanted to travel and nothing would stop me.

Chapter 6 – The Symbols

I visited several places in Europe but the internship was about to finish. I really wanted to travel more so I did everything I could to prolong the internship. There were many big airports close to the city where I was living (Bratislava). For me, that only meant more options to travel. I managed to get an unlimited contract with the company I was working for. I saw it as a big opportunity to travel even more so I started to make bigger plans. I set a goal for myself. At the time, I thought the goal was too big but I did it anyway. I even talked to my friends about the goal. I wasn't sure if I would be able to do it but talking about it would help me to visualize it better. I wanted to visit at least 100 countries. I would travel alone, using only a backpack. I would stay with local people and I would learn about the world as much as possible.

I started to travel to the typical European destinations. Like many tourists in Europe, I was fascinated with the cities and their history. I liked the architecture of many buildings, especially because they had a lot of symbolism and I didn't know anything about it. I collected flags from all the countries I visited. I noticed that in some flags, and many symbols of European countries, they had animals, mainly eagles and lions.

There were many definitions of what these symbols could mean - courage, strength and many others. But there was always a lion with a crown. Some European leaders, as part of their job, have rituals where they show respect to a crown. This also happens in few countries outside Europe. In many cases, these leaders don't know why they have to do it. They just do it. There are still some countries that have kings and queens. This is because of the European influence, when England colonized many countries around the world. The queen of the United Kingdom is also the queen of Canada, Australia, New Zealand, and other countries. I never understood why there are still queens and kings in modern times. And I never understood the symbolism related to a crown, queen, or king. Also, I noticed that other symbols have appeared in many cultures of the world, like pine cones.

Another common symbol is called the fleur-de-lis. This symbol is in almost every symbol of any queen or king in our history. And you can find it in many churches around the world.

I thought deeply about the lions. They are everywhere, almost in every empire of our history. They are in movies, like The Lion King. I found it funny that the animals were showing respect to the lion, even though the lion will eat some of them. I even found it funny that the coat of arms of Finland looks like a lion killing himself.

I didn't know why so many countries still used the Latin language if it was used only in the Vatican City and the Roman Empire a long time ago.

I thought that maybe the animals could indicate where these people came from. Maybe the eagle and the lion could be related to a mythology that I didn't know. The eagles and the lions are mentioned in many cultures around the world - even in Mesopotamia, the first human civilization. I didn't know much about the history of the world, but I knew more about the history of Mexico.

In the Mexican flag there is an eagle eating a snake. The Aztec people had a god who told them that someday they would see an eagle eating a snake, and that was the symbol for them to build their city. This city is now Mexico City.

In primary school I had to learn the history of Mexico, including the history before the Spanish people came. There were many civilizations and many of their gods were related to snakes. The snake is also mentioned in many cultures around the world, in ancient texts and even religions. There are dragons in many Asian cultures. Sometimes they can look like snakes. For example, this is the flag of Bhutan, a small country in Asia.

In Europe, dragons often appear in legends and sometimes in symbolism. For example, the flag of Wales has a dragon.

Also, some monuments in Europe have gargoyles that look like dragons.

The dragons have been in many ancient and modern cultures around the world. Even today there are many movies or TV series with dragons, and usually they are related to a king or queen.

I didn't have any idea about the relationship between these animals and the symbolism. Even my European friends didn't know. Most of them just told me that they grew up with these symbols so it was very normal for them to see them. I totally understood them because it was the first time I paid attention to the eagle and the snake on the Mexican flag.

I visited every big city in Europe. I was mainly focused on famous cities - Paris, Rome, Venice, London, Dublin, Barcelona, Florence, Prague, Vienna, Budapest, Madrid, Amsterdam, Istanbul, Munich, Athens, Berlin, Copenhagen, Brussels, Moscow, and many more. I felt like an expert on traveling and many friends started to ask me how to do it. My ego was very high, but in reality there was nothing special about it. I was just saving money and booking cheap flights. I was spending time checking flights all the time. And somehow I always managed to take days off from work.

I wanted to visit all the countries in Europe and I had only a few countries left. Greenland was one of them. Although Greenland is part of the American continent, this country is part of Denmark. I wanted to go. There are no big cities in Greenland so it was not a typical tourist destination. I went and it changed the way I see the planet.

Every time I traveled, I was mainly focused on the architecture of the buildings, the monuments in the cities, museums, and all the typical tourist attractions. But I ignored many places in nature. Greenland changed me, and it changed me forever.

Greenland is unique. Since there are not many buildings and no roads, you can appreciate the pure nature, the mountains, the snow, the icebergs. Something was different about Greenland. I felt like I was on another planet. There were no plants like in other places in the world. Also, in Greenland I saw the *Northern Lights (Aurora Borealis)* for the first time. I saw all the colors, the same colors as in the rainbow. I was able to hear the light. I didn't know this was possible, but I did. I heard the *Northern Lights*.

I researched about these lights. The first thing I noticed was that these lights are the electromagnetism of the planet. The Earth behaves like a magnet, with the north and south poles, so the lights are the electromagnetism of the planet. That's why they appear in the north and south poles of Earth.

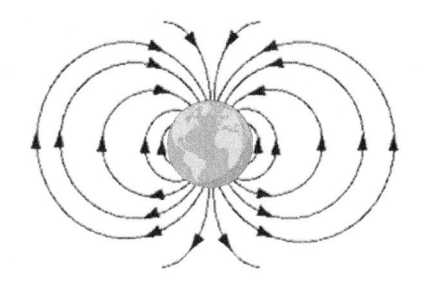

And thanks to this we can use the compass because it points to the Earth's magnetic poles. This movement reminded me of Marko Rodin's coil.

It was so interesting for me to be in a place like this, where you can enjoy nature and see these lights. After this trip to Greenland I started to appreciate nature much more than before.

In Greenland, I was told that old people living there say that something unusual has been happening for quite some time. The sunrise and sunset used to be in the same location for many years, but they could see the sunrise and sunset were changing their location. They could use a mountain as a reference. I didn't know what that meant, but it was interesting for sure. It took me few years to know why this was happening. I will talk more about it later.

There was another interesting thing about Greenland. There are the Inuit people (also known as Eskimos) - the original people from Greenland. They look similar to Asian people and they all live in the North Pole (Greenland, Canada and Alaska). I met some of them. They are very nice people. Unfortunately, I didn't know much about them. The only image I had about them was the one I got from school and movies, where they are shown as people living in igloos and not very interesting. I wondered why schools don't teach much about other cultures in the world.

The history of the world is told from a certain point of view. For example, we learn much about the Roman Empire but not much about the other empires. I thought that maybe this was because the Roman Empire was the most important, but this is what I was told. Maybe other civilizations had more impact on human evolution, but since we didn't get the proper education about it, we don't know.

There were many other civilizations around the world and I could see that the history of the world was focused mainly on certain things. Whenever there is a war, the winner writes the history according to their point of view.

In Mexico, I grew up thinking that the civilizations before the Spanish people came were not very developed. This is the image I got from school and mass media. These old civilizations are famous for knowing many things about the universe, but I grew up thinking that they are not as advanced as the Europeans. I liked Europe very much, but I started to pay more attention to other cultures. I wanted to know if there were things in the history of the world that we're not told. I really didn't know. But, for the first time ever, I started to doubt the history of the world as I was taught.

While traveling in Europe, I found many interesting places. One example is Transnistria, a region between Ukraine and Moldova, where they declare themselves a country. They even have their own currency. When I was there I felt like I was stuck in time. The place looks like a typical place from the Soviet Union. At least that was my idea about the Soviet Union because I used to see it in books.

Another interesting place was Belarus, a country in Europe that is completely different from the rest. They have had the same president since 1994.

In Bulgaria, I was driving a car. I was trying to turn right but there were many cars on my right side. I asked the person in the car next to me if he could give me the opportunity to turn right. He moved his head from one side to another. I thought he was saying, "No." Then I asked another person and he did the same. I asked a third person and the same thing happened. Later, I realized that in Bulgaria when you want to say yes, you move the head from one side to the other. And if you want to say no, you move the head from up to down, which is the opposite of most countries in the world.

The most shocking cultural difference I saw was in Iceland. Some people leave the babies outside the stores while they are shopping, even during winter. They do not take the babies with them, they leave the babies outside the store where anyone could take the baby. But nobody does.

In the countries closer to the North Pole, it's very interesting to experience how the Sun doesn't set during summer and you don't see the Sun during winter. That is because of the way the Earth rotates around the Sun. It has a little tilt.

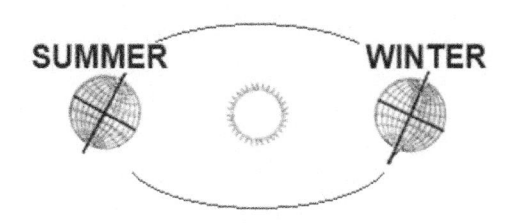

Also, I found it interesting that flying from Europe to America is shorter than traveling from America to Europe, because the Earth rotates to the right and an airplane must deal with the rotation of the Earth.

After a few years of living this way, saving money and traveling every time I could, my life was changing. I was different. I felt healthier than ever, even though I was not eating meat. I felt like I was learning so much about the world and myself. I could see that by traveling alone I was getting to know my body much better. I was more aware of what my body and mind needed. I was able to analyze my own thoughts - the good ones and the bad ones. I started to see that I was understanding myself better even though I didn't know who, or what, I was.

During all the time living in Europe, I never got sick. I did not have doctor appointments, even though it was mandatory by law. Maybe I was healthy because I never drank alcohol and I was actively playing football. I started to think more seriously about my health. I wanted to know when I was last sick. I had a conversation with my family trying to figure it out, but we realized that I was never sick, never. At least we don't remember.

There was a time when I had to have a medical check. It was mandatory for my job. The doctor said that I was very healthy. I asked the doctor if it was related to the fact that I am very active. She said, "It could be that, or maybe you just have positive thoughts." It was funny that a doctor said something like that. So I took it as a joke. Whatever it was, I was thankful for it. But in fact, I always believed that being sick was not for me. I was very active, and I didn't want to stop doing things, so I never imagined that I could be sick. I never believed that there was a relationship between thoughts and health, even if a doctor said it. A few years later I would realize that thoughts are totally connected to our health.

Chapter 7 – The Atoms

Most of the time I met normal people and had normal conversations. In this book, I am focusing on the stories that helped me to understand the world in the way I understand it today.

While traveling in Europe, I heard several stories that were unusual. Since not many people know about these stories, I thought people were making things up. When I heard these stories for the first time, I was not paying close attention. I believed that these stories were not important. But without knowing, these stories would help me to understand other important things in the future.

In Bosnia and Herzegovina, some people talk openly about a pyramid in that country. The pyramid is hidden under grass. If you look at it from the distance, it actually looks like a pyramid, but there are not many scientists talking about it seriously. Some people say that there is more than one pyramid, and that the pyramid is connected to other pyramids around the world. The pyramids and other sacred places all over the world are creating a special energy around the planet, and this energy is keeping us alive. These people believe openly in aliens, and they related them to the construction of the pyramids. Not only that, they believe that this information is not so openly public because there are people in the world trying to hide information about what is really happening in the world.

This sounded for me like a conspiracy theory. I believed that the history of the world could be different than the one we know. But this was too much for me.

In Serbia, there is a similar story of a pyramid in the mountains called Rtanj. This one is a little bit harder to see. It is interesting that it has similar geometry compared to one pyramid in Mexico.

In Romania, there is a big rock that looks like the sphinx in Egypt.

I didn't understand the meaning of the pyramids or anything related to them. I could not deny that I had a weird feeling when I was on the top of the pyramid in Mexico, but I didn't believe in these weird stories. If there was not a scientist talking about it seriously, I wouldn't consider it as something real. After some research, I found out that there is no scientifically documented connection between these places and the stories.

Later, I realized that there were also hidden pyramids in Slovakia. In a small town called Rudňany, there are some hills, thought by some people to be pyramids covered with grass and trees. I went to see them and they looked like actual pyramids. When I arrived, there was a group of people talking about a cave. This cave goes to the center of one of the pyramids. I was lucky - the person who discovered the pyramids was there and he invited everyone to go inside the cave. I went to the middle of the pyramid and I didn't feel anything unusual. But two unusual things happened in the cave.

There was a dog, a very friendly dog. After few minutes of walking inside the cave, the dog suddenly stopped. The dog was behaving differently. Then, the person who found the pyramids said that the dog was standing exactly in the middle of the pyramid. Then, this man took a little machine that measures ion density from his pockets.

When there is air pollution, especially in big cities, it means that there are many positive ions in the air, but negative ions in the air are good for the human body. Negative ions can be found in nature, especially close to the ocean, mountains, waterfalls, and in crystals.

When we were inside the pyramid in Slovakia, and we were getting closer to the center of the pyramid, the machine started to register a huge number of negative ions. If the machine is correct, it means that this is very healthy for humans. Why is nobody talking about this?

Inside the atoms, there are electrons (-), protons (+), and neutrons (without charge). For now, let's focus only on electrons and protons.

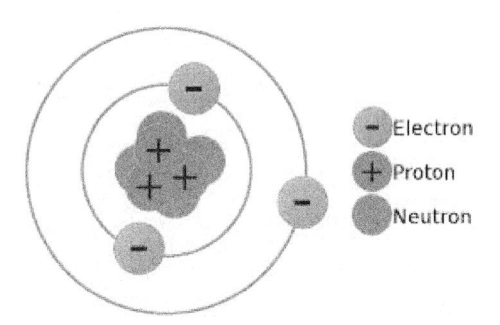

Atoms sometimes have more protons, and sometimes more electrons, but usually, they have the same amount. When an atom has more protons or electrons, it has a charge, or ions.

After hearing all these stories about the pyramids in Europe, I thought that these people were followers of something like a religion to support their belief in the mystical aspects of pyramids. I thought that spirituality was the antithesis of real science. I thought that I was just randomly meeting weird people, but it was just the beginning.

Chapter 8 – The Desert

I started to travel to places outside Europe. I started with Morocco. I didn't speak Arabic and my French was not good. It was not easy to find people speaking English. Sometimes in Europe it's the same, but you can always find a way to communicate. Morocco was different. The language was not the biggest difference. The way they think is very different. It was a little shocking.

When I taught at the high school, I learned that when I wanted to explain something I had to do it in a way that the students would easily understand. I had to use words and things they can relate to. This helped me to communicate easier with people, even in other languages. But when the other person understands the world differently, first I had to learn how they see their world so I could communicate better with them.

In Europe, there are some differences between cultures and languages. Languages not only influence, but define our perception and set the boundaries on how we look at things. For example, in some languages, especially in Finnish, there are many words to describe "snow". In Spanish and other languages there is usually only one. Also, the gender of some words can change between languages, so we relate to them in different ways. For example, in German, the word "key" is masculine, but in Spanish it's feminine. In Russian, the days of the week have different genders. Monday, Tuesday and Thursday are masculine, Wednesday and Friday are feminine, and Sunday is without a gender. So when Russians talk about Wednesdays and Fridays, they could describe them with words that are related to feminine things. There are many differences in

Europe, but Morocco was totally different for me, even though it is very close to Spain.

I was fascinated with this feeling. I was in a totally new environment, outside my comfort zone. As usual, I was staying with local people that I met on the internet. In the mornings, when I was waking up and realizing that I was in a totally different place, I felt like I was in a video game. I played video games when I was a child but I never played video games during my adult life. This may sound funny, but I really felt like I was in a video game. I imagined that everything around me was like a new level in the video game and I had to get used to this new level in order to play there.

I had to find a different way to communicate. I tried to learn a little bit of Arabic. I was used to reading from left to right so it took me a while to get used to reading from right to left. I started to pay attention to their clothes. They were very different. They looked very comfortable. I liked to walk down random streets and see how they lived. I was used to wearing clothes that are more common in Europe. I could see people look at me on the streets. I looked different than them. I didn't want to be different. I wanted to be like one of them, at least for few days.

In Mexico, I grew up thinking that using gel in my hair to style it would make it look good. I grew up seeing men with gel in their hair so I thought that it was the way hair should look. Also, influenced by TV and other people, I wanted to wear the type of clothes I saw on those people. When I moved to Slovakia, having gel in my hair was considered very weird, and the clothes they usually wore were a little bit different. I probably adapted to something in between.

In Morocco, I looked weird to them. I wanted to be one of them for a few days. I wanted to understand how they live and why. Since I was staying with local people, I had many questions for them. They were very nice people and they made me feel part of them. I started to wonder how my life would be if I had grown up there. I would probably be dressed like them, and I would probably be a Muslim.

I started to think more about myself. I had questions like, what makes me look good? Why do I wear the clothes I wear? What makes me think that the clothes I wear look good? It doesn't matter what I wear, I will always look weird for someone, somewhere in the world. Also, it doesn't matter what I say or do. Someone, somewhere, will think that I am weird. It was the first time that I asked myself these questions. I didn't take them seriously at that time. I thought they were just philosophical questions. But they would help me in the future. Since that day I started to dress simply, only with comfortable clothes.

My last day in Morocco, I wanted to walk down random streets so I could see how people lived there. I was taking pictures. I saw a wall with some letters in Arabic. I found it beautiful so I took a picture of it. Right after I took the picture, a man came running to me and he was trying to hit me. He was saying something in Arabic. I didn't understand, but I could see that he was very angry. Some people walking on the street saw him and they came to stop him. One of them spoke English so he explained to me what happened.

He explained to me that the man was very angry because I took a picture of his wife. I checked the picture on the camera and I realized that there was a woman walking when I took the picture. Even though she was completely covered, the man was very angry at me. He also explained to me many things about Muslims. I realized that I didn't know so much about Muslims. If I really wanted to understand other people, I would have to understand how they think and what they believe. I grew up in a Christian family but I would not consider myself a follower of any religion. I started to be curious just because I wanted to understand people.

I had a long conversation with my new friend. He told me that Muslims believe in Jesus and other people mentioned in other religions. He also says that Muslims believe that the Christian Bible and other books were corrupted or mistranslated. He mentioned that the Archangel Gabriel talked to Muhammad, and then Muhammad wrote the messages in the Quran, the sacred book of Islam. I didn't know that Muslims believe in angels and Jesus. What he said about the books being corrupted or mistranslated was the only thing I could believe. I think this was the first time I started to be a little bit curious about religions.

I also visited other Muslim countries in Africa. There was a specific place that I really wanted to see. I wanted to see what it looks like where the Sahara Desert meets the Atlantic Ocean. The country of Mauritania would be the perfect place. This country requires a visa for almost everyone in the world and the visa process is not easy. There was an exception. There was a list of countries that could obtain the visa at the airport if you fly directly to the capital city called Nouakchott. I was traveling with a Mexican passport and Mexico was on the list so I got a flight ticket to Nouakchott.

As usual, I was always contacting people before arriving in any country. When I arrived in Mauritania, my new friend was waiting for me at the airport. I told him I wanted to see where the desert meets the ocean so he took me there. When we arrived, it was not what I expected. There was some trash in the sand. My friend told me that it was because of people. He said that if I wanted to see cleaner sand I would have to go to the north, closer to Western Sahara.

Western Sahara used to be part of Morocco; it was occupied by Spain but they left the territory. Western Sahara was recognized as an independent territory but Morocco claimed it back. Now, Morocco occupies Western Sahara. The African Union is similar to the European Union. The African Union asked Morocco to leave Western Sahara, but since Morocco said that it should be returned to them, they didn't want to leave. Morocco is the only country that is not part of the African Union because of this conflict.

I wanted to go to Western Sahara. The easiest way to get there was by car. My friend helped me to arrange it with a local person. There is a road going through the Sahara Desert all the way to Western Sahara. It would take one day of driving to get to the place I wanted to go.

I got into the car with the other three people. My friend was not there so I had to find a way to communicate with these people while on the road. The driver was from Mauritania and he spoke only Arabic. Another person was from Morocco so he spoke Arabic and French. They saw my passport so they knew that I was from Mexico. The other person was from Mali, and he spoke only a little bit of French. I didn't speak French. I knew just a few words. The French language sometimes can be similar to the Spanish language so I was able to understand French if it is written out. I wanted to talk to them, but the language barrier made it hard. Every time the driver or the guy from Mali said something, the guy from Morocco would write it down for me in French so I would understand. But there was no way for me to talk to them.

We went through the desert for many hours. There was nothing - just sand and the road. During the night, we suddenly stopped in the middle of nowhere. It was completely dark. The only way to see was with the lights of the car. They explained to me that we had to sleep there. I was sleeping on the sand in the middle of the Sahara Desert. I couldn't sleep. I was amazed. I was looking at the stars. There were so many stars that I hadn't seen before.

The next morning, we arrived at the border of Western Sahara. I was surprised that the police officers were speaking Spanish to me. After they checked our passports, the police said that the guy from Mali was not allowed to enter Western Sahara. The police said that he was probably trying to move permanently to Morocco, therefore he was not allowed to cross the border. We had to continue without him.

Later, the guy from Morocco wrote to me in French trying to explain something. He said that the guy from Mali was probably rejected because he was not a Muslim, and sometimes the police can be arrogant. I told him that I was also not a Muslim, but he said that I come from a catholic country and it was accepted.

Using the little French I knew, I asked him if he knew the religion of the guy from Mali. I am not sure if I understood completely because he wrote it in French, but he told me that in Mali there are some tribes who have uncommon beliefs. Then he wrote to me that I should probably know because I am Mexican. I really didn't understand the relationship between Mali and Mexico, so I asked again more seriously. What he wrote to me didn't make sense at that moment, but later it would help me to understand many things.

He wrote to me that there are some groups of people in Mali called Dogon. The Dogon people live in houses very different than the rest of the people in Mali. They have masks, symbolism, and they know many things about the universe. He said that he was comparing these people with the Mayan in Mexico.

A group of people called Berber live in North Africa. They have different skin color - they are whiter. They have their own language. But they are accepted as part of the countries in North Africa. Many people don't know the origins of these people.

When I came back home, I researched the Dogons and found many interesting things about them. The Dogon people from Mali refused to convert to Islam. They decided to live in high, elevated places to protect themselves and be away from the rest of the people in Mali.

The Dogon people have very different traditions than other people in Africa. The Dogon people say that long time ago they were contacted by intelligent beings who came from somewhere else, who taught them many things about humanity and the universe.

The Dogon people don't have a written language. They don't have telescopes or any kind of technology. But they knew detailed information about planets and stars, even before scientists discovered them. A long time ago, even before scientists realized it, the Dogon people knew that the Sun is the center of the solar system and not the Earth. They also knew about the rings of Saturn. They knew about the planet Jupiter and its moons. They knew that the star Sirius was in orbit with another star, much smaller, with big mass, and not visible from Earth. Scientists discovered it around 1970, and they called it Sirius B. The Dogon people knew all this a long time ago. They say that they got the information from intelligent beings who came from somewhere else. They say that these beings were amphibious so they could live in water and on land.

I have met several people who told me that they had dreams with some beings who look like half human and half frog. They called them the frog people.

In Slovakia, I heard tales of amphibious beings called *Vodník*. They described them as green creatures that live under the water. These creatures could change the shape of their body to appear like a normal person. For some people these creatures are good, and some people describe them as bad. Similar stories exist in the Czech Republic, Slovenia, and many places in Eastern Europe. In Russia, they have a creature called *Rusalka*. In Germany, there is *Wassermann*. In Greece, they have the *Naiads*. In England, they have *Jenny Greenteeth*. And even the Aztecs in Mexico have a creature called *Ahuizotl*. And there are many more in other parts of the world.

These stories are considered to be myths so there is no official information confirming the existence of these beings. I don't know if these stories are just myths or if they are based on true stories. But some years later I would have to deal directly with some amphibious beings.

Chapter 9 – The Geometry

My daily life was very similar to almost all of my friends. I had an office job, I played sports in my free time and I went to night clubs on the weekends. Probably the only difference was that I did not drink alcohol, I was not going to restaurants, and during my free time I checked cheap flights and more options to travel. I was obsessed with traveling.

I visited many places in Europe several times. There were some cities that I knew very well and I didn't need a map to know how to move around. One of these cities was London. I feel better when I am walking around the places I visit, and if I can, I avoid local transportation. I feel like I can see more this way. While walking for many hours in London, I arrived at Buckingham Palace, the place where the royal family lived. I just knew that this place was famous and I wanted to see it. After taking some pictures of the palace, I started to look for a place to sit down. There were many tourists. I needed a place with less people so I could relax. I was very tired after many hours walking and the only place I found was a park next to the palace so I laid down on the grass.

Not so far from where I was there was a couple having a snack. They were speaking Portuguese. Because of their accent, I knew that they were from Brazil. The Portuguese language is similar to Spanish. I learned some Portuguese before so I was able to hear all of the conversation. Even if I didn't want it, my brain automatically registered what they were saying. I was alone with my head on the grass. They were talking about the royal family. I thought they were saying nice things about them. They were using the word "esquisito" in Portuguese, which is very similar to the word "exquisito" in Spanish. But then, I remembered that these words have opposite meanings.

The word "exquisito" in Spanish means exquisite, or related to something good. The word "esquisito" in Portuguese means weird. I realized they were talking about the Royal Family as weird people.

I always saw the royal family as special people because they were the descendants of previous kings and queens. I grew up seeing them on TV and they seemed to be important for many people. But the Brazilian couple were making fun of them. I didn't like the way they were talking about them, especially about the queen. In the same conversation, they were switching topics as if they were related. They were talking about the royal family, South America, pyramids and aliens. I believed that this couple were the weird ones. I was interested in South America and pyramids, especially after my experience with pyramids in Mexico and Europe.

I didn't understand the relationship between all these topics, but for them it was like a normal conversation. I don't remember the whole conversation because I was not really paying attention but I remember two things they said.

They said that there were hidden pyramids in Peru and Brazil. I could believe this. I was already aware of hidden pyramids in Europe so I wouldn't be surprised about hidden pyramids somewhere else. I was not able to believe the second thing they said. It was too weird for me. They said that the royal family were aliens that looked like humans.

A few weeks later I went to Egypt. I wanted to see the pyramids of Giza. Egypt has a lot of history and I wanted to learn as much as possible. I researched as much as possible about Egypt so I could be more informed. According to scientists, the pyramids were built as tombs for pharaohs (leaders of ancient Egypt), around 2560 BC (around 4,580 years ago). There are many theories, but this one is more official and more acceptable. Some people believe that they were built more than 10,000 years ago, and others believe that they were created by aliens.

In Egypt, staying with a local person, I shared a room with a traveler from Taiwan. He was traveling the world on a low budget. He said that he had already been doing it for 5 years and he would travel 3 more years. He explained to me that he saved money for several years and he sold everything he had. He was going to Latin America after Egypt and he was learning Spanish. He asked me for help with the Spanish language but it was his last day in Egypt and we didn't have time. I just knew that his name was Chi and he was from Taiwan. I thought I would never meet him again.

I spent all my time with my host. He took me to the pyramids. I wanted to go alone but he told me that there were many people who would try to trick me and take extra money from me at the entrance. I didn't believe him. It was a famous place and many tourists came to see it. It would be very uncomfortable for tourists if they had to deal with scammers. He took me there by car and we had a hard time getting to the entrance of the pyramids. There were so many people trying to scam tourists. I was with a local person and it was hard to manage. My friend told me to ignore everyone. I believe many tourists would have a harder time trying to get to the entrance.

My friend took me around the pyramids. He told me everything he knew about them. There was nothing unusual. He told me the same things I read on the internet. I asked him if he knew about hidden pyramids around the world but he didn't know anything about them. My friend was going to Alexandria, a city in the north of Egypt. I asked him if I could come with him and he said yes. We drove for a few hours. We stopped in several towns because he had to meet some people. Eventually we arrived in Alexandria. He told me the story of this city. I heard about this city before but I had to admit I didn't remember anything. In school, world history was the hardest subject for me.

My friend said that there is a famous library in Alexandria. This library was very old and used to be the biggest in the world. A lot of information from the ancient world was stored there. But the leaders of the Roman Empire burned the library and information from the ancient world was lost forever. I asked why the Roman Empire would do that. He said that they were probably trying to hide the knowledge and implement their own version of history. This made me think a lot. There was a big chance that everything we know today was influenced by the Roman Empire.

In Europe, there are symbols of the Roman Empire in many important buildings. First I thought that these buildings were old and therefore they kept the symbols from the Roman Empire. But some of the new buildings also have these symbols. The castle of Bratislava, where I was living, had the logo of the Roman Empire. This building had been reconstructed many times.

The symbols of the lions can be found also in Egypt. I asked my friend if he knew something about it but he didn't know anything. I told him that I had seen lions in a lot of symbolism in Europe but I didn't know it was also present in Egypt. Maybe there was a relationship. I also noticed something else that I saw often in Europe. Obelisks.

There are obelisks in Egypt and in many places in Europe. I saw obelisks in Rome, the Vatican, Paris, London, and many places around Europe. Also, I knew they were in Washington D.C. because I saw them often in movies.

My friend also didn't know about these obelisks around the world so I thought it was just a coincidence. Another thing that I found interesting was that the United States Capitol Building in Washington D.C. has a similar architecture as the one in Rome. I knew that there had to be something related between Egypt, the Roman Empire, and Washington D.C. I wanted to know more but I was not willing to spend time researching so I ignored it.

I left Egypt and I went to Turkey. When I arrived in Turkey at the airport, I saw several socks on the floor. It looked weird. It looked like someone was drying socks. I looked at the person next to the socks and noticed that it was the guy from Taiwan, the guy I met in Egypt. I said, "Chi?" He looked at me and said, "Hey, finally you can teach me Spanish." It was a nice coincidence. He had problems with his flights and he was in Turkey waiting for a connection flight to South America. I helped him with Spanish and he told me about his adventures around the world. I asked him about the socks. I asked if he didn't care about other people. He told me that after many years of traveling he learned how to ignore what other people may think about him. It made sense. He was not bothering other people. At that time, I would not have been able to dry socks at the airport. I would probably feel ashamed of what people could think about me.

He was not taking pictures during his trips. He wanted to experience everything without spending time taking pictures. I loved pictures so it was hard for me to understand him. He was not taking pictures but he was drawing often. He showed me some of his drawings. One of the drawings was of the Egyptian gods. I asked him if he knew the symbolism of these gods. What he said would help me in the future but at that time I thought he was just trying to be funny. He said that he believes these beings are not symbolism. He believes that these beings are real physical beings.

Every time I went to a new place I asked about pyramids, obelisks, lions, and eagles as symbolism or any other unusual thing. Egypt had all of that. Even the Sphinx looked like a lion. Turkey was not an exception. Some people say that Mount Nemrut is a pyramid even though it doesn't look like the others. There is a statue of a lion next to it. The Roman Empire used to have obelisks, lions, and eagles in their symbolism. Turkey used to be part of the Roman Empire so having lions, eagles and obelisks was expected. I realized that all these symbols have been used since the first civilizations in Mesopotamia.

I wanted to learn more about the Roman Empire. Ancient Greece existed before the Roman Empire and since I was going to Greece I thought it was better to start studying about ancient Greece.

The first thing I found fascinating about Greece was the distinct symbolism. The symbol for Greece was the dolphin, very different compared to symbolism in the Roman Empire. I became interested in the philosophers Socrates and Plato. Socrates wanted people to think for themselves rather than just repeat information, and developed the Socratic Method. Socrates was considered one of the best philosophers of all time. By using his Socratic Method we can start to question what we know about humanity.

Ancient Greek philosophers knew more than 2,000 years ago that the Earth was spherical. But we didn't rediscover it until around the year 1520. That is why the Spanish who discovered America were trying to reach India. They already knew that Earth was spherical. But they didn't know about America.

According to science, the different human races around the world are caused by a big difference in genetic material. A few years ago they found out that this was not true. The difference in DNA between two Africans can be more different than the DNA of a European compared to an Asian. So the theory that humans evolved from apes could be wrong. It is, after all, only a theory.

We also believe that dinosaurs had tough, leathery skin, like some depicted in the movies. But scientific evidence says that the dinosaurs had feathers, like birds. We can be wrong about many other things.

For the first time ever, I opened to the idea that even the aliens may exist, especially because we used to believe that

Earth was the only planet with water. But this has been dismissed by scientists since they have discovered water on other planets and moons.

Socrates believed that the way we think could be manipulated without us even knowing. He made it very clear in his quote, "True wisdom comes to each of us when we realize how little we understand about life, ourselves, and the world around us." It seems that he knew many things but he didn't want to tell people. He wanted people to think for themselves.

Socrates was killed by the rulers of ancient Greece and Plato was concerned about his own life. I always wondered why these people with great ideas get silenced.

Plato said, "There will be no end to the troubles of states, or of humanity itself, until philosophers become kings in this world, or until those, we now call kings and rulers really and truly become philosophers, and political power and philosophy thus come into the same hands."

Plato talked about a city called Atlantis that existed in the Atlantic Ocean. There is no scientific evidence for the existence of this city. What was very interesting to me was that Plato described many details of Atlantis as if he lived there. Plato described Atlantis as a beautiful place with a great civilization. But then something happened. The people became corrupted and greedy, and when the gods saw this they decided to destroy Atlantis. Then big waves came from the ocean and Atlantis sank into the sea. Plato said Atlantis was not a metaphorical place. He said Atlantis was a real place.

He talked about mathematics and geometry, and he related them to the experience of our reality. Plato believed that the soul is immortal and many other things I didn't understand at that time. He talked mainly about five figures. We know them as Platonic solids.

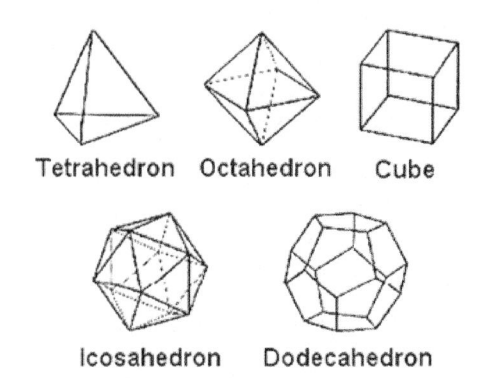

Tetrahedron   Octahedron   Cube

Icosahedron   Dodecahedron

In each figure all angles are equal, all faces are identical in form and all corners have the same number of faces. I will not talk about the details of these figures. You really have to love mathematics and geometry in order to understand completely these figures. If you really want to understand more about these figures you can study sacred geometry. The relationship between these figures and reality is incredible.

Plato talked about something called Allegory of the Cave. Imagine that there are three prisoners living in a cave. They have been there since they were born. They don't know anything about the outside world. They are always facing a wall in the cave and they cannot turn around. The only thing they see is the wall of the cave. There is a fire behind them.

From time to time there are people or other objects passing close to the fire and their shadows are reflected inside the cave. The prisoners recognized the shadows as real objects, and eventually they give them names, believing that they are real. Suddenly, one prisoner is allowed to leave the cave. He goes outside the cave for the first time. His eyes hurt because he has never seen so much light. He is disoriented. Eventually, his eyes adapt to the environment and for the first time he sees the real world. He realizes that everything he saw in the cave was a shadow. Now he can see everything with more clarity. He realizes that the Sun is the source of the light in the world outside the cave. The prisoner returns to the cave and shares with the other prisoners what he discovered. But he is no longer used to be in the darkness and he cannot see the shadows the same way he did before. The other prisoners think that he has become blind and stupid because he left the cave. They don't want anyone to leave the cave again.

Plato used this as an analogy with his students and people in ancient Greece to describe what a philosopher is. I believe that the meaning of "philosopher" in ancient Greece was different than how we understand it today. If Plato were alive today, he might be considered a lunatic or conspiracy theorist.

Not many people understood Plato in ancient Greece. Even today many people wonder what he was trying to say. What I understood from Plato's analogy was that humans live inside the cave right now. What we see around us are the shadows. If this is true, I want to get out of the cave and see what causes the shadows. I didn't know where to find the exit of the cave, and I couldn't even imagine how real objects might look.

When I read about Plato's analogy of the cave, I thought again about the idea of living inside a video game. I imagined that I was the main character in the game and someone, somewhere, had the control and was using my body to explore this world. In the video game, there are other people and these people have someone controlling them. It is something like a multiplayer video game.

So, in this case, the shadows in the cave can be the things we see in our daily life, or in this video game. If I wanted to see the real objects I would have to see the world outside the video game - outside the screen.

I really imagined that I was in a video game. Especially when I was traveling to a new place and the environment was completely new to me. Since I was traveling alone, nobody could judge me for my crazy imagination. Sometimes I even imagined that I was trying to communicate with the controller.

Sometimes, especially when I had to drive a car, ride a bike, or even run, I played music in the background. But it wasn't normal music. Usually, I played music from the video games that I used to play when I was a child. This way I would feel more like I was in a video game. I was always ashamed to share this idea I had about the video game but after reading Plato's analogy I felt more confident. Maybe I wasn't so crazy.

Socrates, the teacher of Plato, studied in Egypt. This means that ancient Egyptians knew many things that maybe only some people know today. It was clear to me that there were people from the times of ancient Egypt who knew many things about humanity. Probably even before Egyptians, the Sumerians knew these things. Probably there was knowledge about humanity that people tried to share with others, but for some reason these people were silenced. If this was true and they were silenced, who would do that? Why? We are all human after all. We can grow together.

I wanted to see the world outside the video game. I didn't know where to go or what to do. Maybe I had to find a way to communicate with the person who had the control.

It seems that geometry is related to nature in so many ways. I wasn't sure why. But it was very interesting that it can be found in so many places in nature, from the shape of molecules to big pyramids. Also, geometry is found in some touristic places like the Giant's Causeway in Northern Ireland, the Hexagon Pool in Israel, the Svartifoss Waterfall in Iceland, Devils Postpile National Monument in USA, the Prismas Basalticos in Mexico, and many more.

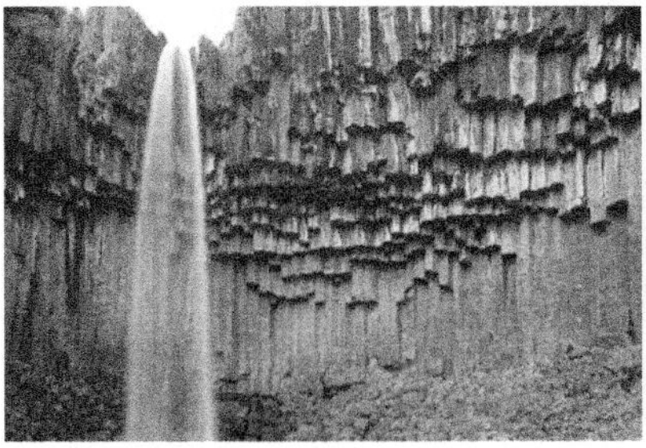
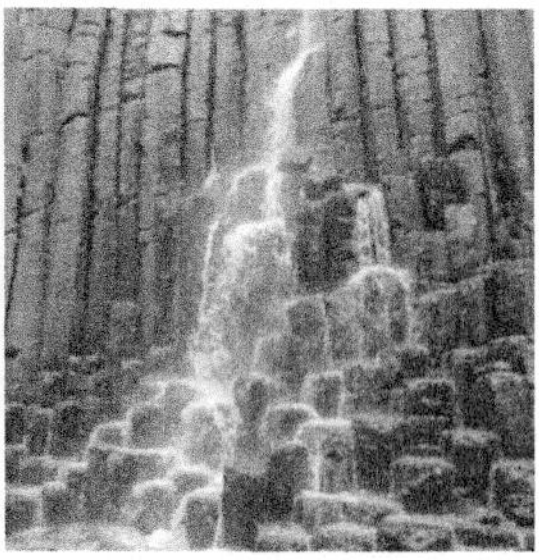

Chapter 10 – The Circles

I want to remind you that everything in the book is to help you to remember who you are and it is intended with love. Some information might be uncomfortable for some people. After reading the whole book, I hope you feel it is pure love.

Many times, while searching for cheap flights, I found very cheap flights to several destinations around Europe. In many cases, the flights were during the weekend. I could spend every weekend in a different place and I didn't have to take days off from the office. I spent many weekends traveling.

On one of these trips I went to London. I knew the city so I wanted to see other places around the area. I heard of Stonehenge, a place with some rocks in an interesting formation, not so far from London.

This place was famous, so I wanted to see it. But I really didn't know so much about this place. The first time I was in London I met somebody who was coming back from

Stonehenge. This person told me that it was a magical place and that people with magical powers built it a long time ago. For me, it was just some rocks so I didn't pay attention. But this time I was more open to new ideas so I researched.

I read about the Celts. There are many theories about where the Celts came from. Some scientists say that they came from Central Europe. Other scientists say that they came from the Middle East. Descendants of the Celts now live in Ireland, Wales, and other parts of the United Kingdom and France.

The Celts had a very interesting religion, but almost all the information about it was destroyed when the Roman Empire conquered them. They converted the Celts to Christianity and destroyed almost all evidence about the Celtic religion.

In Celtic cultures there were people called Druids. They were religious leaders, judges, political advisors, healers, and much more. The Druids believed that all humans are interconnected. They also believed in reincarnation and that we can become immortal. They believed that all humans have a special connection with nature and the planet, and they referred to the planet as Mother Earth. They healed people with magic. They attributed their magical healing powers to Mother Earth. There is not much information about the druids. Almost all evidence of their existence was destroyed by the Roman Empire. Most of the information about the druids has been passed down in stories.

The Roman Empire conquered three continents. They destroyed or changed many civilizations including their culture, beliefs, and traditions. This means that much information was lost. The only continents that the Roman Empire didn't conquer were America and Australia. But these two continents have been conquered by Europeans in the last centuries so there is a chance that right now we are living in a world mainly influenced by the Roman Empire. After the Roman Empire disappeared, many things have changed. But the information from the other cultures disappeared or they are not taken seriously, like the ancient cultures in America.

Some people still follow some Celtic traditions. Some of these people meet in Stonehenge every solstice. There are two solstices during a year - one in summer and another one in winter. The summer solstice is the longest day of the year because the Sun stays visible for a longer time compared to any other day of the year. The winter solstice is the opposite. It's when the Sun is visible for the shortest time during the year. When I was on the top of the pyramid in Mexico, it was winter solstice.

There are many places similar to Stonehenge. Most of them were destroyed. Many people believe that these monuments were built by the druids. The monuments similar to Stonehenge are also related to the location of the Sun, Moon, and stars. They are in Mexico, Egypt, and many other places.

Close to Stonehenge and other places around the world, some figures appear on the ground. They are called crop circles. These figures can be created by humans and many people have proved how they do it. Sometimes these figures even appear on snow or ice. Most of the figures are created by pushing down the grass, but there are also figures where the grass grew up forming the figure. The figures have interesting geometry and sometimes Celtic symbolism. These figures started to appear around 1970 and some people say that they were created by aliens.

In Europe, some people follow old religions. Some of these people are called Pagans. The word *pagan*, for Christians, is related to something bad. This is because the Roman Empire didn't want to accept any religion other than Christianity.

Christianity (and all its branches) is the most common religion in the world. Islam is the second most common religion. I grew up in a Christian family and I believe that religions can help some people. However, whoever controls the information around Christianity has a big influence on many people in the world. They have changed the Bible several times. In 1684, the Vatican removed many books from the Bible; deciding what many people believe. This is a big responsibility. Unfortunately, we don't have access to the information that has been removed from the Bible. This information is archived in the Vatican.

When the Roman Empire left Britain, invaders called the Saxons, from what's now Germany and Netherlands, came to Britain. The Saxons were also Pagans, like the Celts, so almost all the information related to them is lost. The only way people know that they existed is because of stories in books. Some of these books mentioned a character known as King Arthur. He was a leader from Britain who fought against the Saxons.

Eventually, the Saxons invaded Britain. *Anglo-Saxon* is a term we use for the people who lived in Britain after the Saxons arrived. *Saxon* refers to the people we know today as German-Dutch. *Angles* refers to the people in southern Denmark. The name *England* came from the word *Angle-Land*, and the English language was formed around this time.

The Roman Empire was over, but Christianity was not. So Christianity was re-introduced in England and almost everything Pagan disappeared or was silenced. And with the arrival of Christianity, all dragon mythology was gone.

The stories of King Arthur say he was in Britain fighting against the Saxons. He had a round table located in a castle called Camelot, somewhere in Britain, where the knights had discussions about all kinds of topics. Everyone was equal. A very famous object mentioned during this time was the *Holy Grail*. For many people the *Holy Grail* is represented by a cup - a real physical cup like the ones used for wine. For some people, it symbolizes the descendants of Jesus, or descendants of families during the time when Jesus lived.

Whatever it was, there was a lot of symbolism. It seems that for the Roman Empire symbolism was important. It made me think about the eagle and the lion. They are present in some parts of Europe, the United States, and other parts of the world. The symbol of the Roman Empire was an eagle, and maybe it's somehow related to many places in the world today. The Persian Empire existed before the Roman Empire and it also had eagles and lions in its symbolism. Even the first civilization, the Sumerians, had eagles and lions.

I started to be more open to the idea that the world today is still connected to the first civilizations, and somehow this has been kept secret. The Roman Empire destroyed many documents related to other cultures. Probably other empires also destroyed information - information that we will never know.

When I went to Stonehenge, I walked. I didn't have a car. You can see the stones from the street. The main entrance was too far and it would take me a long time to get there so I decided to jump the fence. I felt confident jumping the fence because I got the tickets for Stonehenge on the internet, so I felt like it would be okay. I saw the rocks so I walked towards them. When I was getting close the rocks, the police stopped me. They said that I was in big trouble. I told them that I already had a ticket I got on the internet the previous night. They told me that in that case it was not so bad. But they mentioned something interesting. Something I never heard before and there is no information about this on the internet or any book I know. They told me that if I wanted to see Stonehenge I should walk in the same direction as everyone else and never the opposite direction. This is how people walk around Stonehenge:

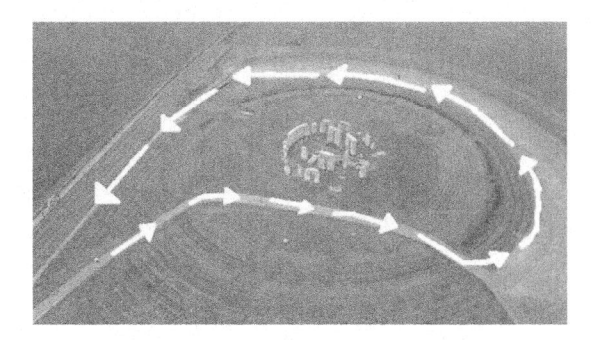

I asked why the direction was so important. The police officer said it was important for the United Kingdom. I found this weird. I thought that it was made this way so everything would be more organized for the visitors.

I knew that Muslims in Mecca, Saudi Arabia do something similar. They move in the same direction.

I didn't know much about religions, so I didn't know the real meaning of this. What was important for me at this moment was that the orientation of the movements was important for several people around the world.

At the airport, in London Heathrow, when you have an international flight connection you have to walk through an area with two big pictures on the wall. Two queens are on the wall and there is nothing else in that area. This area could be used for something else but it is used only as a path for people to walk. It is totally unnecessary but you have to walk through that area, and you have to walk in a circle going in the same direction as in Stonehenge.

The Celts used to walk around monuments but in the opposite direction. I started to notice that symbolism was very important. I always thought that symbolism was important only for old civilizations but I started to believe it was important even today.

I don't watch the news but from time to time I see information shared on the internet. Around the same time when I had these thoughts I saw on the internet that a group known as ISIS was destroying some places in the Middle East. These people destroyed ancient places and burnt libraries with a lot of documents. This was a confirmation for me. Whoever these people were, or whoever hired these people, knew what they were doing. This was a confirmation for me that something had been kept secret to the public. And whatever it was, it was related to the history of all humanity.

There was a time when the Roman Empire had its own religion. Before Christianity, the Roman Empire believed in many gods. Like other cultures, they offered sacrifices of animals to their gods to keep them happy.

When the Roman Empire still had their own religion, Judaism and Christianity were becoming popular. These two religions had something in common - they were against sacrifices. Eventually the Roman Empire accepted Christianity and it spread all over the Empire. But Christianity changed through the passing of time.

It seems that many wars, if not all, have been related to religion. Why is religion so important? It had to be something bigger than just a belief.

Because I grew up in a Christian family, I went to church when I was a child. My family is very respectful of beliefs. When I was 13 years old, I told my family that I didn't want to go to church and they respected me. Something that I remember from the church is that they ate bread and drank wine from a cup. The bread represented the body of Jesus and the cup of wine represented the blood of Jesus. The cup could symbolize the *Holy Grail*, or the descendants of Jesus, and they were drinking the blood of Jesus. Obviously this is full of symbolism. Many people have different ideas about the meaning of the symbols so there is always more than one interpretation. Symbolism is a huge topic, and we might never obtain a single correct interpretation, so I will not talk much about this topic. For me, it is important to know that symbolism has been, and still is, very important around the world.

Chapter 11 – The Dragons

I visited almost every country in Europe. There was only one country left - a small country in the Mediterranean Sea called Malta. This is one of the smallest countries in the world, so I thought that there would not be much to learn about Malta. I thought it would not have an impact on me. I was so wrong.

When I arrived at the airport in Malta, many people started to look outside the window. The queen of the United Kingdom was there. She was going to a meeting with many other leaders of the world. The queen used to live in Malta a long time ago. This was special for some people on the plane. I didn't know she would be there and it was not important to me.

Malta, like many other countries in Europe, has underground cities and ancient temples. I went to visit these temples. Some people compare some temples in Malta with Stonehenge. They don't really look very similar but I found them interesting anyway. I went to the temple called *Mnajdra*. There were no people - just a family walking around the temple and the security guard.

I was walking around the temple until I got close to the family. There were two children and they were playing. One of the children stepped on my feet accidentally. The father looked at me and apologized. I told him that I was okay and I was happy to see the children play. He smiled and started to talk to me. They were from Pakistan and we started to have a typical conversation.

After a while I asked him if he knew anything about the temples. He said with great confidence that he knew many things. I asked him to share whatever he knew with me. He looked at me and smiled. He asked, "Do you want to know the official story or a weird story?" I said, "The weird story sounds interesting." I knew that these temples were among the oldest monuments in the world but nothing else. He told me that during his free time he researched UFO phenomena. I told him, "Look, a few years ago I would have laughed, but right now I am open to anything." What he told me helped me so much in the future.

He was in that temple because he heard from another researcher that it used to be inhabited by aliens. He said that these aliens were very similar to the velociraptors in the movie *Jurassic Park* and that they were very smart and more advanced than humans. I said, "Wait, you said aliens. These beings are more like dinosaurs." He told me that there are so many types of aliens in the universe, not just the small gray aliens we see in the movies.

At that moment I remembered something I saw on TV when I was a child. In Mexico, there was a famous TV show called *"Otro Rollo"*. It was a live TV show and they always had interesting guests. One day they presented a person named Jonathan Reed. This person said that he had a direct encounter with an alien in a forest close to his house. He managed to capture the alien and kept it in his house for a few days until the alien disappeared. He filmed the alien before it disappeared and the videos were shown on live TV. The alien was small and green. It was not a gray alien like the ones in movies.

He also said that the alien had a bracelet which was used for teleportation. He brought the bracelet to the TV show but he didn't use it. He said that he would use it again on live TV. He mentioned that the government was trying to capture him and take all the evidence.

A few years later, after the TV show in Mexico, I checked on the internet to see if he actually used the bracelet on live TV. I found a video on the internet where he was on a TV show in Canada. He used the bracelet on live TV. He put the bracelet on his hand and he explained that he had to wait for the connection to be made. He mentioned that the connection was not made by him - it's made by the aliens. After the connection is made, he explained that he started to feel something in his heart. Then, a few seconds later, his body became light, pure light. You could see the light floating in the TV studio and then the light was gone for a few seconds. Then the light started to appear somewhere else in the studio. The light moved back to the place where he was sitting and his body appeared again in front of everyone. When he became light, there was no audio in the video. I read somewhere that this could have been caused by the changes in the electromagnetism in the room.

When I saw that video, I was not sure if all that was real or not, but this time I was much more open to the idea of aliens. I thought that all videos could be fake but if at least one video is real then the aliens are real.

I don't even remember the name of the man in Malta but I am very thankful for what he shared with me. At that time, I was not sure if I could believe him or not. But a few years later I would understand much better.

I asked him if he knew about this person called Jonathan Reed but he didn't know. Then I said, "Wait a minute, I saw people talking about these dinosaur aliens. They are called *Reptilians*." He explained this too. He told me that the reptilian beings were not the same as the velociraptors.

They were very different. He said that there were many types of reptilians and not all of them caused problems for humans. I read about reptilians before but I thought that it was just a conspiracy theory.

It was the first time I talked about this subject seriously. I was not scared. Even as a joke I told him, "So once we know about all the alien races, then racism on this planet will be nothing compared to the universe." He told me that almost all aliens are very peaceful and that we will never hear about them on mass media.

I asked him, if these reptilian beings were real, why didn't we ever see them? He said they try very hard to remove any evidence of their existence, but they are mentioned in ancient civilizations. I asked him, where? He said that in many civilizations they were represented as snakes or dragons. In this moment all the ideas about symbolism came to my mind. It reminded me of the voodoo religion from Western Africa. Its followers believe in spirits in the afterlife. They have a god with a shape of a snake. There are stories of snakes and dragons all over the world, in ancient and in modern times. Everything that this man was telling me sounded very crazy but it made sense.

I asked him if he has seen any aliens. He said, "No, but the Queen is in Malta right now." I think he was trying to tell me that the Queen was an alien but I didn't want to ask any more. I asked him if he had directly seen any aliens because I hadn't. He said that he knew someone who translated an interview with a reptilian being. A person in Sweden had an encounter with a reptilian being. They had a conversation and the reptilian being was open to talk and answer any question. Eventually they ended up having an interview.

The reptilian being was a female. They don't have names like humans do, or humans cannot pronounce her name, but she could be called Lacerta. This being was described as a humanoid reptilian who belonged to a race we call alien, but Lacerta said they have been on Earth since before humans. She mentioned that many old civilizations knew about them and mentioned them in their texts. The Christian Bible mentioned them as snakes, but because of misunderstandings they were shown as evil creatures. She said that humans were genetically engineered by aliens called *Ilojiim* who left the planet around 5,000 years ago. The reptilian beings lived underground and the way they measure time was different than humans. She was a student of social behavior. She agreed to the interview to see how humans would react.

Lacerta said that many lights in the sky are not flying objects or UFOS but some of them are. Some of these objects belong to other species but the ones in the shape of a cigar belonged to them. They had special ways to hide their ships. They were usually around the North and South Poles. She said that their symbol was a dragon with seven stars. The stars represented the seven planets and stars they colonized in the past but are now abandoned. She said that humans were programmed to ignore the existence of reptilian beings. They have underground farms and they eat fruit, vegetables, and even raw meat. They cannot live without meat as some humans do. She said that some human scientists have found bones that belong to them and the scientists thought they were from dinosaurs. She said that the dinosaurs were not killed by an asteroid, but that most of them died because of a war between two races on Earth at that time.

She said that Earth is not hollow with an internal sun as many humans believe but there are underground cities connected by caves in many places around the planet. She said that when they are on the surface, humans cannot recognize them. They use telepathy to make humans believe they are seeing normal people. She talked about planes and dimensions. Some aliens live in different dimensions. She said that the reality we live in is not what we think. She ended the interview saying that humans should not believe everything from politicians, scientists or the history of humanity.

I don't know if this interview was real or not but the information provided made sense to me. Meeting this man from Pakistan was weird and nice at the same time. If I had met him a few years before, it would not have had the same impact on me. I felt like everything was happening at the right time. Otherwise I would not be able to understand anything. I was not totally convinced about the existence of aliens but I was much more open to the idea than before.

I returned to Slovakia from Malta. I lived close to a famous church. Many people called it the blue church. I started to notice that this church had a lot of symbolism, including some symbols from Malta and some symbols that appear on American currency. These symbols are also used in England, Rome, Israel, and even in ancient societies.

I didn't know how all these places were linked, but something was clear to me. There was a relationship between all of them.

At that time, I was teaching Spanish to some friends. One day, a friend asked if I could teach Spanish to a kid, and I accepted. My friend took me to the kid's house, and I was talking to the mother. She used to live in Barcelona, so she was able to speak Spanish. Eventually, we became friends. A few weeks later I realized that the parents of the kid used to be the owners of a national television station. And the father of the kid used to be a leader of a political party.

One day when I was talking to the mother, I asked her if there were things that were not allowed to be said on TV or things hidden from the public. She said there were many things hidden from the public but it was mainly because there could be fines or penalties, but she didn't say from whom. I asked them directly if they believed in aliens and she said "absolutely". I asked her if they could share with me anything to help me understand the world better. She told me the answer was not simple. If I wanted to understand the world as it is now I should study ancient civilizations, and I should believe in aliens because we were created by them.

This was another confirmation for me that I was not crazy for believing unusual things. I knew there should be a connection between ancient civilizations, aliens, the way we perceive reality, history, religion and science. I just didn't know what.

I prepared for the next trip. I wanted to know more about ancient civilizations. I started to study them. I knew that there was a big chance that the information available about old civilizations was altered but I wanted to know whatever was available.

I wanted to go to Iraq where Mesopotamia used to be. I needed a visa for Iraq. I checked the options and I decided to go to Iran where the Persian Empire used to be. I could get a visa when I arrived at the airport in Tehran, the capital of Iran. When I arrived in Iran, I went to get the visa. Everything was fine. They asked me where I would sleep. I told them that I had a friend there. They asked me for details of my friend, especially the phone number. I told them everything and they called my friend. It was 3am so my friend didn't pick up the phone. The police in Iran told me that my visa was rejected because I wasn't able to prove that my friend would host me. Because of the rules, I was supposed to be sent back to the place I came from, which was Belarus. I didn't have a visa for Belarus. I tried to explain this to them, but those were the rules.

I was sent to Belarus. The police were waiting for me at the airport. They took me to a room and talked to me only in Russian. I didn't understand everything but they didn't care. Sometimes the Russian language sounds similar to the Slovak language so I was able to understand a few things. They left me alone in the room. There was only a bathroom and a place to drink water. I thought I would be there for a few hours. I tried to talk to them but they ignored me most of the time. They asked me to buy a flight ticket to a destination where I don't need a visa. They took me to a travel agency at the airport. The only country available where I didn't need a visa was the country of Georgia.

I got the flight ticket to Georgia but it was in two days. I had to wait. I didn't have food, only water and a bathroom. I would have to survive with this for two days. I tried to talk to the police and explain to them that I didn't have food but they ignored me. I thought this was not legal but there was nothing else I could do. I decided to relax and find a way to handle the hunger. I thought this experience would be like a nightmare but it turned out to be a great experience.

I was alone with my thoughts. I thought about what was happening. It was happening and there was nothing I could do about it. I could take it as something good or bad - it was up to me. I started to analyze my own thoughts and saw that something is considered good or bad depending on how I interpret it. Whatever is happening is already happening and it's up to me to see it as good or bad. I started to think about what I consider bad and what makes me think that something is bad. Maybe I thought it bad because I learned that from society.

A person's definition of good or bad could be defined by their culture. It starts with the family, but the family learns from the people around them. A culture is a collection of ideas shared by a group of people. So who decides which ideas are accepted and which ones are not? What about my culture? After several years of living in Slovakia and traveling to many places, I felt like I didn't have an identity. Which culture do I belong to? If a culture is based on ideas, maybe I am just a bunch of ideas about who I believe I am.

I thought that all these ideas during these two days were just philosophical questions. When I think about philosophy, like in ancient Greece, I think of it as something that cannot be considered seriously, not as serious as theoretical physics. Some theories in physics are considered facts, and facts have been proven wrong in the past. So, if we think about something deep, like understanding who we are, it's considered philosophy. Some things that could explain our existence are categorized as philosophy. So, if scientists try to explain who we are, it will not be in the category of physics, it will be considered philosophy. Philosophy for Plato in ancient Greece was not the same as it is now; ancient philosophy is something like theoretical physics today. If we relate "philosophy" as something not serious, then anything considered philosophy would be considered not serious.

If a group of people starts to define a word as bad, eventually we will see anything related to that word as bad. But what influences a society? Family, friends, school, mass media and many other things. But family and friends learn from the same culture. So whoever decides what is in mass media, schools, and other things influences a society.

I didn't know how to meditate but those two days were like a long meditation. All the ideas I had during those two days would help me in the future. This experience in Belarus could be considered bad, but for me it was good. Maybe I needed an experience like this and the only way to experience it was by putting myself in that position. So I didn't see it as something bad. I saw it as something I needed.

I went to the country of Georgia. The people in this country were very welcoming. Since I wasn't prepared to go to Georgia I hadn't contacted anyone in advance. I stayed in a hostel. In the hostel I met a family from Australia. At that time, they had been traveling the world for ten years. So the two children in the family were born during the trip. These children were incredibly open and smart. They could speak many languages and they knew much about many cultures.

I talked to the family. It was great to hear their stories. They saw so many places and met so many people. They had so much to share. They both worked online and the children attended online school. I asked how it was possible to live like this for ten years. They really believed that it was possible, therefore they did it. When they said that I totally understood them because I was never sick, and I think it is mainly because I never believed I could be sick. I didn't know how it was possible but it happened.

Every time I met people who travel often I asked if they had seen anything unusual while traveling around the world. They said no. I really thought they would say yes. They had great stories but nothing unusual. I asked them if they had noticed hidden pyramids anywhere in the world. They said they met people who believe that when you are inside a pyramid the energy there is different. The tombs in Egypt were made for people who wanted to keep their bodies mummified so the body can be preserved. Eventually the spirit would come back to Earth and take the body to heaven. This is something similar to what Jesus did during the resurrection. These people believe that the energy inside the pyramids would help them take the body to heaven in an easier way.

The father of the family told me that he didn't believe in that but for me it was all very interesting. In the north of Georgia, there are some ancient structures. These structures are tombs but they are not pyramids. They are called dolmens, or portal tombs, and they can be found in many places around the world.

I didn't believe in heaven or anything like that but that was definitely an interesting theory.

After an amazing time in Georgia, I returned to Slovakia. I didn't feel comfortable with what happened in Iran. I decided to go back to Iran but this time, to avoid problems, I would have the visa before arrival.

I arrived in Iran without problems. The first thing I noticed was that people in Iran are incredibly nice. It was hard to find people who speak English. Even though I did not speak their language I could feel how nice they were to me. I felt welcome all the time. I felt so good that I even fell asleep in a park. One evening I was tired after a long walk so I took a rest in a park. I was so tired that I fell asleep and woke up in the morning.

In Iran the main religion is Islam but it's not the same Islam as the other Islamic countries. There are two types of Muslims - Sunni Muslims (the majority) and Shia Muslims (mainly Iran). I knew many Sunni Muslims but I was curious about the Shia Muslims. The main difference between these two groups is that Shia Muslims (Iran) believe that all successors of Muhammad must be direct descendants of Muhammad's family. The Sunni Muslims (the majority) believe that the successors can be elected by the Islamic people.

Iran has a different calendar than to the rest of the world. Most of the world has the Gregorian calendar which started to be used in the 16th century when a pope introduced it in Rome. Iran rejected this calendar. So in Iran, talking about days of the year could be a challenge.

I was curious about Iran. I visited several cities and towns but I was mainly focused on the ancient sites of the Persian Empire.

When I arrived at the ancient sites there were not many tourists, but there were some tour guides who spoke very good English. I spent all day with them. I asked all kinds of questions but nothing they said was out of the ordinary. I was already so used to hearing unusual stories that I was probably always expecting them. But this time nothing was unusual so far.

I was at the airport in Shiraz in the south of Iran. I was going back to Europe. While sitting on a chair waiting for my flight. There was an old man sitting next to me. He looked at me, smiled, and with fluent English he asked me if I had a good time in Iran. I said yes. I told him that I was very interested in the ancient sites. I asked him if he knew anything about the Persian Empire that was not included in the tours. He said that he knew only the basics about the Persian Empire. Later, on the plane, he was sitting in the same area as me. When they served food I ate everything except the meat. I didn't know what to do with the meat so I offered him the meat. He looked at me surprised and told me that he also doesn't eat meat. There was an empty seat in front of him so he invited me to sit there. We talked mainly about food. Then, after a few minutes, his face was more serious. He asked me, "What do you want to know about the Persian Empire?" In that moment I realized he was not an average person.

I didn't know who he was or what his job was but it appeared to me that he knew things. For a moment I felt uncomfortable and I tried to get back to my place. He noticed it. He got closer to me and tried to make me feel comfortable. He told me that the reason he didn't want to talk to me was because he thought I was a typical tourist. But he liked the way I thought so he was more open to me. I felt more confident so I asked about his job. He worked for the government of Iran. I asked him if he knew about any hidden pyramids in Iran. He said there was something like a pyramid called *Chogha Zanbil* but it's not hidden. It's just very old.

This place is very close to Iraq so it's related to Mesopotamia, the first civilization.

I thought he knew many things so I shared with him what I knew so maybe he could confirm my theories. He was not aware of many things I said except for one thing.

I asked him if he knew anything about some humanoid reptilian beings. He said, "Ooh, so you know about them. Yes, I know about them too." I asked him how he knew about them. He said that he didn't know so much about them. He knew more about the "Tall Whites" because they were on the news in Iran. I said, "The what?"

I said, "Wait, I know about amphibious beings, reptilian beings, smart velociraptors, small gray aliens and even plasma beings in Mexico, but not Tall Whites." The Iranian news said some extraterrestrial beings called "Tall Whites" were leading some parts of the United States government behind the scenes. He told me this with a lot of confidence like talking about something normal. I asked him why they are called this. He said because they look like humans but very tall and very white. I asked him if he knew about more extraterrestrial beings. He said that probably there are many and most of them are helping humanity but they are not supposed to interact with people.

It was too crazy to be real. When I returned home I was not sure about what to believe. I asked several friends if they could believe something like this. Nobody believed anything. I was a little bit divided. Part of me believed it and the other wanted to completely ignore it. It felt like a forbidden and unmentionable topic. If I did talk about it, they might say I was crazy. Still, for some, talking about drinking beer at the weekends was totally normal. To me, talking about alcohol was boring! Whilst I respected their decision to drink alcohol, it seemed to me that they could not accept that I thought and felt differently so I started to spend more time alone.

I noticed that I started to look at symbolism differently. Every time I saw something that looked like it might be symbolism I tried to connect it with something else. Many times I thought that I should just think normally like anyone else. I couldn't.

I played semi-professional football in Slovakia and the name of my team was "Dragons". I started to think about it. I was there when we chose the name for the team. There was no symbolism behind it. We just liked the name. I thought that maybe it was the same with the symbolism all over the world. I really didn't know what to believe.

The next story might sound funny. This is exactly how it happened so I will share it.

One night I was trying to get to sleep but I just wasn't sleepy. I tried to read something or watch videos on the internet. As a child I used to watch TV and things on the internet and sometimes I like to remember the old times, so from time to time I like to watch TV that I used to enjoy when I was little. One of these is programs is *The Simpsons*.

At that time, *The Simpsons* was becoming famous on the internet for their predictions. Many things that happened in the episodes of The Simpsons happened in real life a few years later. There are many examples of this. For example, they predicted that Trump would be president of the United States. They predicted problems when people tried to vote in the 2012 elections in the United States. Problems in the Greek economy. Problems related to corruption in *FIFA*. A Nobel Prize winner. Scientific discoveries. And many technological devices that didn't exist then but do now. The Simpsons were predicting many things several years before they happened. For many people, including myself, this was just an interesting coincidence.

While I was watching an episode of The Simpsons that night there was a part in the episode were two politicians were talking in front of an audience. Somebody got closer to the politicians and removed their masks, showing their real identity. The politicians, in fact, were aliens disguised as politicians. More specifically, the aliens were reptiles. Then the aliens started talking to the people saying that they had to vote for one of the two political parties. They were involved in both parties so no matter who the people vote for the aliens were involved.

This was very interesting. After everything I experienced, and now watching this, I started to believe that this was something serious. I started to take it more seriously. I wasn't able to talk to anyone about it but somehow I knew it was real. This sounds like *The Simpsons* convinced me, but I believe it was something bigger than that. I asked myself if everything I was experiencing was real.

I knew there were many non-human beings. I wanted to meet the ones helping humanity but I didn't know how to find them or how to contact them. They were not supposed to contact people.

A few years later I met them. I met some of the beings helping humanity. They were amazing. I will talk about them later.

Chapter 12 – The Cells

I always had a fascination for Africa, especially Sub-Saharan Africa. I went there several times to different locations. One of the things I found fascinating was the diversity in Africa. While traveling in Africa, I met other travelers. In most cases these were Europeans. We traveled together for a while in Africa. Some African people could not see the difference between my European friends and me. I have brown skin and my European friends are white. Some African people asked us if we were brothers. At first I thought that it was a joke but, in fact, some of them thought we looked similar. I totally understand that because my European friends and I didn't recognize the differences between the African people. We could just say they are all Africans. But there are many differences. Some African friends told me that I should pay attention to the shape of the faces. Africans can tell who is from West Africa and who is from East Africa, or they could even be more specific and guess which country they are from.

I started to think about my body and the people in Latin America. I didn't see it before but suddenly, after being aware of the differences in Africa, I was able to see the differences between Latin people. Some people even look Asian but I never noticed before.

Africans are more genetically diverse than the rest of the world combined. If we compare the DNA of a person in West Africa to the DNA of a person in East Africa it will be more different than comparing any African DNA with any other DNA in the world. This is amazing. Basically what I understood about this was that no matter how similar we think we could be, inside we are totally different.

I thought about what makes us human. A human being and a chimpanzee have very similar DNA but chimpanzees are not considered human. We even have similar DNA to a mouse. Maybe the idea that we were related to aliens was not so crazy.

When I was in Uganda I stayed with a family who told me about the Pygmies. The Pygmies are humans with different DNA. They are shorter than an average human. They exist in many places in Africa, but also in Asia and Australia. These people have different names but scientists have discovered that all these people are related. If these people are located in many places around the world, there should be a part of history that we are missing.

I went to the rain forest, somewhere between the Congo and Uganda, because I wanted to see how gorillas lived in the wild. In the forest, I saw small houses that seemed inhabited. Some Pygmies were living there. I saw them and I couldn't believe it. They have normal bodies like any average human, but much smaller, usually smaller than 1.50 meters (4.9 feet). Their bodies are not deformed or unusual. They are just smaller. I didn't know about them and suddenly, in the same week, I met them and learned so much about them. I talked to them thanks to a translator in the region.

Somehow, I knew that meeting the Pygmies would help me to understand other things but I would have to wait a few more years to understand them. According to scientists, the Pygmies originated in Africa then eventually moved to Australia. But the rest of humanity was so different than the Pygmies. People in the Netherlands are on average the tallest people in the world, and they are so different than the Pygmies. The human evolution theory doesn't sound right.

At least it didn't sound right to me after meeting the Pygmies. There had to be something that made us so different. Perhaps the idea of alien intervention didn't sound so crazy after all.

Human cells usually contain 46 chromosomes. From these 46 chromosomes, 44 are called autosomes, and two called sex chromosomes. These last two chromosomes define the sex of a person. Males have X and Y, and females have X and X.

Each human cell contains 46 chromosomes, or 23 pairs of chromosomes. There are cases where one of the 23 chromosomes, instead of dividing into two, divides into three. These cases in humans result in down syndrome. People with down syndrome don't experience ego, which is amazing. They enjoy things without competition. Every little moment is huge for them. They are really happy. We can learn a lot from them.

While traveling in Africa, I met several scientists and doctors. Most of them were researching diseases. These people told me very similar things but the one I remember most was in Malawi because I was given a lot of information. I stayed with a doctor from the Netherlands.

Malawi was one of the countries with more cases of malaria and other diseases in Africa and in the world. The doctor told me he went to Africa originally to investigate diseases. As a doctor, he felt ashamed to tell people that some diseases have no cure. He knew how to cure people with certain diseases but he was not allowed to do it. He told me that the cures for many diseases have existed for many years but they are not approved by any institution, making it illegal to use them. He even created his own products but he was not able to get the patent.

Usually, when I met interesting people with interesting stories I asked for unusual things. But in this particular case I didn't ask for unusual things. He told me everything because he deeply believed it. He believed that pharmaceutical companies knew about the cures but for some reason they don't want to approve them or talk about it. He even believed that some diseases in Africa are there on purpose but he didn't know why. He told me this because most of the diseases affect mainly African DNA. He even gave me some of his products. He told me how to use them in case I got malaria while traveling in Malawi. But I should be careful when leaving the country because the products were illegal. I told him that I avoided vaccinations because I believed that I could not be sick. He said that thoughts are related to some diseases. It was not the first time a doctor told me this. Every time I said this to any of my friends who were doctors they said I was just lucky.

I have a big problem with mosquitos. Wherever I go they follow me. Even if there are people around me, mosquitoes usually bite only me. I took his products but I didn't use them. I threw them away when I left the country. He advised me to avoid getting many vaccinations because some of them may cause harm in the long term.

I have several friends who are doctors. I asked them about all of these unusual cases of forbidden medicines. There were divided opinions. Some doctors said that it was possible. Some doctors didn't believe any of that. But most of them had something in common. They say that in most cases they don't cure patients - they just help them to heal. Patients cure themselves because the body has everything we need to be healthy.

Something I learned from these doctors is that our cells regenerate themselves very often. Old cells are replaced by new cells. Some cells are replaced in only a few days. This means our DNA is regenerating the information contained there. If we could have access to our DNA and change the code, we could delete certain problems from the root so they will not appear in the body. In other words, if we have a problem in our body, the problem could keep appearing because the DNA would regenerate also that problem. The solution would be to go to the DNA and change it there so it doesn't regenerate it again. The doctor I met in Malawi believed that somehow thoughts are related to our DNA. He believed that I could be healthy just because I believed so.

Another doctor I met in Africa talked to me about healing with electricity. This doctor was from China so I asked him if this had something to do with acupuncture. He was talking about a different type of electricity. He was talking about electromagnetism in the human body and it is somehow related to the electromagnetism of the planet. He said that working with this energy, we could heal ourselves from many things. We could even regenerate organs. This doctor also talked to me about cancer. He said that most doctors are trying to kill the cancer cells, when in fact these cells are part of us and should be treated differently using methods that already exist.

These affirmations were too much for me to believe so I wanted to prove him wrong. After research, I found out that actually he was right. Several doctors in the past, including very respected doctors, have talked about cell regeneration in humans. They openly say that humans could regenerate organs, including bones, like some animals do - especially salamanders. But I didn't understand why we don't use this now.

My personal point of view was that probably doctors were attached to what they have learned and they didn't want to try something new. Or perhaps they were not allowed. Otherwise, they could lose their license. So the problem was not with the doctors. It was with people who tell doctors what to do. This is similar to the school system. Teachers are told what to teach and that they should stick to the program. This is similar to mass media. They are not allowed to say certain things. The problem is not science. The problem is the people who tell the world what science is. The only area that is not controlled by governmental institutions is the church. They don't even pay taxes. So my thoughts about it got stronger. I believed that religion was something bigger than just a belief. And I wanted to find out if I was right.

I knew that something was happening in the world. Something was hidden and most people don't even know. I remember saying out loud, "I don't know what is happening in the world, but something for sure is hidden. I don't know what that is but I want to know no matter what."

Chapter 13 – The Download

I went for a trip to India. I wanted to see the amazing tourist attractions. At the same time, I wanted to know more about the culture. Some people advised me to be very open-minded because India was very different but I was ready for anything. I was used to seeing all kinds of things when traveling. Sometimes I had to sleep in airports while waiting for the next flight. Once I slept in a train station because the train departure was very early. A few times I slept outdoors when I was very tired. So I was ready for anything.

When I arrived in India, I found amazing people. I wanted to know more about their culture, religion, traditions, food, history and the nice people there. I tried to learn as much as possible. I had a great time in India. I went to several cities and I saw everything I wanted to see. I learned a few things about the culture in India but not as much as I wanted, but I was happy with that. After seeing all the places I wanted to see in India, I was ready to leave. I already had prepared a trip to Mount Everest, in Nepal. I was more excited about going to Mount Everest.

During my last day in India, I met a couple from Australia. They said that they were traveling around spiritual places in India. I ignored them. But they insisted that I should visit some of these places. I told them that I didn't have time. They talked to me about a place not so far from where we were located. The place was called Pushkar. They told me it was a magical place.

I didn't know about this place and I was not really interested. The couple were very insistent that I should go to this place. I really didn't want to go but since I had a few hours before my flight to Nepal, and that place was very close, I went.

I arrived in Pushkar but I didn't see anything special about this place. There was a market so I walked around but I didn't want to buy anything. I didn't know why the couple said that it was so special.

After walking for a few minutes, I started to feel something. I had to admit, there was a nice feeling in my body - something like the feeling I had when I was on the top of the pyramid in Mexico. After a few minutes I was still feeling it. I couldn't deny it. I stopped for a while and I started to talk to a woman selling something, just to have a conversation. After a few minutes talking, I asked her, "Can you feel something?" She said, "Probably you are feeling the lake." There was a lake in the middle of the town. She showed me how to get there. I couldn't deny it. I was feeling something similar to what I felt on the top of the pyramid in Mexico.

I sat down by the lake. I was there for a few minutes before a man came up to me. I thought he was asking for money but after few minutes of trying to understand what he wanted from me, I realized that he just wanted to tell me that I was in the right place at the right time. At least this is what I understood from his broken English. He just told me this and he left.

After he left, I started to have a great feeling around my whole body. It was much stronger than before. I tried to find a logical explanation, but I didn't know what it might be. For a few seconds I thought that maybe this was something spiritual and I didn't have to understand it. I think this was the first time I experienced anything spiritual, if only for a few seconds.

A few hours later I went to the airport in New Delhi. I was ready to go to Kathmandu, the capital of Nepal. I organized everything in advance with a travel agency on the internet, so I already had arranged a flight from Kathmandu to Lukla, the closest airport to the Mount Everest. My plan was to hike from Lukla to Mount Everest.

I arrived in Nepal but many weird things started to happen. The person who was supposed to wait for me at the airport didn't arrive. I called him. He said that he was having a lot of difficulties getting to the airport. First I thought he was trying to trick me, but I knew he was a reliable person. He was a friend of several friends and he was highly recommended. In the end, I don't know why he had problems getting to the airport and he couldn't meet me. I didn't pay anything in advance so I decided to look for other options.

I found some people organizing trips. I asked them to take me to Lukla but the people working with them were having difficulties booking flights. I could not fly to Lukla that day. I tried again the next day but I started to have problems with my cards. I tried to withdraw money. It was not working. After trying many options, they asked me to wait till the next day.

The next day my card was working but they had problems with their booking system so I had to pay with cash. I went to withdraw the money but there was a problem with the amount of money I could withdraw. I tried to fix it but after many problems with the bank I wasn't able to fix it that day. I didn't know what to do. I waited another day. The next day, there were no flights available. I didn't have many days left so I decided to skip Mount Everest.

I visited several places in Nepal. I even got a flight somewhere else just to see Mount Everest from a distance but I didn't go there. After visiting many beautiful places in Nepal, I was ready to go home. I felt like I had enough of Nepal and I was just waiting for the day of the flight back home.

I walked around the streets and I met a guy who said he was from Poland. We talked about Nepal and the beautiful temples. Then he talked to me about Kumari, a little girl who is considered a living goddess in Nepal.

Just after few hours of talking to me about her, we saw her. We were walking around the streets and then I saw a man carrying a little girl. There were a lot of people following them. I saw cameras and people trying to reach the girl. I was standing next to a chair and the man with the little girl came straight to the chair next to me. The little girl looked at me and then she sat down next to me. I was not sure what was happening so I decided to get away from the people. Then a woman came and put a red dot on my forehead. The little girl was Kumari, the living goddess of Nepal. My friend took this picture a few seconds after I was in front of Kumari. As you can see in the picture, Kumari was looking at me for a while.

My friend from Poland was excited to see Kumari. All the people were touching her feet. They said it was good for the soul. I just wanted to leave. My friend went to kiss Kumari's feet so I waited for him. Then he came and asked me to kiss Kumari's feet. I didn't want to but I knew my friend would insist for a long time so I went to kiss her feet. Actually I didn't kiss the feet. I just pretended. When I was in front of Kumari, she looked at me in the eyes. Again, I felt energy like on the top of the pyramid in Mexico.

I told my friend that I felt something. It was very unusual for me but for him it seemed to be normal. We left Kumari. We started to talk about temples. My friend asked me which temples I visited so I told him. Then he said, "You are missing one temple. You have to go. It is on a hill. It's called the Monkey Temple. It has this name because there are monkeys."

I told him that I was not interested. After seeing many temples in Nepal, I decided to skip that one. But he said that I should really go to this temple. It seemed that almost every person I met was pushing me to do things I was not planning.

My Polish friend took me to the temple. We went to the top. Then he said that he wanted to be alone so he left. He left me there alone. I didn't know what to do so I was just walked and took pictures. Then the most amazing thing happened. I was there, walking, and suddenly I started to feel a beautiful feeling around my body. It was something like what I felt on the top of the pyramid in Mexico, but this time was much stronger than ever. At the same time, I felt like I was receiving a lot of information through images and feelings. Everything happened in less than one second but I felt it much longer.

I didn't know what was happening but at the same time I understood everything. The beautiful feeling in my body stayed with me. I started to see everything differently. At the same time, I knew many things. I just knew them but I didn't know how I knew them. I got all the answers for all the questions I had but all the information was inside my body. I didn't know how to use words to describe them but I knew the answers. All the questions I had about hidden things in the world, I knew them all. But I didn't know how to use words to describe them. I just knew it.

I tried to remember if there was something besides the images and the feelings I got, but there was nothing except for something I heard with voice. I remembered that there was a voice saying, "Focus on love."

Somehow, I knew what the voice meant but when I tried to explain it to myself I didn't have words to describe it. But

I certainly knew the answer, for sure I knew it. I knew all the answers I was looking for. They were just inside my body.

I realized that I started to feel the people around me. I could easily tell who was happy or sad just by being close to them. I didn't have to look at them.

I was not able to explain with words what happened but I knew all about it. I also knew that this was supposed to happen at some point in my life. This was something I decided to experience. I knew this a long time before it happened. I knew it even before I was born.

When this happened, I didn't have the words to describe it. Now I know. That is why I am putting everything in this book. What happened in Nepal was something that happens to some people in one way or another. It is something that we choose before we are born. You can also choose to experience it during your lifetime. We don't remember right now because we lost our memories when we were born. But before we were born, we knew what kind of life we would experience. We chose it this way and we knew that we would forget. It is part of the experience we chose before coming here.

The place where it happens is not so important and it can happen several times during our lifetime. Everything comes at the right time - just as the guy from India told me. What I experienced is called a download. The same way you download information from the internet, you can download information from the universe into your body.

Chapter 14 – The Lights

I went back to Slovakia thinking that everything would return to normal but the feelings and the knowledge stayed with me. It was undeniable; something in me changed. I was so happy and thankful because I was able to finally understand many things I wanted to know. But since I received the information through images and feelings I didn't know how to say it with words.

I talked to a few friends about it, trying to express with simple words what I have learned. I knew it was very important information and I knew it could help people to understand many things about the world and about themselves. Every time I tried to talk about it I couldn't find the words, but I was sure about what I knew.

The reaction I got from my friends was not what I expected. Most of my friends that I shared the information with thought I was crazy and that all these things were not possible. Maybe it was because I was not able to explain it properly and with evidence. I didn't know if evidence existed and I didn't care. I was sure about what I knew. For me, it was very obvious. But everything was inside my body. I was not able to share it properly. I couldn't understand why I never saw it before, and I couldn't understand how nobody else noticed it before. Or maybe some people knew it and nobody was listening to them.

During the experience in Nepal, I saw some images of myself talking in front of an audience. I knew that I would talk about this information in the future. But in the images I saw, I was not alone. There were people presenting with me.

I saw a different version of myself with different ideas and goals.

Somehow I also knew that my life was taking a different road. I knew that most people would not understand me and that I would have to change the people around me. I knew that I would meet people who would understand me and they would help me to understand more.

I knew that the information was not so important. It was just a way for me to work better with my own body and the energies around me. I remember the voice I heard during the experience in Nepal, "Focus on love."

I was so sure about what I knew. I had no doubt. I couldn't explain it but I knew I was right. The conversations with my friends started to be boring to me. I was not interested in the same things anymore. In many cases, I could see how people were hurting themselves with their own thoughts. But I was not able to explain to them what I saw. Also, I was able to feel people. I knew that in many cases they were saying one thing but feeling something else. I realized that many people lie to themselves and others. I just knew it. This led me to spend more time alone.

Eventually, I started to be alone all day. I had an office job but my job only involved talking to a few people through email. So there were many days when I didn't say a single word during the whole day.

During my free time I was always alone, thinking about what to do. I wanted to do something, something big. I was alone most of the time but I didn't feel bad about it. I enjoyed it because I felt better when I was not feeling other people's energies.

I started to feel sad every time I was around people. I felt terrible for feeling like this. I thought I would not be able to be close to another person. I tried to spend more time outdoors. I was concerned that I would feel depressed if I was always alone in my room. Every time I went outdoors, I had to be careful and avoid many people.

While walking on the streets, I could feel when someone was having a good or bad day. I just had to be close to them. I felt this as if I was the person having a good or bad day. The feeling was close to my heart. But after few seconds feeling this, I realized that the feeling was not me, it was someone else. In the beginning, it was not easy to recognize when the feeling was coming from someone else. After a while, I got used to it and learned to sense the difference between my feelings and the feelings of someone else.

I was sure about what I was feeling but I tested it anyway. Sometimes I got close to people just to see if I could feel something. I remember one day, while I was walking around a market, I stopped to see some articles on a stand. There was an old lady behind me. She was talking to another person. Suddenly I started to feel a very strong, sad feeling. I knew immediately that I would not feel that way just like that so this feeling was coming from someone else. Since I was close to the old lady, I was sure that it was her. I got closer to her but I realized she was speaking Hungarian, a language I don't understand. I was sure that she was sad but I was not able to confirm it since I didn't know what she was talking about and I was not able to ask her. I really wanted to know so I asked people around me if somebody spoke Hungarian. I found someone who could translate for me. We came to talk to the old lady and she confirmed it. She was very sad because some family members were having a difficult time. Somehow, I managed to make her feel better. At the same time, it was a confirmation for me that I could sense other people's feelings.

I did similar things many times to train myself and recognize when the feeling was coming from me and when it was coming from another person. I realized that I was able to feel more when there was a big change. For example, the feeling was stronger when someone was very sad or very happy. Something very easy to recognize was when there was a mother with a baby. The feeling coming from the mother usually is a very strong, good feeling. This was because the mother has a lot of love for the baby. This reminded me of what I heard in Nepal, "Focus on love."

I also noticed that my reactions were different. Whenever something happened, good or bad, I stayed in the same state of mind regardless of what was happening in front of me. This helped me easily recognize other people's feelings because their feelings had no emotional impact on me. This led me to recognize which feelings originated with me, and which originated from other people. I felt like everything happening in front of me was something that would happen anyway, but my reaction to it was up to me. Again, I felt like I was in a video game. And it doesn't matter what happens in the video game, it was just a video game. It was just an experience, not something real.

In the mornings, when I woke up, the first thing I saw were geometrical figures. I was able to see my room but also some geometrical figures around. They were not physical. They were only in my mind. I could see them, but I knew that they were just in my mind. There were many figures and they were full of colors. This was happening almost every morning and I could see them only for a few seconds right after I woke up. Also, sometimes I would see a net made from hexagons. Many times I woke up before the alarm rang, so the first thing I did was to check through the windows to see if the Sun was up. Many times I saw the green net of hexagons outside, through the windows. There was a building outside of my window, and because I saw the net every morning, I thought that the building was green. One day, when I was totally awake, after several weeks of seeing the green net in the mornings, I observed the building in front of the window. It was actually gray but I always thought it was green. The way I was seeing reality was different. I wasn't sure if what I was seeing was physical or just in my mind.

If I told someone that I was seeing things differently in my mind, many people would think I was having hallucinations. But I was sure that everything was fine and it was meant to be that way.

I knew that many people were able to see things that most people don't see. If the person talked about it, this person would be taken to the doctor. Most doctors learned that these things are hallucinations and therefore they have to be cured. Most of the time these people get medications to stop seeing what they see. I knew that doctors would not comprehend any of this because they didn't have experience or knowledge to provide a basis of understanding. With the experience in Nepal, I knew that many things were manipulated - many things in all fields. I was sure that the Earth was being manipulated.

One evening, I was sitting on my bed. I thought about everything that was happening. Suddenly, two lights appeared in my room. They were floating and moving towards me. One light was purple and the other one was blue. Both lights were around the size of a football. The purple one was a little bit bigger than the other. The purple light started to talk to me. It didn't with a voice. It was internal - like telepathy. The lights were there to help me. I asked them who they were. They told me that they were angels.

When I received the download in Nepal, I knew that many types of beings exist. Some of them are invisible to us. But I didn't know what they look like. I never felt comfortable with the word *angel* and the angels knew it. They told me that since I didn't feel comfortable using the word *angel* I could call them whatever I wanted. They really didn't care. Only the purple one was talking. Somehow I knew it was a female. At least I visualized it as female. She told me that new people would come to my life and they would help me to understand what was happening. She also said I should not research any information because there was a lot of misinformation everywhere, even on the internet. She told me that I should meet my guides.

Every person has guides, or helpers. Our guides are non-physical beings that are assigned to us before we are born to guide us through life. They are with us at any moment, and they help us when needed, even if we are not aware of their existence or their messages.

The angels told me that my guides would help me to research what I need to understand. They said that first I had to learn how to recognize when my guides were talking to me. I had to find the difference between my own thoughts and something generated externally. Then, abruptly, they left.

I wasn't sure how to find the difference between my own thoughts and something external. The only thing that came to my mind was that I could do something similar to what I did when I was feeling people. When I was feeling people, I had to train myself to identify when the feeling was mine and when it came from another person. I tried to do the same with thoughts.

I started by observing my own thoughts. Every now and then, I stopped everything I was doing and I observed what I was thinking about. Sometimes it was something stupid but that was the thought I was having and I paid attention to the thought. It was hard for me to observe my thoughts. It took me a lot of practice but eventually I was able to be aware of my own thoughts.

Very often I stopped what I was doing and I asked myself, "What was the last thought I had?" Sometimes I knew what I was thinking. Sometimes I didn't remember. I kept doing it often.

After a while I was more familiar with recognizing my own thoughts and continued practicing. In fact, I still do it. I stop whatever I am doing and I observe the last thought I had. Sometimes I realize that the last thought was unusual - something that I would usually not think. So I tried to find the root of that thought.

I tried to observe the previous thoughts before the unusual thought. Sometimes I thought about something that led me to another thought, then to another thought, and eventually I got to the unusual thought. There was a sequence taking me to the unusual thought. For example, if suddenly I stopped and observed my last thought, I might realize that the last thought was "dog food". I didn't have a dog so why would I think about it? There was nothing around me that could make me think about dog food. Then I observed the previous thought before dog food. I realized that before, I thought about a friend. This friend once told me something about a dog. When I thought about dogs I thought about another friend who liked to feed street dogs. So in this case, there was a thought sequence leading me to the unusual thought.

I realized that this happens often. One thought takes us to another thought and we always relate one thought with another. There are some cases when the unusual thought has no relationship with any previous thought, or with anything around us. When this happens, there's a big chance that the message is coming from someone else - in most cases your guides. My guides didn't tell me how to do this. It came to me naturally. But I believe that somehow they were guiding me without me realizing it.

The lights appeared to me again, in the same place, in my room. Again, only the purple one talked. She told me that I was doing it correctly, but I should practice more and more until I am aware of my own thoughts all the time. I told them that it's not possible to be aware of your own thoughts all the time. They said it is possible but most people are thinking all the time. I should think less. They said thinking is an activity - something you use when you need it, but when you don't, you don't have to use it. I asked them how to do that. They said that there are many ways and meditation is a very good one. I told them that I didn't know how to meditate but they said that they would teach me in the future. I asked them if they were real or only in my head. They said that they didn't really have a form but they appeared to me as light because it was the easiest way for me to recognize them at that point. She told me that someday I would not be able to see them because it would not be needed. She said that every person has at least two guides and sometimes they talk to people. But since people are thinking all the time, people are not able to hear them.

I practiced the thought exercise more and more. Eventually I was able to catch some thoughts that were not coming from any sequence of thoughts. So I knew it was a message, probably from my guides. The thought was always related to a feeling. I knew it was them when the feeling was good.

After learning how to catch the external thoughts, or external messages, I started to follow them. Sometimes the messages were weird. For example, if I was walking on the street, sometimes I got a message to take a different road, a much longer road. Sometimes I followed the messages and sometimes I did not. But I noticed that in most cases, when I followed the messages amazing things happened, like meeting amazing people, or just witnessing something nice. Sometimes nothing happened, or at least I was not aware of what happened.

The lights appeared to me for a third time. They didn't say anything but I knew that it would be the last time. I told them I was ready to hear my guides more often and I wanted to understand more with their help. The lights told me that my guides would help me to find only accurate and useful information. There were many ways to meditate and I would learn them in the future. They showed me one meditation that day.

I asked them to show me a physical form other than light so I could understand better that I was talking to real beings. They told me that we could do that with a meditation and I would be able to see them. But I would be able to see them according to what my brain would understand. I don't know why I always felt uncomfortable with the image of angels. Maybe because I related them to the church and I was not a religious person.

They told me that I should lay down, close my eyes, and breathe normally. Then I should focus my attention on my nose. I should imagine that I was the oxygen coming in and out. I should not see the air as something external to me. It was part of me. I was the oxygen and the oxygen was me. After one minute doing that, with my eyes closed, I should imagine that I was looking at the walls of my room. I should visualize the colors on the wall. Then, after a while, in my mind, I should change the color of that wall. I could choose any color I wanted and visualize the new color. I could change the colors of the walls as many times as I wanted. Then I should focus my attention on the door in the room. I should visualize the door closed. And in the corners of the door I could see the light coming from the other side of the door. That light was them. I should invite them in. I should say mentally, "Please come in. You are welcome here," so I did. And in my mind, I saw the door opening slowly. There was a bright, white light on the other side. Then I saw them. The purple light became a beautiful woman. She was full of light. The blue light was behind the purple one. I was not able to clearly see the second person but I believed it was male.

Later I opened my eyes. The lights were not there anymore but I knew it was okay. This was a very personal and very important moment for me. I decided to share it as it was because it may help you someday.

After few days, I was able to catch some messages from my guides. Sometimes I asked myself something in my mind and they replied. Sometimes they did not reply immediately. Sometimes it would take few days to get an answer and sometimes I never got an answer. Probably I was not ready for that answer.

Once I was able to keep a communication with my guides. I asked them if the angels really look like the way I saw them. They told me that the only reason I saw them this way was because my brain related them to this shape, so that was the image I got from them at that moment.

I was ready to research information with the help of my guides. I wanted to know as much as possible but I spent almost all my time in the office and I didn't have time to research. At that time, I was programming an application on the computer. Sometimes I made simple mistakes and my guides told me there was a mistake. I was not sure how they could know about programming. I asked them if they knew about programming. They didn't know but they have access to another part of my brain. This part of my brain was able to see things even if I was not aware of it consciously.

I was very busy with work. I wanted to research but I didn't have time. I started to say out loud, "How I am supposed to research if there is no time for that?" Then the magic started.

I was at the office and I got a phone call. It was my manager. He was a very serious German man. He said that he was coming to Slovakia the next day and he wanted to talk to me. I thought that I would be fired. The next day we had a meeting. He said that for the next months I would not have much work to do but I had to stay in the same position. He advised me to work on personal things in the meantime. He also said that I would have to move temporarily to Croatia, then to Italy, but just to meet some people. I would have a lot of free time during this period as well. He advised me to use all my free time to do personal things. After leaving the meeting room, I heard my guides tell me, "Here you have it."

It was unbelievable. This was really happening. I followed his advice and I researched all the time with the help of my guides. In fact, I also researched at home so basically I was researching all day. My guides told me what to read and what not to read. There were times when they asked me to buy a book and read only two or three pages of that book.

There were many things that my guides didn't want me to read. I asked them why. They said that in many cases the information was not true and it could confuse me more. In other cases, the information was provided with an intent to scare or confuse people. So pretty much everything on the internet was not allowed for me. Only a few things were allowed. My guides told me that I should focus on messages delivered with love. I asked them if it was like the message I heard in Nepal. They said yes. I asked them if my experience in Nepal was something they did. They said that I did it. I did it to myself and I chose it that way before I was born.

After researching with my guides, I understood that the message "focus on love" has nothing to do with romantic love. Love is the way you experience something - the way you experience life. I visualized it like in the video game. You are full of power, so you go everywhere confidently. But instead of killing people in the video game, you share experiences with other characters. It's like a multiplayer video game where every character sees the world the way they want to see it. Even though they are in the same video game, they experience it in a different way. Love would be one way of experiencing the video game.

While researching, I realized that a lot of information on the internet was based on fear. In many cases the presenters were trying to cause fear and panic. Sometimes they just wanted attention. That was why my guides didn't want me to focus on them. Something that I found very frequently on the internet was people focusing on alien disclosure. I asked my guides many times about this and they told me very clearly that this was not going to happen, at least not anytime soon. I still see this often on the internet and usually many people follow this kind of information. In the end it's only entertainment.

The information shared with love is related to the person who shares it. A person who sees the world with love wants to share love - the way they experience life. Usually, a very good person thinks that everyone else is a good person. They experience life with love, so they see love everywhere. In other words, every person will follow what matches their energy. Please focus on love.

After a few months researching, I learned a lot. I was able to explain things using words that most people would understand, although not everyone believes it. I read articles and watched videos on the internet of amazing people who shared my perspective. It was great to know that I was not alone, but most of these people lived in other countries.

My manager came to Slovakia again. There were changes in the company. I had to report to a different manager. At this point, I was not interested at all in my professional career. I was totally focused on my personal development. I accepted the changes in the office. I had a new manager and a new desk. I asked my guides what was happening but they didn't say anything. The next day I went to the office and moved my personal things to the new desk. I noticed that all the desks in my old department were empty. I went to human resources to ask what was going on. They told me that the whole team was fired. But since I was already on another team, nothing would change for me. They told me that I should keep doing the same as before, at least for a few more months, so I kept researching with my guides.

I wanted to meet someone in the same city who would understand me. After some time, I found a person - a journalist who knew many things thanks to some contacts she had. We became good friends. She even wrote some articles about my trips. But we were not able to talk about spiritual things. She told me that she doesn't talk about these things in public because many people were not prepared. From time to time she tried to talk about them in some articles but she was very careful because she didn't want to lose credibility. After she wrote an article about my trips, many other people were interested in sharing my story. I was invited to be on TV in several countries. I also had interviews for newspapers and magazines. I wanted to talk about my experience in Nepal but I noticed that most people working in TV didn't have any idea what I was talking about. I tried a few times to explain everything with simple words but they just thought that I was talking about philosophical things. And probably they thought that I was crazy.

Communicating with people was difficult for me because every person sees the world in their own way. For example, if I wanted to say something about dogs (and I love dogs), what I mean to share is the feeling of love. If the other person doesn't like dogs, it can be interpreted as something not nice. In other words, I wanted to share a feeling converted into a word. The other person understood it according to their belief system. Therefore, we never communicate exactly what we want to communicate. This is usually why there are many misunderstandings when having a conversation.

In many cases, when there is a problem in a relationship, the problem is seen differently by every person. For example, a couple wants to solve a problem. Let's say that the woman wants to talk about it. She loves him. She wants to solve the situation so she wants to talk about it. This is her understanding of showing love. The man is different. His understanding of love is listening. If he has a problem, he wants to be heard. So if there is a problem, his way of showing love is listening to the woman. The woman may expect the man to talk because for her talking about the problem means love. But for him, listening without saying anything means love. So everyone sees the world in their own way. We never talk about the same thing because we talk using words and we relate the words according to our belief system. And every person has a different belief system.

Even though I was able to communicate with my guides, and there was evidence for almost everything I knew, there were times when I thought that everything I was experiencing was not real. There were times when I had doubts. One day I decided that it was enough and I would ignore all the information I received. I would ignore my guides and I would be just like any other person. Probably I would feel better this way. That night I had a dream. I still remember every detail of it.

In the dream I was running around some cornfields. I was running with a friend. Then we saw a couple also walking in the fields. After a while, we realized that the couple was following us. It looked like they were trying to hurt us. We started to run and the couple ran behind us. There was a big house and we decided to go in. Inside the house, there were many people. All of them were acting as if they were filming a movie but there were no cameras. These people knew that I was there but they were ignoring me. They kept acting, in every room of the house. I tried to talk to them. They looked at me and ignored me. They kept acting. I didn't understand why they didn't realize they were acting. I tried to explain that they were acting but they ignored me. Then I saw a very attractive woman. She was also acting. She was extremely attractive to me. I approached her. I wanted to tell her that she was acting but when she got closer to me I realized that she was more attractive than I thought. I didn't care that she was acting. I started to act for few seconds with her. Then the couple who was following us found a way to get into the house. We started to fight. I don't know how it happened, but I killed one of them.

I tried to get out of the house but it was not easy. All doors and windows were locked. The windows were covered with wood so I was not able to get out. After a while, I found a window without wood and I left the house. I was getting away from the house when I stopped for a while to wait for my friend. An old man approached me and said, "You know everyone is acting. You don't have to act anymore even if the woman is very attractive. When you are acting, you are even able to kill. You don't have to act." I wanted to get away from the house but I didn't want to leave without my friend so I started to shout his name "Victor". Then I woke up.

Since my childhood, I have had dreams where someone is trying to kill me. Most of the time I can fly in my dreams, so usually I just fly away from them. But this dream was different, very real, and I was not able to fly.

I don't have a close friend named Victor and I don't know why I said that name in my dream. But I took that dream as an analogy to understand that many people in the world are acting and they don't even know it. After that dream, I realized that what happened to me was important. I felt like it was my responsibility to share it and help others to wake up from acting. In other words, I should talk to the characters in the video game. I should tell them that we are inside a video game and we can communicate with the controller.

I realized that there was no way back. Once you know that you are acting you cannot act anymore.

Chapter 15 – The Skin

When I researched with the help of my guides, I discovered that several experts in physics believe we live in a holographic world, in a simulation, like a video game. I wasn't so crazy after all.

Also during the research, I read about Inge Bardor, a Mexican girl who was able to see with her skin. I knew this was possible but I didn't know anybody who was able to do it. She could read newspapers with several parts of her body. When someone gave her a picture, any picture, she could say what was in the picture. She had done it in public many times. People usually covered her eyes to make sure she was not able to see anything. She could say who was in the picture but also, she could say who took the picture, when, where, what time, and the past or future of that person.

Another thing that Inge Bardor was able to do was something called remote viewing. She could see objects that are in other places. She could see details of these objects even if they were on the other side of the world. It's like moving your mind to another location and being able to see objects there. It can be anywhere in the world or in space. Some governments know about this and use it to spy.

Remote viewing allows us to time travel, though not in the same way we see it in the movies. You cannot travel in time with your body but you can see into the past or future

Something similar to remote viewing is astral travel (or astral projection). It's when your spirit leaves your body and goes somewhere else. The spirit experiences other places. This is not a dream. The easiest way to determine whether you are astral traveling or dreaming is if you look at the clock. During an astral travel, every time you look at the clock you will see the same numbers. During a dream, you will see different numbers every time. Some people practice astral traveling, although I don't recommend it. If you don't know what you are doing, you may not know how to get back to your body. Some people, when they are astral traveling, see a silver cord connecting the body and the spirit, therefore they know how to get back to their body.

When I read about Inge Bardor, I immediately felt strongly that I should contact her. I hesitated, but the next morning I wrote to her. I told her that I was fascinated with her work and I would like to learn more if possible. I also told her that I could help her if she needs help. When I wrote to her I thought she would never reply. But she replied immediately. She said that she wanted to talk to me. We ended up having a conversation the same day.

I talked to Inge Bardor. We talked about many topics. It was great to talk to someone who understood everything I knew. I felt awesome. We talked like old friends. Then she said something I didn't expect. She just wrote a book. She wrote it in English and it had to be translated into Spanish. Also, she needed to create a new website and other things related to computers. She asked me if I had experience with any of that.

I had detailed experience with everything she told me. It was like a huge coincidence, or maybe she already knew it all. I told her that I wanted to help her with everything she needed. I felt like it was the right thing to do. I knew that she knew a lot of people so I asked her why nobody else is helping her with this. Many people wanted to help her but she was not able to work with any person. She was able to work only with certain people - people with a specific energy. She said that I had a good energy and she wanted to work with me. I took it as a huge compliment, especially because it was coming from someone like her.

After that meeting we met several times. We became good friends. We worked together on several projects. I also learned many things by working with her. I felt much more confident than before. I felt more prepared to share this information with whoever was open to it.

While working with Inge Bardor, I got to know many people who worked with her. They were amazing people and they understood everything I knew. One of the people working with Inge Bardor was a famous person called Drunvalo Melchizedek.

The first thing I read about Drunvalo Melchizedek was that he also talked to angels in the form of light. This made me curious about him and his life. I asked my guides if it was okay to read about him. I didn't even finish the thought in my head and they already said yes.

The first thing I noticed was that Drunvalo Melchizedek was not a normal person. I have some memories from some previous lives and some people I know also have some memories of previous lives. But Drunvalo Melchizedek had many more memories than an average person. I asked my guides why he was so different and they told me that he was not a human.

While researching Drunvalo Melchizedek's life I realized that he was a "walk-in". Basically, this happens only to a person who has a special agreement that was signed before birth. There was a person named Bernard Perona. He was born as a baby in a human body. Then, at some point, the spirit of Bernard Perona left the body and he allowed another spirit to come in. This new spirit was Drunvalo Melchizedek. This is not very common, and it happens for very specific reasons. Drunvalo Melchizedek came to Bernard Perona's body to help humanity.

I learned so much from Drunvalo Melchizedek. As I mentioned before, when I was traveling in Mexico I saw some orange lights in the sky. I mentioned that some people called them plasma beings. Drunvalo Melchizedek was in direct communication with these plasma beings. He said that they were very advanced beings who live underground close to crystals and they were helping humans. The orange light was not a UFO. It was light coming from the physical body of the being.

They used the energy around their body for transportation and they were telling humans how to do it as well. Several people had met these plasma beings and they said the same thing about them. They were very advanced beings who were teaching humans how the human body and the universe worked.

The plasma beings used to have physical bodies like humans do now. But they learned that they are pure light. Eventually they found the way to become light without the need of having a physical body. These beings are teaching humans the same because humans are also pure light. But since we don't have this information we are not aware of it.

Not having the knowledge makes it harder for us to understand that we are pure light. My guides told me many times that humans are pure light but I wasn't sure what they meant. I thought it was something symbolic but now I understand that they really mean that humans are literally pure light.

Drunvalo Melchizedek also talks about numbers and geometry and how it relates directly to our physical reality. This made complete sense to me because every morning I saw geometrical shapes. I always had the feeling that these geometrical shapes were the real world. In other words, if we could see the code of the video game it would be something like the geometrical shapes. He also talks about a special geometrical shape. He calls it the Flower of Life.

This figure can be found in many structures of ancient civilizations, even in hidden pyramids. It contains amazing mathematical and geometrical properties. According to Drunvalo Melchizedek, many things related to our reality can be found in this shape with mathematics and geometry. The number 1.618 appears many times in the Flower of Life.

I will not talk about more details because there are so many. What is important to say is that mathematics and geometry can explain our physical reality. This is similar to what Plato was trying to explain in Ancient Greece. All the platonic solids can be found in this figure, and many other figures.

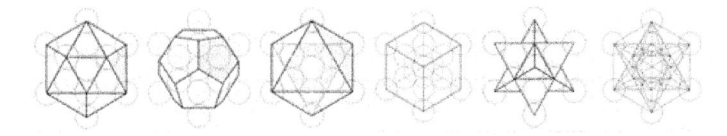

The Flower of Life also contains the shapes in which the cells of a human baby are divided.

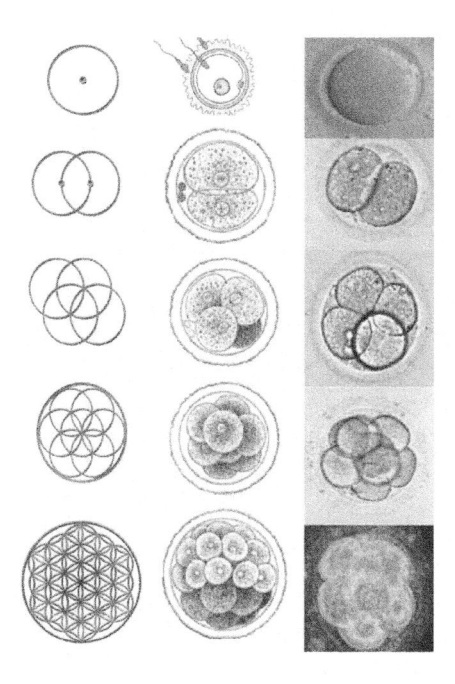

153

Drunvalo Melchizedek says that a star tetrahedron can be found around every person, and it should be rotating. But because most people are not aware of it, it doesn't move.

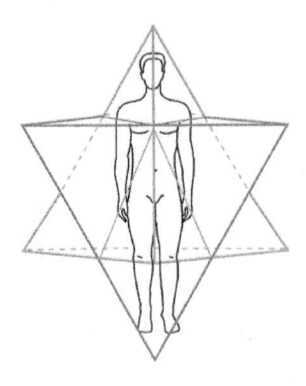

Drunvalo Melchizedek also says that the energy around the human body runs in the shape of a torus. This is a torus:

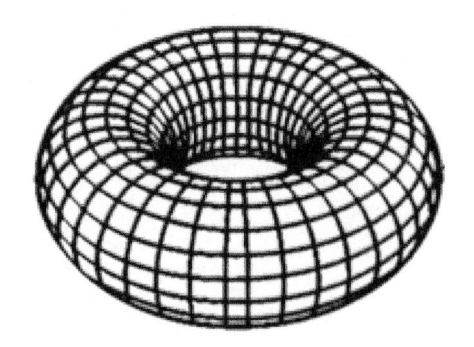

It is a very similar shape to Marko Rodin's coil. In fact, Drunvalo says that we have two tori around the human body, and the field is created by the heart. The star tetrahedron and the energetic fields are not visible, but they are there.

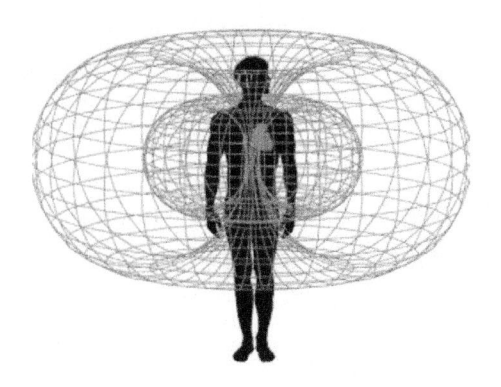

So basically our human body is a perfect example of how free energy from the universe works.

When I was close to people I could feel them. This is because I was inside the field of energy around their body.

I asked Inge Bardor how she could read information from people. She told me that she had access to the person's energy field and a lot of information is there. She said that this energy runs around the human body in the shape of a torus.

Information about the Flower of Life has been present in many monuments about the world. I have seen it several times during my trips. Many ancient civilizations knew about it. The information was kept as secret in the modern world until Drunvalo Melchizedek wrote several books about it. If you really want to learn more about this figure and its details you should definitely check the work of Drunvalo Melchizedek.

One day, when I was doing my research, I watched a video of Drunvalo Melchizedek talking about Inge Bardor. He said that during a presentation, Inge Bardor and another person had a misunderstanding. Inge Bardor wanted to be nice to this person so she said, "I am going to give you a beautiful gift." She pointed to the clouds with her finger, she moved the finger up and down, and the cloud started to divide. She split the cloud into two parts.

After I watched this video, I called Inge Bardor immediately. I asked her if the story about the cloud was true. She said yes. I asked her if she could teach me how to do it and she said, "Sure, it's very easy." She told me the following, "You have to imagine that you are the cloud. There is no separation between you and the cloud. You and the cloud are one. Then just decide to split."

Right after she told me that, I went to the window and I saw a cloud in the sky. I knew that I really had to do it properly so I put all my focus and intention into the cloud. Once I was convinced that there was no separation between me and the cloud, I started to imagine that I was splitting. I followed her instructions and it worked. The cloud split in two.

When that happened, I was not surprised. I didn't tell anyone. I just knew that it worked that way. I knew that we could do this with many things. A few days later, I split a cloud again and it worked exactly the same way.

After that, I felt like I could do it any time. I started to think I could demonstrate it to my friends. But my ego started to be involved. I tried a third time but it didn't work. I knew that it would never work if the ego is involved. I never tried again after that. I was happy with splitting the cloud the first two times.

Chapter 16 – The Words

When I got the download in Nepal, I was not able to communicate properly what I knew. I didn't have the words. After several years of research with the help of my guides, I felt more confident and ready to share the information. I will share it with you here.

At this point, you may have realized that the name of the book and its chapters are very general. This was done on purpose. There is no hidden message or anything secret. I want to share everything as clearly as possible. I have done it this way so there is no judgment of the titles without reading everything first.

I was advised to give this book a simple, clear title so it can reach more people. It's not intended to reach millions. It is intended to reach the people who can appreciate it. As I said at the beginning, not everyone will accept my story. If only one person gets benefit from this work it was worth it. This book has helped me to put all my thoughts together so it has already been worth the effort. I hope you can get something from it as well.

I will share a few things that many people may already know but some others may not. I will share it anyway. Please take this information with love. It helped me so much and I hope it can help you too.

Humans are not the body or the brain or anything physical. If you want to visualize a human being in a physical way, the closest thing would be pure light - literally. Humans are consciousness or awareness. You could also say that we are souls or spirits.

We are the observers. For example, sometimes when we are dreaming, suddenly we wake up and realize that it was a dream. Waking up doesn't mean that the dream was not real. This physical world seems more real than the dream, but both are real because we are the experiencer - the observer. During the dream we are experiencing another reality without our body, but it is still us. We are experiencing that reality at that moment. When we wake up, we are experiencing this physical reality using the body. We are the observer and the experiencer. We never die. We live forever. We may experience different realities but since we are the experiencer we literally never die.

Imagine that the physical body is like a battery similar to the one we use for electronics. The battery is made so electricity can run through it. The human body is like this. It's the vessel that we are using to experience life. However, in this case, we are not the battery. We are the electricity running through the battery. We are all the same energy. We are just having individual experiences using our body. The electricity is running so fast that it is, in fact, everywhere at the same time.

As you can see, the electricity that runs through the battery is everywhere. It is the same with consciousness. It is everywhere - even in space. The whole universe is a conscious being and we are part of it. In fact, we are the universe. In other words, the electricity running through the battery is the same electricity running through every battery. We are all the same energy. We are just having individual experiences.

The planet is also like a battery because we are the children of Mother Earth. Our bodies are an extension to her. The magnetic north and south poles are like the poles in the battery. The energy runs all the way up. Then from the outside it goes down then all the way up again. We can see the electromagnetism entering and leaving the planet close to the north and south poles in the *Aurora Borealis*, or *Northern Lights*. The movement of this energy forms a torus similar to Marko Rodin's coil. We could say that we and the planet are free energy devices. We just need to allow the energy to flow through us.

There is another type of coil that has so many benefits for the human body and the environment. It's called an Acu-Vac coil.

This coil has been used to clean the pollution in cities and to heal the human body. It changes the energy wherever it is used. Eventually, it changes the physical reality around it.

We are all the same energy. There is no separation between us and other living beings. We may have different bodies, but we are the same electricity running through different types of batteries. Even our guides and other beings are the same energy. Or if you want to look at it in a more religious way, God is everything and everywhere. God would be the electricity and we all are God. We are not part of it - we are it.

Since you are God, you are a creator. You can create anything - literally. You can attract anything you want into your life. Many people know this as the law of attraction. This is because time and space don't exist. We experience time and space but they are not real. Also, we understand time as something linear. There is no time. This concept can be very hard to imagine but I will explain it using an analogy that my guides showed me.

Imagine that you are a little fish. There is nothing around you. You cannot see anything. It's just you, swimming in the middle of nowhere. Suddenly, a drop of water passes in front of you. When the drop of water passes in front of your eyes, you are able to see the world inside that drop of water. It passes very fast, but you saw something for a very short time. Then another drop of water passes in front of you. Again, you are able to see something. Then several drops of water pass in front of you, one drop of water after the other. Every time a drop of water passes in front of your eyes, you are able to see something. So when several drops of water pass in front of you, you are able to see several realities. The reality in one drop was very similar to the previous one. They are not exactly the same, but very similar. Now, imagine that there are many drops of water passing in front of you, one after the other. Now you have something like a movie passing in front of your eyes. This is similar to our reality.

Imagine that we live in a river and there are millions of drops passing in front of us all the time, one drop after the other. Every drop is very similar to the previous one so we don't notice the difference. The current in the river is very fast so there are many drops passing in front of us all the time. There is nothing we can do about it. The drops are always moving.

Einstein's theory of relativity says that if you move at the speed of light time will stop. Imagine that the fish starts swimming in the same direction as the current in the river. If the fish could swim as fast as the speed of the current, the fish would stay in the same drop all the time, therefore time would stop for the fish, although time really doesn't exist.

In our reality, what we see is not a solid physical world. There are millions of parallel worlds and they are passing in front of us right now. In other words, the world you experienced one minute ago is not exactly the same world you are experiencing right now. It may look very similar but it's not the same.

Every reality you can imagine already exists somewhere in a drop. If you want something, you don't have to attract that drop (parallel reality). You have to move there.

Since we are the electricity running though the battery (the body), we have to change the energy in our body so we can move to that reality we want. Energy is just vibration so we have to change the vibration in our body.

When we are born, our body starts to develop a certain vibration. During our childhood, the vibrations increase. Eventually at some point during our adult life, our vibrations stop increasing. This happens to many people and they keep this vibration in their body for the rest of their lives. Some people continue to increase their vibrations during their adult life. This is when they keep themselves active and experiencing new things. This also happens after big changes in their lives and they are forced to change their lifestyle. That is why is important to keep trying new things even during our adult life. We should keep developing our imagination all the time. We can do this by doing activities where we use our creativity. We should be like children even during our adult life. We never stop being children, we just learn how to behave in front of others. Even in the Bible, Jesus told his people that they had to be like children.

One day I was walking on the street. I was talking to my guides. I asked them if they could better explain to me how realities work. They told me, "Look at this car. Look at it." I didn't see anything unusual. It was a normal car. Then my attention went to the front part of the car. Something unusual was there. The brand name of the car was Volvo. I noticed that the logo of Volvo was different. There was an arrow in the logo and I didn't remember seeing that arrow before.

My first thought was that the company changed the logo at some point. But my guides told me that the company didn't change the logo. I was in a different reality now. In this new reality, the logo has an arrow. The memories I have of the logo without an arrow were memories from a different reality, where the logo was without an arrow. But right now I was in a new reality where the logo has an arrow. In this new reality, the logo always had an arrow.

I checked on the internet for the history of the Volvo logo. I realized that the arrow was always there in this new reality.

| 1930 | 1959 | 2006 | 2014 |

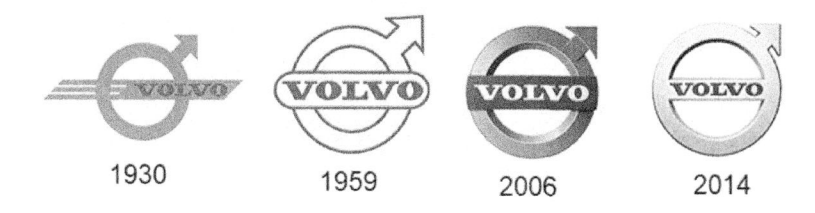

I remember the logo without an arrow but it is because I was in a different reality.

In other words, a few years ago I was in a drop (reality) where the logo of Volvo did not have an arrow. Then, after some time, I moved into a different drop (reality) to the point that I arrived at a new drop (reality) where the logo has an arrow. Since we move through realities all the time and we don't even notice, I never noticed this small change.

I noticed that some people on the internet talk about changing realities. And some people don't know why this is happening. Nelson Mandela, the former president of South Africa, died in the 80s. This is how many people remember it. Many people remember watching the news reports saying that Nelson Mandela died in the 1980s. In 2013, the news said that Nelson Mandela just died. Many people were confused. They remembered Nelson Mandela dying in the 1980s, but now the news said that he died in 2013. This is because many people were experiencing a reality where Nelson Mandela died in the 1980s. They moved through realities, and eventually, they moved to a different reality where Nelson Mandela was still alive and died in 2013.

After this, many people started to notice changes in their realities. Some people thought that they were remembering incorrectly. Some other people were convinced that something weird was happening. Many people started to notice similar cases and they started to call it the Mandela Effect.

Something similar happened with the logo of Coca Cola. Many people remember the logo of Coca Cola having a hyphen (-) between the words Coca and Cola. It was something like this: Coca-Cola.

Then they found out that the logo of Coca Cola was different. It never had a hyphen (-). Instead, there was a dot. Many people don't remember a dot because they were in a different reality. Right now, if you check on the internet for the history of the logo of Coca Cola, you will realize that the hyphen was never there. It has always been a dot. So when people saw the hyphen symbol, they were in another reality, not this one. This one has and always had a dot. Because we move through realities, sometimes we don't notice. Many things you remember from your childhood don't exist in this reality now. It could be anything - even people. We are all creating this together. We can move to any reality we want. It already exists somewhere. So if we are experiencing this reality now it's because we are creating it together.

It doesn't happen only with the logos. It happens with movies, songs, people and even countries. There is a famous story of a man who arrived at an airport with a passport from a country called Taured. The passport seemed to be legit because it had stamps and visas from many countries. The man claimed that he was from Taured, a small country between Spain and France. He showed them on the map, but he pointed at Andorra. Indeed, Andorra is a small country between Spain and France but Taured isn't the name of that country. The story says that the man disappeared after being locked in a room for interrogation.

I don't know if this story is totally true or not, but I wouldn't be surprised if something like this happened.

The best example for me is from the movie Snow White. In the movie, I remember when the witch was talking to a mirror. The witch said, "Mirror, mirror, on the wall, who's the fairest of them all?" Many people around the world remember it this way, even in other languages. But now, in this reality, it says something else. It says, "Magic mirror on the wall, who's the fairest of them all?" There are many examples of these changes in realities and they happen often. So, literally, you are not the same person as yesterday or a few minutes ago. Everything that really exists for us is in the now.

In the future, this will happen again and again. People are doing it with their thoughts. For example, if a lot of people start to remember a global event like September 11th, there is a chance that something related to the history of the event will change. Or in other words, we will move to another reality where it is already different.

A very good way to move to a different reality is to start visualizing yourself there. Not in the future - now. There is no past. It is just a memory of what we experienced. But we are not the same person anymore. We are literally a new person. If we believe that we are still the same person as before, it will be difficult for us to keep moving to a new reality where we are a new person. It's important to visualize yourself as if it is happening now. If you visualize something in the future, you will be acknowledging that you don't have it now. Therefore, you will keep attracting the lack of what you want.

When I moved the cloud, I had to become the cloud because we are the same consciousness. The planet is a conscious being - literally. Mother Earth is alive. Our human bodies exist because of her. This concept may be difficult to understand. This is because we have learned that the only living beings on the planet are humans, plants, and animals. But in fact, the planet is alive and we are alive because of her. Animals are alive because of her and plants are alive because of her. There are other things that are alive. For example, crystals are alive.

Crystals are formed in rocks. The planet is a big rock. The planet has several layers in its interior. The crust of the planet contains many crystals. In other words, if you could look at the planet cut in half, you would see that you could find crystals of all kinds just a few kilometers under the surface.

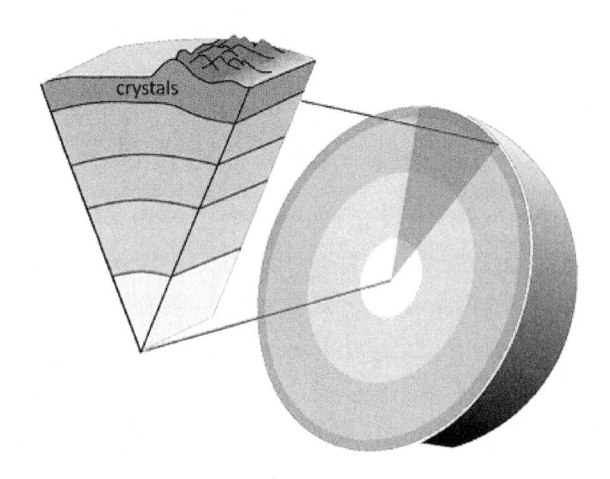

You can talk to crystals if you learn how to do it. You can do it by feeling them. It's like talking to someone who does not speak a spoken language. They talk to you all the time, but since we don't understand their language we think they are not talking.

Sometimes we can be lazy and just expect that everyone has to speak our language or communicate in a spoken language because we are used to it. But communication can be done in so many ways. A person who is not able to speak tries to communicate. They have to learn a specific language to communicate with other people. If someone wants to communicate with them, it's necessary to learn the same language. This happens with the crystals. We have to learn their language, which is not a spoken language. To speak with the crystals, you have to stop thinking so your mind is not busy with other things. Talk to the crystals. They are very conscious and they are very smart. They have so much knowledge and you can learn so much from them. Crystals and dolphins are some of the best teachers with a physical body that you can find on Earth.

When you talk to crystals, wait for some feelings, images, smells, or even words. It may take you some time to listen to them, but the more you interact with them the easier it becomes.

The human body is made mainly of carbon and oxygen. That is why it is so important to learn to breathe properly and breath consciously, being aware of your own breath all the time. Humans and animals are made mainly of carbon and oxygen, but life also exists in bodies made of silicon. Silicon is the element next to carbon in the periodic table of elements.

Silicon can be found in rocks and crystals. The crust of the planet contains rocks and crystals, so therefore, bodies made of silicon are also alive. Most scientists believe that what makes something alive is a body that can move, grow, reproduce, and die. But there are animals that can live forever, like the jellyfish. They don't die.

Some humans have special conditions that don't allow them to move, grow, or reproduce. It does not mean that these humans stop being alive. Many scientists don't talk about consciousness because it is something that scientists are not sure how to explain. Consciousness is a forbidden topic in the scientific community. There are scientists who talk about consciousness in a very scientific and serious way, but they aren't recognized as legitimate, even if the information can be proven.

Mother Earth is a big crystal. You can communicate with Mother Earth. She is alive and she knows many things about you. She talks to you often. She talked to me when I was a child, when I wanted to leave my house. She really loves you. If you are alive right now it's because of her. This may sound weird but I am not exaggerating. Once you talk to her you will understand.

In the north of Mexico, huge crystals were found underground. These types of crystals can be found in many places around the world, but they will be found when Mother Earth feels like it's the right time. If they are found, it's because Mother Earth allowed it. Otherwise, it would never happen.

Crystals can save information. This is probably hard to understand. Imagine you take a USB memory to someone in the last century. They will not be able to read it. Crystals are similar. You have to learn how to communicate with the crystals to get information. The Mayans were doing this. There are 13 famous crystals where the Mayans saved information about our history. Many people know them as the crystal skulls.

During my childhood, I was not interested in the history of ancient civilizations in Mexico because deep inside, I didn't believe in the official story. If they had told me about Atlantis in primary school, probably I would have found it much more interesting.

Under the Sphinx in Egypt, deep inside underground, there is also information about our past. This information has been kept there for more than 12,000 years. Someday humans will have access to this information and the history of humanity will change forever.

The Sphinx is looking east towards the Orion's belt.

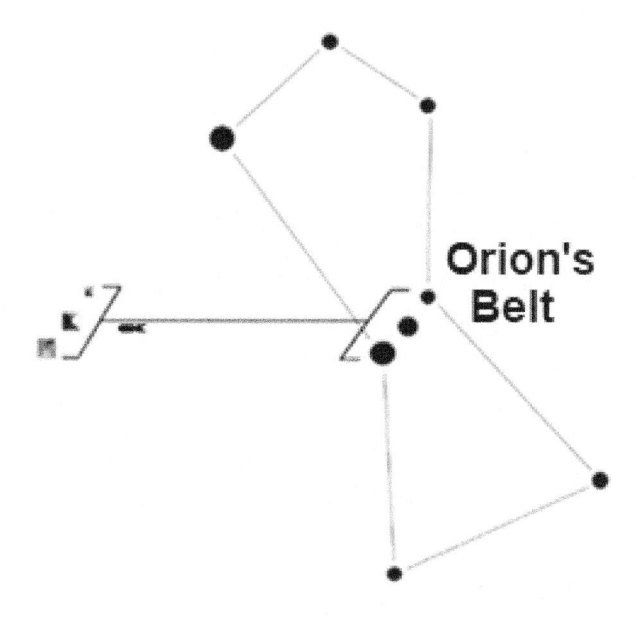

When the Sphinx was built, we were transitioning from the Age of Virgo to the Age of Leo. That is why the Sphinx looks like a lion, its related to the Age of Leo.

It takes around 26,000 years for the precession of the equinoxes to make a complete round. The 26,000 years are divided into 12, so around every 2150 years, there is a new Age.

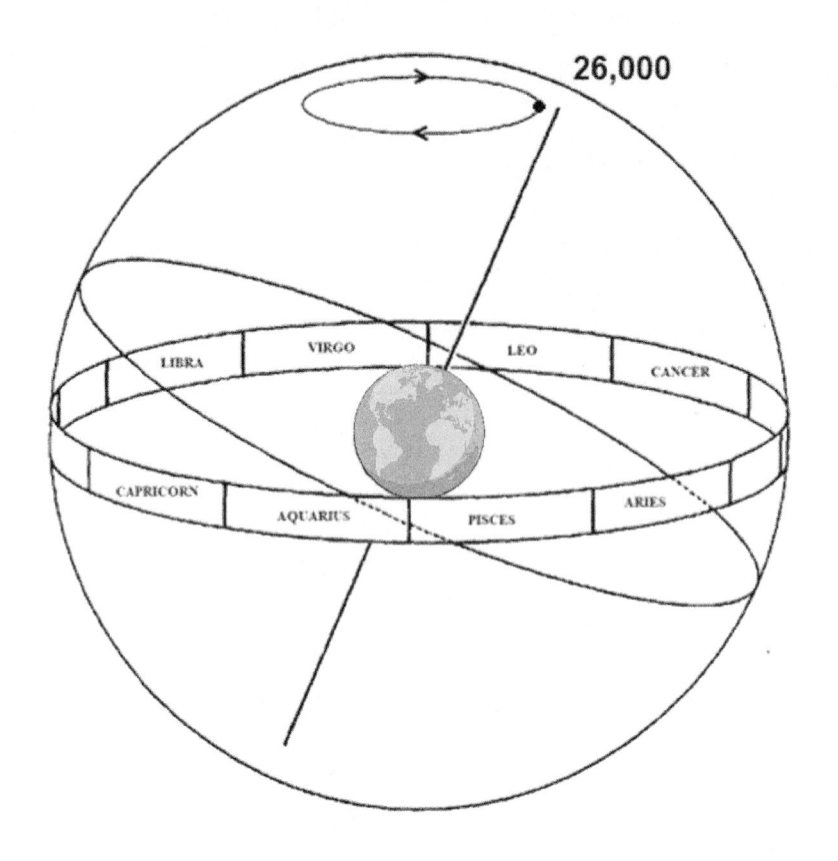

We are moving from the Age of Pisces to the Age of Aquarius. Many people who are into spiritual beliefs are known as New Age people. This name comes from this concept.

The church mistranslated this concept from ancient books and they presented it as the end of the world. This was used to cause fear. There is no end of the world. It's the end of one Age and the beginning of another one.

We are not able to retain so much information today because we are always distracted with the world around us. Most people get influenced by many things happening around them. This is because most people believe that our thoughts happen automatically and we don't have control over them. This is not true. We can control our thoughts all the time.

We forget things easily. This is something normal in humans. If you really want to remember something, it is better to write it down somewhere where you will remember. As I said at the beginning, I decided to write this book to put all my ideas together, but also because I don't want to forget.

Many people believe that we should feel good or bad according to our experience. For example, if you see someone have an accident we should feel bad. If we see someone beautiful we should feel good. In other words, many people believe that our emotions depend on what we experience. This is not true. It's the opposite. Our experience is directly created by our emotions. We can control our emotions therefore we can alter our reality.

Our thoughts create a vibration in our body. We understand vibrations as feelings. Feelings are just the translation for the vibration we are currently experiencing. There is no difference between thinking about something and doing it. In both cases, you create a vibration in your body. This energy stays with you regardless if you do it or you just think about doing it. There are high vibrations and low vibrations. Fear is the lowest vibration and love is the highest.

If you are scared, your reality will be different. You don't trust many people. You are in need of safety. Therefore, your priorities are different. When you experience love, you see everything as beautiful. You can even do things that you would never do otherwise. The physical reality around us is the same as for other people, but the way we experience it changes.

So, in few words, thoughts create the feelings in our body, and the feelings change our reality.

Feeling good or bad is our response to things, not a result of what we see in our reality. Let's say you are watching a horror movie. When you watch the movie, you may get scared of what you see on the screen. If you look at the situation, the movie is not sending you the feelings. Your thoughts are creating the feelings because you relate what is happening in the movie to something scary. So when your thoughts create your feelings, your reality is affected. But the movie itself is not doing anything to you. It's just a screen.

The same happens in our daily lives. What we see is just a screen. What we experience is a reflection of our thoughts. If we can control our thoughts, we can more easily have the experience we want. Also, we have to learn how to stop thinking. We can think when we need it and stop thinking when we don't. Meditation is probably the best option to stop thinking, although it can also be used for many other things. Sometimes we think that we are not thinking, but we are. Once you stop thinking, you will be somewhere else and you will see and hear things that are not from this physical world. You will probably hear your guides.

When I say the word love, I am not talking about romantic love. I am talking about unconditional love for all life. Many times, in a relationship, love is conditional. Couples love each other as long as they do certain things. If one person does something the other doesn't like, the relationship is over. It was conditional love.

The best examples of unconditional love are when you see your baby for the first time, and the unconditional love we receive from a dog.

If you have a partner, this may be interesting for you. When you see your partner and you experience love, it's not because your partner is sending you love. It's because you are using the image of your partner to allow yourself to experience love. This is similar to when you watch a movie.

In the same way that there are vibrations in the human body, there are vibrations in the universe. The human body can see only the vibrations that are inside our visible light. We don't see UFOs because they have different vibrations and our eyes cannot see them. Sometimes they change their vibrations and we can see them, but eventually, they change their vibrations again and become invisible to us.

We can visualize this as if we are watching TV. If we change the channel, we see another show. But this doesn't mean that the previous channel disappeared. It is still there. It's just that we are not tuning into that channel. This is similar to our reality. There are several channels available to us, but we are tuning into only one of them.

Before we start talking about dimensions, there is something we have to clarify. I will be using the word "dimension". This word does not refer to the concept related to quantum physics. String theory is a theory that attempts to reconcile gravity and quantum mechanics. The term "dimension" is used in this theory, but it is not the same "dimension" I am referring to. There is also the superstring theory that talks about 10 dimensions. M-Theory talks about 11 dimensions. In these theories, you can find the word "dimension". It talks about dimensions X, Y, and Z as the first three dimensions we see in our physical world with the 4th dimension being time. The concept of dimension I am going to be using is not the same as the one used in these theories.

Although, there is something interesting about string theory and M-theory. They say that everything in the universe is made of strings. If you go deep into the smallest particles, you will find strings of energy vibrating. The universe is in fact made of vibrations, but these vibrations are not physical.

In the universe, we perceive 12 dimensions. Inside every dimension, there are 12 mini-dimensions. You can visualize it as a building of 12 floors. Every floor is a dimension, and inside every floor there are 12 rooms, totaling 144 rooms.

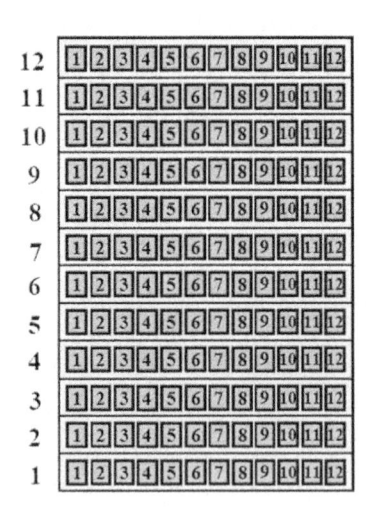

Floor	Rooms
12	1 2 3 4 5 6 7 8 9 10 11 12
11	1 2 3 4 5 6 7 8 9 10 11 12
10	1 2 3 4 5 6 7 8 9 10 11 12
9	1 2 3 4 5 6 7 8 9 10 11 12
8	1 2 3 4 5 6 7 8 9 10 11 12
7	1 2 3 4 5 6 7 8 9 10 11 12
6	1 2 3 4 5 6 7 8 9 10 11 12
5	1 2 3 4 5 6 7 8 9 10 11 12
4	1 2 3 4 5 6 7 8 9 10 11 12
3	1 2 3 4 5 6 7 8 9 10 11 12
2	1 2 3 4 5 6 7 8 9 10 11 12
1	1 2 3 4 5 6 7 8 9 10 11 12

Right now, we are on the 3rd floor in the room number 4.

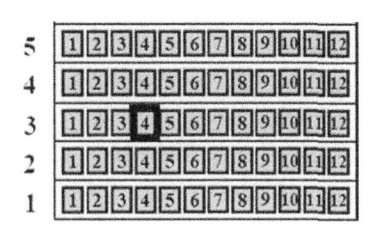

5	[1][2][3][4][5][6][7][8][9][10][11][12]
4	[1][2][3][4][5][6][7][8][9][10][11][12]
3	[1][2][3]**[4]**[5][6][7][8][9][10][11][12]
2	[1][2][3][4][5][6][7][8][9][10][11][12]
1	[1][2][3][4][5][6][7][8][9][10][11][12]

Some people refer to the floors as dimensions or densities. Some people use the same words to refer to the rooms. This can cause confusion. To avoid confusion, I will refer to the floors as dimensions and I will refer to the rooms simply as rooms.

Right now, we are in the 3rd dimension, room number 4. Everything around you, everything you can see with your eyes - your house, the table, the sofa, the sky, this book, even your own body, is part of the 3rd dimension, room number 4.

We (humans) used to live in the 4th dimension. We made a lot of mistakes when we were living there so we had to learn from our mistakes. The only way to learn was to come here to the 3rd dimension, room number 4. I will talk more about it later. For now, it's important to know that we used to live in the 4th dimension.

Moving from one room to another might be possible for us to do, but we would need technology that alters frequencies in our reality. Many beings can move between rooms. It is about frequency. They can change their frequency and they become invisible to us. Or in other words, they will be outside our visible light. Some governments have done experiments with this. In 1943, the US government tried to change the frequency of a ship. They did it. The ship became invisible for a while. It's known as the Philadelphia Experiment.

Moving between dimensions is different. Only very advanced beings can do it.

The universe is like a school. Basically, we have to experience all levels and learn how to love everything in the universe. This is probably hard to understand but everything is related to energy. Since many people are not used to feeling energies, the only thing we can use to understand it is unconditional love.

When we die, our spirit goes back to the 4th dimension, room number 10, where we used to exist. But right now we are learning a lesson so our bodies exist in the 3rd dimension. Some people may refer to the 4th dimension as heaven. Our spirit moves between the 3rd and 4th dimensions. Moving our spirit with our bodies between these two dimensions is a very different thing but it is possible. I will talk about it later.

Every time we come to the 3rd dimension, we take a new body. We are born here as babies. Every time we come to the 3rd dimension, we forget about our life in the 4th dimension. When we are children, during our first four or five years here, we still have some memories but eventually we start to forget. We are supposed to forget our life in the 4th dimension because it's part of the lesson.

When we die and we go back to the 4th dimension, we recover all our memories. We evaluate our experiences and we decide to come back again. Usually, in the next life, we choose to be born in a place and with people who help us to keep learning. We choose our family and we choose the place we want to be born. We come to learn love. For example, if you didn't learn to love animals in the previous life, you may choose to come the next time as a farmer. We also can come as male or female, depending on what would better help us to learn the lesson. We choose our parents. Everything is under agreement. Our mother agreed to help us to develop our human body inside her body and to eventually be born.

When you die you don't suffer. In fact, it's a very beautiful process. I have memories of some times when I died in previous lives. It feels as if suddenly you are floating in a very soft material and there is nothing to worry about. You just relax and you feel like everything is fine. It's really a very peaceful process.

Many things that you do during your life are things that you wanted to experience. These experiences may help you learn a lesson or you may need them to get some skills that you will use later. For example, in my case, I decided to be a teacher to get experience talking in front of people. I know that I will be giving presentations in the future where I will be talking about what I am writing in this book. Also, I moved to Europe so I could learn languages and because I used to have lifetimes in this part of the world with some tribes called the *Cotini* and *Boii*. The *Cotini* people used to be in the area now known as Slovakia. And the *Boii* people were in the area that is now the Czech Republic. The region called *Bohimia*, in the Czech Republic comes from the name *Boii*.

The *Boii* and *Cotini* were Celtic groups that lived in Europe before the Roman Empire. We believed in spirits and life in other dimensions. We didn't have temples, nature was our temple.

In Slovakia, some coins from the Celtic groups were found, they are called *Biatec*.

Many coins were found with different names and figures. The name *Biatec* is the most common name, therefore the coins are named this. It's believed that Biatec was the name of a king. There is not so much information about the Celts because the Roman Empire destroyed almost everything about them, but *Biatec* was not a king. Some of these beings were not humans, and they were represented as animals or symbols.

Some of the beliefs from the Celtic culture were given to us by beings from other dimensions. There are similar figures in England and Peru, these figures are ancient geoglyphs.

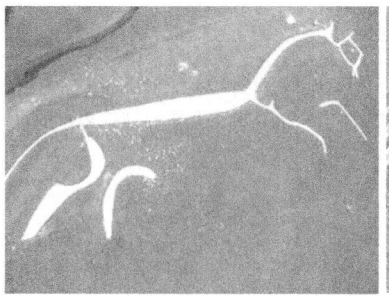

These geoglyphs are huge and they are visible only from high altitude.

I have dreams in which people are chasing me because they are memories from the times when I lived with the Celts. The Roman Empire was trying to take me.

The way we experience life in the 4th dimension is a little bit different. We see the world there is as if we were looking in all directions all the time, not only in one direction as we do here in the 3rd dimension. In the 4th dimension, we can see in all directions. That is why our understanding of time and space is different there. That is why we can see the future there.

Some aliens live here in this 3rd dimension, but in the rooms next to us. Some others live in other dimensions. When we think of an alien or an extraterrestrial, we usually think of a small gray being with big black eyes. This type of alien is just one of many. There are many aliens with many different bodies. Some aliens are very similar to humans. Some other aliens don't have bodies - they are just light. "Being" is probably the most accurate way to refer to them in English.

There are many beings in this dimension, on this planet. There are several reasons why we don't hear about them often. One of the reasons is because we have received manipulated information about our history and current events. Another reason is because they are not supposed to contact us. We have to learn our lesson alone, without their help.

There are many universes. There are so many universes that it's totally outside our imagination. The word "multiverse" would be more appropriate. The universes are different from each other. If we imagine that every universe is a building of 12 floors, our building would be only one building in a huge city full of buildings. These buildings are not connected. There is no black hole or wormhole, or anything physical that can connect one universe with another. The only way to connect these universes is with a very high level of consciousness. We would need many millions of years of evolution just to understand it. We would have to have millions of years of experience in all the dimensional levels, and then we would be able to have the knowledge to understand and move to other universes. Right now it's impossible for us to understand life in other universes.

Some humans on Earth have already been in all dimensional levels but they have decided to be here right now. In other words, their spirit has been in all dimensional levels but they have decided to come here and be born as a human. When this happens, they usually don't lose their memories from previous lives and they remember everything from all the places they have been. This happened to Drunvalo Melchizedek.

In this universe, the 4th dimension is less physical than the 3rd dimension. In the 4th dimension we would see ourselves more as light and less as a physical body. The atoms are more separated. Separation of the mind also exist in the 4th dimension. It means that we have two hemispheres in the brain. Our brains and bodies are a little bit bigger in the 4th dimension. We can play a little bit with our bodies, we can modify the shape. Many beings, when they arrive there, realize that they can modify their bodies. They can change it to the shape they want. They can become a woman, then a man, then an animal, until eventually they understand that it's a normal thing.

The 5th dimension has only a little bit of physicality. It's almost pure light. The 6th dimension and up are pure light. These dimensions are very difficult for our minds to imagine.

I will mention more things about the history of humanity later. For now, I will mention a few things that will help us understand why we are in the 3rd dimension.

Humans were created by two alien races, one race is called the *Elohim* (some people call them *Anunnaki*) and another race that came from the star Sirius. This happened in the 4th dimension, more than 200,000 years ago. The *Elohim* were more involved than the beings from Sirius. The word *Anunnaki* can be confusing sometimes. Some people use this word to describe the beings who created humanity, and other people use this word to describe other beings. To avoid confusion, I will use the word *Elohim* to talk about the beings who created humanity. This is the name used for these beings in the Hebrew Bible.

The *Elohim* came to Earth through portals, not with UFOs. The stone formations like Stonehenge are portals. The *Elohim* came through one portal in South Africa. They were not allowed to create a new race. It was forbidden but they did it anyway.

Many scientists believe that all humans came from Africa because the oldest bones have been found there.

We lived on Earth in the 4th dimension along with the races that created us and others. Eventually, we started to evolve very fast. We were at the best moment of our evolution. We had some problems with other beings on Earth. These beings wanted to control humans but we were very advanced and could protect ourselves. These beings started to manipulate the leaders of humans until eventually, we started to have problems in our society. These problems became so great that we started to have wars between humans.

We came to this 3rd dimension and we had to learn our lesson as a society. We had to do it without help. That is why aliens are not supposed to help us directly. Also, the planet Earth has cycles. Every cycle is around 26,000 years. We had to learn our lesson before the end of the cycle. The cycle finished in December 2012. When we came to the 3rd dimension, we had around 12,000 years before the end of the cycle. The last ice age happened around this time. Humans lived in caves until around 6,500 years ago. Many beings modified human DNA during this time and created the different races around the planet. We used to look like indigenous people. Then the first civilizations appeared.

We had to learn our lesson alone and we had already passed the test. We made it! This is thanks to some indigenous people around the planet who took care of the energy of the planet. Also, some spiritual people have been doing amazing things for humanity, even though most humans are not aware of it. This is because the information available to most humans has been manipulated.

When we came to this 3rd dimension, it was different. It was not what we see right now. It was the first time that humans were in this dimension. Some very advanced beings saw this, and they gave us a very beautiful gift. These beings are the same beings from Sirius who were involved in the creation of humanity. Without this gift, we probably wouldn't have made it to the next level. They created a hologram around the planet - an illusion. The world we live in is not real. Everything around us is not real. It looks real. It feels real. But it is only in our mind. It was a beautiful gift for us so we could experience this dimension in an easier way.

Now that we passed the test, many things are going to change on the planet. They are happening right now. As you can see, the population on Earth has increased dramatically in the last decades. Also technology has increased more than ever. This is part of the change. I will talk about these changes later. These changes are very beautiful, and we should be celebrating now. These changes are so beautiful that many beings came from many places around the universe to experience it directly.

Dolphins and whales are very smart and conscious beings and they have a very special relationship with humans. They are not from this planet. They are from the star Sirius. The spirit of the dolphins and whales went to several places in the universe and asked for help. Many souls came to Earth to have a human experience, and just by coming here, they are improving the energy of the planet. These souls are some of the children born after 1970, and they are known as *crystal children* or *indigo children*. Most of these children came in 1985. I was born in 1985, and I have dreams with dolphins and whales often. I came here to help because they asked me to do it.

I knew that I would forget. I volunteered to come and forget. But before coming here, I wrote everything on a rock. Sometimes I have dreams that I am writing and reading what I wrote on the rock. This is not the first time I've come here. I have been here many times - 562 lifetimes to be precise.

All the souls of humans come from somewhere else in the universe. In other words, we are all aliens. You have to experience at least 8 lifetimes in a human body to be considered a human - at least 4 as man and at least 4 as woman.

If you have a child, and your child feels like he or she is not from this planet, it's probably because your child is one of the souls who came to help humanity. Your child may say many unusual things when they are young. If this is the case, help them to remember why they came here. They probably came to help humanity. Just be aware that once they remember why they came, their whole life will be focused on that mission. They may not have a normal life. They will have a very interesting and amazing life. They knew it before they came here. You can help them to remember.

The increase in the population of the world in the last decades is not normal. Many souls from many parts of the universe are here to help. Just by being here they are helping tremendously.

Some planets are not visible in this dimension. For example, you may come from a planet that is located inside a star and this star is not visible in this dimension. It doesn't exist for us in this dimension, but it's there.

Whatever happens in another dimension affects this dimension as well. All of the universe is connected. One good example would be the pyramids. They were built in the 4th dimension and eventually they appeared in the 3rd dimension as we know them. There are many pyramids around the world. They were created by advanced humans from the 4th dimension before we came to the 3rd dimension. They knew we would come down to the 3rd dimension and they knew that we would have only a limited time to learn our lesson. So they built the pyramids because they concentrate energy around the planet.

When we were living in the 4th dimension, there were other beings living on the planet. One group of these beings were causing a lot of problems. After we came down to the 3rd dimension, some of these beings managed to still cause problems from the 4th dimension, and some of them are also here in the 3rd dimension.

I will call them *"Problematic beings"*. These beings capture some leaders in this 3rd dimension. And through some rituals and extreme torture, they remove the spirit from the leaders, and bring the spirit of a problematic being in, something like a "walk-in". This is similar to what happened to Drunvalo Melchizedek, but in a negative way. This is how they come here. Many leaders around the world have human body, but their soul is that of a *problematic being*.

They have been causing problems since we came to the 3rd dimension. They have been in communication with many ancient civilizations. Since we lost our memories, we didn't know who they were. They took advantage of this and presented to us as gods. Some of these beings have an appearance like humanoid reptiles. That is why old civilizations talk about snakes and dragons.

When the first civilizations started in Mesopotamia, these *Problematic beings* began communicating with humans, specifically in the city called Babylon. They contacted leaders and convinced them to rule according to what they wanted. The soul of some *Problematic beings* came into some human bodies and have been leaders of the ancient societies until modern times. Some *Problematic beings* are here with their reptilian bodies. They have been manipulating humanity. Some people have recovered their memories from the 4th dimension. They have been keeping the knowledge in secret because the *Problematic beings* are trying to silence people. Even though the *Problematic beings* have been trying to manipulate the information, there have always been people who remember. There are more and more people remembering now.

The *Problematic beings* started controlling humanity in Babylon. The official history of the world begins in Babylon or Mesopotamia. Even if you check the English language today the word baby is related to a beginning - related to Babylon. The word victory is related to the name of a queen – Queen Victoria. The souls of Kings and Queens are the souls of *Problematic beings*. There are many words in Latin and Latin-based languages, related to them. For example, in French you have *"Je suis"* which means "I am", which relates to Jesus. Symbolism is everywhere.

Problematic beings were in communication with the leaders of the Roman Empire, and are still here working with several governments, corporations, and religious leaders. Many of them operate from the 4th dimension and some of them are here in the 3rd dimension. The reason we don't know much about them is because they have been destroying evidence and misinforming us. They ridicule anyone who talks about them. They also ridicule anything that could help humanity to remember who we are.

I don't want to focus too much on them because actually there is nothing important about them. They have been making it difficult for us to evolve as humans. But we don't have to focus on that. We always manage to keep evolving. Also, we have so much help from many amazing beings who have been helping us since we were created. They are still here - they are just not allowed to contact us directly.

Sometimes, a person decides to come to the 3rd dimension and live only for a few days. They may decide to be born in extreme poverty or with walking or speaking difficulties. Sometimes they do it this way because it helps the family or people involved. Usually they come to unify a family or make them experience certain things, mainly related to love. We tend to believe that this is something very sad but if somebody has a lifetime that is difficult, it was chosen this way. The person may not have a conscious memory of that, but the agreement was made. Otherwise, they wouldn't be here in the 3rd dimension right now.

Some people commit suicide. If it was not in their agreement, they would go back to the 4th dimension and they may decide to come back to another experience where they would learn to appreciate life in the 3rd dimension. When a person kills another person they go back to the 4th dimension and usually agree to come and have several lifetimes together, probably as family members or close friends, until they learn to love each other.

Some of our family members or close friends have lived several lifetimes with us in the past.

Some ancient civilizations found the way to go back to the 4th dimension. They were able to take their bodies with them. That is why some civilizations disappeared suddenly. Many old civilizations understood the world and the universe better than we do today. But because of the manipulation of information, we are supposed to believe that they were just uncivilized.

Jesus and many other beings were trying to teach this in one way and another. Jesus didn't want followers, he wanted people to be like him. In the Bible, there is not much information about Jesus from when he was around 12 years old until he was about 29 years old. During this time, he went to India. His uncle Joseph of Arimathea helped him. Jesus learned from his teacher Mahavatar Babaji, in the Himalayas Mountains.

Then he went back to the Middle East to teach people there. But the information has been manipulated by the Roman Empire. The information we now see in many religions has been manipulated to the point that it's not completely understood. The *Problematic beings* have presented themselves as the leaders of religions and tell people what is true, just as the Vatican did.

The leaders of Jerusalem didn't like Jesus because they were losing power, after Jesus started to teach people in the Middle East.

The heart is the most powerful organ in the human body. It does amazing things, much more than what doctors think. The heart produces the energy around our body. Imagine that our spirit is a ball of light. This light is living in the brain. When we were in the 4th dimension we used to live in the heart. We can also live in the heart in this dimension. Our spirit can experience everything from the heart. That is why love is so important.

Unfortunately, because of the manipulation, most humans live in the brain. This is in part because the *Problematic beings* don't have emotions. They don't understand the feelings that humans experience. Therefore, they want to force us to experience reality like they do. But our natural state is experiencing life from the heart. We are emotional beings and they don't understand that. Experiencing life from the heart means that you can experience life without ego, or at least being aware of your ego, and not allow it to control your life.

Chapter 17 – The Upgrade

Living consciously means that you are aware of your own thoughts and breath. You think, eat, walk, speak and do everything consciously. You will have a huge feeling of freedom when you live consciously. Living consciously is like being a new version of a human, like an upgraded human.

You can start by being aware of your own thoughts. Everything will be easier after this. When you breathe, focus on your breath. Imagine that you are the air coming inside your body, and the air leaving your body. Imagine that there is no separation between you and the air.

When you eat, feel the food. Visualize how the energy of the food is consumed by your body. Try to eat only vegan and unprocessed food. Do not kill any living being. Do not eat meat. It has a very low vibration. Everything related to death has a low vibration. You need high vibrational food. This means food that comes from nature, without chemicals. Eat food that is touched by the Sun in a natural way. Processed food loses energy. Eat mainly unprocessed food. Drink only clean water and avoid any artificial drink. Avoid any kind of addiction - alcohol, cigarettes, coffee, sugar, drugs and porn. They will alter your brain and make it harder for you to live consciously. Listen to your body.

Eat less. We tend to eat too much. The human body only needs a little bit of food. If you want to talk to your guides or any other being, you can do it better if you don't eat for a few hours.

Sleep well. When you live consciously, you will start to have more dreams and you will remember more of what happens during your dreams. What happens in your dreams is real. You are experiencing other realities and you may be interacting with other beings. What happens in your dreams may not be exactly what is happening. It will be what your brain understands. For example, you may be talking to a being from another dimension, but since your brain doesn't have a concept of that you may see it as a family member or someone you love. Your dreams can be affected also by the food you consume. Therefore, it's important to eat high vibrational food.

Spend time in nature and in the Sun. The Sun is very important. Whenever you feel the Sun, feel it with all your senses. Be thankful for the Sun and nature. Be thankful to the universe for everything you experience, even the difficult times. Everything is the way it's supposed to be, even if we don't understand why. Just be thankful.

Walk consciously. Be aware of your own body while you walk, while you talk, and while you eat. Feel your body. Be aware of what you are doing all the time. This may be hard to do in the beginning, but then you will get used to it and you will do it automatically. You just need to keep practicing all the time, every day. Eventually, you will do it automatically, just don't stop doing it. Even if you don't see any result, don't stop doing it.

Meditate every day. The same way you eat every day, meditate every day. Make it part of your day. Even if you don't have time, make it a priority. The way you see life will be different after a few months of meditation. It will be easier to be aware of your own thoughts with meditation. Try guided meditations or find someone who can teach you. Try many different options. You may find a good meditation for a while, but then you may not like it anymore. This means that you are growing and you need something more advanced. Do not stop growing.

Do not spend much time with electronics. Whenever you can, leave the electronics for a while. If you work with electronics, do everything you have to do. But once you are done with that, leave the electronics at work.

Avoid the news from TV and the internet. Anything negative will lower your vibrations. Even if you don't watch anything negative, try not to get influenced by people who watch media. It is one thing to be informed, but another thing is to take it in a negative way. Focus on love.

Do not worry about other people. You can advise them and show them how to live consciously. You can be an example for them, but they need to make their own decisions. It doesn't matter what you do, they will decide for themselves. There is nothing you can do about it. You do your job, take care of yourself, and live consciously. If others want to follow, help them. If not, it's okay. They will find their own way at the right time. There is really nothing to worry about. Everyone is here to experience everything and learn.

If we learned how to live consciously, we would be a very different civilization right now. We knew how to live consciously when we were in the 4th dimension. We could create almost anything we wanted just by living this way. The human body is able to create a new human being. We are able to have babies. This is because sexual energy is extremely powerful. If we knew how to use this energy properly, we could do amazing things with it. When a person has an orgasm, the energy runs through the body. We can feel it. But since we don't know how to handle the energy, we just release it. That is why we get tired. We could learn how to keep that energy in the body and create many things with it. But we have to create it from the heart, not from the brain. Unfortunately, we don't have education about energies and sex.

Having sex is not done with the body. It's done with the brain. That is why you can have sex during your dreams. You can connect your brain with your heart. The body of the other person is used as a mental image for you so you can trigger the sexual energy in your body. Some people have sex during their dreams without touching another person. During a dream we are not experiencing the body, therefore the need for physical contact is not needed. In this physical reality, you could trigger this energy without having sex. It can be done by concentrating energy in your hands and placing the hands close to the sexual organ to trigger it. You don't even have to touch the body and you can have an orgasm. The sexual energy, no matter how it's triggered, is so strong that it can create new babies. We could use that energy to create anything, but we have to keep that energy in the body and concentrate it in the heart. You can try, but you and your partner would have to put all the intention in keeping the sexual energy in the body.

Everything is about energy. The *Problematic beings* feed themselves with energy. The energy in the 3rd dimension can be felt in the 4th. They asked old civilizations to make sacrifices so they could get this energy. Many religious leaders rape children because children have pure energy, and sexual energy is very strong. They do this so the *Problematic beings* can feed themselves with this energy.

The *Problematic beings* have to let us know what they are doing, and since we accept it, they do it. Also, they create anything to get approval from people. For example, in order to attack certain countries, first they need the approval of the people. In order to get approval from the people, they usually create a big media campaign. Sometimes it's a real event and sometimes they fake it. They have been doing this the whole time. But they do not have control of the information on the internet. They have tried, but they haven't been able to control it. What they are doing now is trying to confuse people with too much information. They have been trying to attack certain countries, but since they haven't had the approval from the people they cannot do it. They attacked countries in the Middle East easily because people accepted it after September 11th. Sometimes they just want to create fear of specific groups of people. For example, you may notice that in the last years, some people are afraid of Muslims. The *Problematic beings* created propaganda, in part, because they want people to believe that it is okay to hate Muslims. This way, Israel can expand their territory. This doesn't mean that people from Israel are bad. In fact, some have a lot of knowledge of the real nature of humanity. But some leaders in Israel are working with some *Problematic beings*. They are creating fear using propaganda against Muslims. Fear is a powerful weapon but if you don't live in fear they cannot control you.

The *Problematic beings* are not allowed to manipulate us unless we give them permission. Unfortunately, most people do. They let us know everything through symbolism. Most humans give them permission to do many things and we don't even know it. This is done through symbolism and rituals. One example is eating meat. It's a ritual sacrifice. There is no difference between sacrifices in old civilizations and the modern world.

Most people eat meat not knowing that they have been part of a ritual. This is because we have been programmed to see meat as a thing and not as a living being. The difference is in the awareness. If we imagine ourselves eating a dog, most people would feel uncomfortable because we see dogs as beings with feelings. But since we see other animals as things and not as beings with feelings, there is no awareness of the living being. Because of the programming that we have had since childhood, we are not aware of some of our actions. Most animals on farms are not aware that some animals are consumed by humans, and most humans are not aware that some humans are also consumed by others. By eating meat, humans also absorb the energy of death. This is permission for the *Problematic beings* to absorb the energy of the human, but also to consume the human body if needed. Since most humans are not aware of the exchange of energies, they are not truly choosing freely. They are choosing unaware of the consequences. Without awareness, there is no free choice.

In the 4th dimension, we never ate meat. Humans started to eat meat in the 3rd dimension after the manipulation. When I met my guides, I was already not eating meat. Right now, I am in contact with several beings from other dimensions. Some of them have told me that they would not contact me if I ate meat.

Since we never get a proper education about the real nature of our body, we don't understand it. If we could understand that there is energy running through our body, and we could focus on that energy more than the physical body, there wouldn't be many sick people. Most sickness comes from emotional problems. Many doctors know this. The emotions come from the thoughts and the energies around us. If we could learn the real nature of our body, we would not be sick. But this also means no business for some people so they make sure that we don't learn about our real nature and they keep us sick.

Some people in big corporations want to get more and more wealth; they don't care what effect they have on people or the planet. Many times they create a product, then they create the need in the people to get that product. They can create a virus that affects people and they can also create the medicine to heal it. Or they can create conflicts around the world so they can sell guns. Many of the products used by people are not really needed but the need to have them was created.

There is technology that we are not using right now because it could help us remember who we are. This includes free energy, understanding higher consciousness, medicine, and even transportation. Some people control much of oil in the world, as well as banks and many other businesses. They destroy or ridicule anything that can ruin their business.

Energy is very important and most humans are not aware that we could control our energy. A very low energy in our body is fear. We are kept in constant fear mainly through mass media. In many cases, what is reported in the news is not real. Some of it is even staged. The *Problematic beings* keep doing it because they want to keep their control.

Since childhood, we are programmed to be scared of many things. It could be spiders, snakes, or other animals. Some of us get programmed to be scared of darkness. In part, that is why we don't remember who we are. We are manipulated from childhood through fear at school, in the church and in society. We learn that if we don't do certain things something bad will happen to us. This is fear-based information. We are emotional beings, but we don't learn how to take care of our emotions. In part, that is why childhood and puberty can be confusing times.

Kumari, the living goddess of Nepal, is considered to be a goddess until she reaches puberty. Then they find another baby who can be the reincarnation of the goddess. People in Nepal believe that once we start puberty, humans start having problems.

The amazing beings who have been helping us all the time are beings full of love. In most cases, they don't take sides. They love all life in the universe. They love everyone the same way. They are aware of what is happening so they are helping us to wake up from the manipulation.

The angels are real, it was hard for me to believe it, but they are real. They exist in the 4th dimension, rooms 7, 8 and 9. They have always been very close to us. They were our neighbors. They saw what happened when we came to the 3rd dimension and they have been helping us the whole time. Time for them is not the same as it is for us so whenever it's needed, they help us. That is why many people see them during accidents, or during big changes in their lives. They come just at the right time and help, and they try not to leave evidence. They are not supposed to help us but they do it anyway.

There are many types of beings. There a few manipulating information for humanity but there are so many beings who are helping humanity.

The Reptilians, the Amphibians (frog people), the Tall Whites and three more races are the *Problematic beings*. They tell us about their existence through symbolism but most humans don't understand it. It's everywhere around the world.

But there are so many beings helping us all the time. We have so many friends. That is why it's not important to focus on these *Problematic beings*. These *Problematic beings* have decided to experience reality in a different way. They believe that they can be separated from the rest of the universe. Or from a more religious point of view, they believe that they can exist outside all the energy of the universe - outside God. This is not possible, but they believe it. Since they can have any reality they want, they are experiencing a reality where they are separated from the rest. As I said, this is impossible. All beings in existence know this.

We are emotional beings and we can create amazing things with our emotions. They are as powerful as any other thing created with our brain. The *Problematic beings* have been forcing us to experience reality from the brain, which is not natural for us.

By living in the brain, we have been forced to focus mainly on the physical world and we ignore the non-physical world. This is related to ego. The ego exists in our body. We all experience it. But we can control our ego. We could even live without ego. But these beings are trying hard to make us live with ego.

Ego is the main problem in humanity. All types of problems in our society are directly related to ego. Corruption, crime, injustice, and many others originate in separation, which happens when we experience ego.

When we are in a group of people, most of the time we behave according to the personality we believe we have or we should have in this specific group. We are different when we are alone, with family, with our best friends, with our partner, etc. But this is just an imaginary mask that we put on ourselves. We put masks on almost all the time. The only time we are not using a mask is when we are experiencing unconditional love. This is the real us, without a mask on. When we are in this state, the ego is minimized. It is still there because ego exists as long as we are in a human body, but we can control it. When we are using a mask, we are not in control of our ego. Most of the time the ego is controlling us. The personality we have at the moment when we are having a specific mask is just ourselves believing that we are the mask. We can be in any place and with any type of people without a mask and still have similar interactions with others.

There is a part of our brain called "the reptilian brain". This is related to the material world, which is related to ego. When we came to the 3rd dimension, human DNA was altered. The DNA of many beings are in our DNA, including some reptilian DNA. They want us to use this part of the brain which is related to the material world. That is why physical appearance is so important. You can see this in magazines, movies, and mass media in general.

They have been trying to force us to experience reality the same way they do - as separation. But it's not natural for us. That is why we have so much propaganda about separation in the world. Deep inside we know perfectly well that we have to be united, all of us. Even though we have forgotten our memories, deep inside we remember this.

The symbolism is everywhere, in government, religions, cities, history, movies and music. We grew up with them so we don't see them as anything unusual. The news in most places in the world is controlled. The people working in media are told what to say and they don't even know it. If you pay attention, you will notice that the news is the same in many parts of the world, because the scripts are prepared by the same people. It is the same with music. Some singers are told what to sing. You will also find a lot of symbolism in movies. Also, there are messages in movies and songs that our brain cannot consciously register, but our unconscious mind does.

There are smart beings who look like velociraptors. These beings are helping humanity. In the past, we used to have a negative image of velociraptors, especially from movies. These beings are trying to change the image we have about them because they are helping us. In the future, you will see that the image of velociraptors will be more friendly. We may see it mainly in movies.

The symbolism is everywhere. It is not really important to talk about it. It's just important to be aware that it exists. There is a lot of low vibrational energy related to this so I prefer not to talk too much about it, I just want to mention it so we are aware that it exists. Remember to focus on love.

The energy running through our bodies has different names. In China it is called Chi, in Japan it is called Ki and in India it is called Prana. This energy runs through our bodies. There are some points of concentrated energy in our bodies that many people call chakras. There are seven main chakras in our bodies and they are represented by colors from red to purple. These are the same colors of visible light like in the rainbow and the *Aurora Borealis*. There is so much information about chakras but I will keep everything simple. These are the locations of the seven main chakras in the human body:

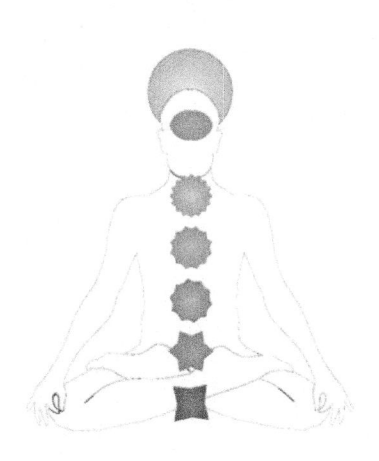

Each chakra is related to a physical part of our body. Starting from the bottom, we have the red chakra which is related to our sexual organs. When we have an orgasm, the energy in our body runs from this place, all the way up. Usually, we let it go. The ideal would be to keep it in our body, especially in our heart chakra. When we have an orgasm, the sexual energy comes from the sexual chakra, which is connected to our sex organs. It passes through all the other chakras and it gets double energy every time it passes through another chakra. 1x2=2, 2x2=4, 4x2=8, 8x2=16, 16x2=32, 32x2=64. So, sexual energy is 64 times more powerful than normal energy. If we just release it, we will be tired. But you can use it to create many things, 64 times faster.

The second one is the orange chakra which is located in the lower abdomen. The third chakra is the yellow chakra. It is located in the upper abdomen. Next is the heart chakra which is green. Many people may think that red refers to love but, in fact, it's green. This chakra is very important. It's related to love and healing. Next we have the blue chakra which is in the throat. It is related to our communication. Next we have the third eye chakra which is directly related to an organ inside our brain. This organ is called the pineal gland.

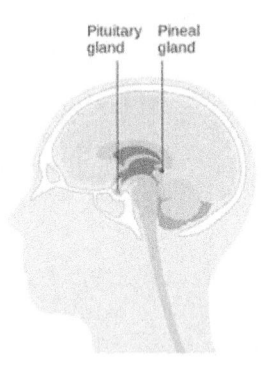

The pineal gland is extremely important because it helps us communicate with other dimensions. It is literally a third eye. But it's not looking in the direction of the other two eyes. It's looking up. Unfortunately, many people don't use it because we aren't educated about it. And eventually, we lost the connection with other dimensions. The food we eat can directly affect our pineal gland. Fluoride in toothpaste is damaging our pineal gland, creating a layer of minerals around it and not allowing us to connect to higher dimensions. Fluoride can be also found in flavored drinks, coffee, beer, some animal products, and even in tap water (water from the city).

With meditation, you could turn the pineal gland 90 degrees and point it to the pituitary gland. You could also do it with a very strong intention. For example, when you want to move your hand, you think about doing it and it moves. There was an intention of moving it. This is similar to the third eye, but since we haven't used it we have to practice how to start moving it. Turning the pineal gland 90 degrees will activate some energy beams in that area and it will create a halo. They could be visible to the human eye. This is what some people call opening the third eye. Jesus is represented with these light beams in some images.

The last chakra is the crown chakra, it is located above our head. There are more chakras and there is a lot of information about them. But for now, this is all we need to know. The chakras in other dimensions are different, but we will focus on the seven main chakras in this 3rd dimension.

Food is energy and it directly affects our body. It's important that we eat organic and unprocessed food and avoid meat or any animal product. Many people think that they like meat but I don't know many people who like the taste of the meat. Most people will not eat uncooked meat. What they really like is the spices added to the meat. The spices come from nature and this is what makes food tasty.

Fruits and vegetables have colors, and every color is related to a chakra of the same color. Fruits and vegetables are there to help us. If you want to improve certain parts of your body, focus on the food with similar colors.

The only reason we eat food is because we are not able to get food from the universe. But some people live without food. In Slovakia, I met a guy named Peter Starec who is known for not eating food. Also, in the United Kingdom, there is a girl named Olivia Farnsworth. She doesn't feel hunger, pain, or fatigue. This is because her DNA is different.

If you have a better knowledge of your body, you can control it better. You can eat less, or nothing. You can avoid any sickness. And you can even control the temperature and weight of your body. The thyroid gland controls your body weight and temperature. The thyroid is physically connected to your heart, the same as the tongue. If you want to meditate, make sure that the tip of your tongue is touching the upper part of your mouth, like it's pointing to the brain. This is because you have to connect your heart and your brain, and the tongue is physically connected to the heart.

Another way of understanding dimensions is with music. Every sound is a vibration decoded by our brain. Visualize a piano. The piano is divided by sections called octaves.

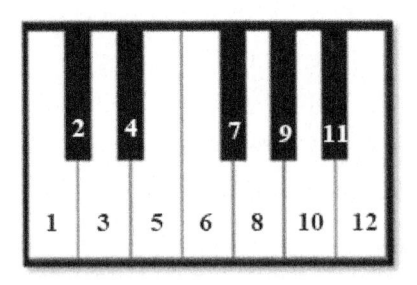

Every octave has 12 keys, and every piano has several octaves (sections). The 12 keys in the octaves have the notes do, re, mi, fa, sol, la, and ti.

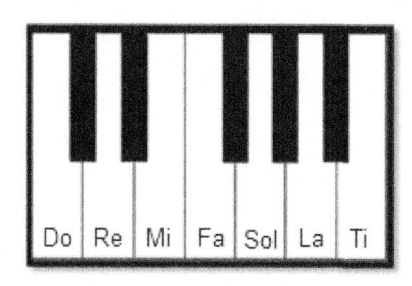

The universe is very similar to the vibrations that we understand as music. Almost all the pianos have 7 octaves (sections), but our universe has 12 octaves (sections) or dimensions. And every key of the piano would be a room.

You can also visualize it as if you are playing the guitar. If you touch the string of a guitar, it will move up and down something like this:

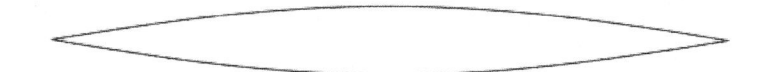

If you could put your finger in the middle of the string, and move both sides of the string it will look something like this:

Let's say that we are able to do the same, but with 12 fingers. It will look something like this:

Let's imagine that this is what the full set of strings looks like. The 12 parts of the string would be considered different frequencies. In music, these frequencies are called overtones. Using the analogy of the building, every overtone can be represented as the rooms. So we can say that the universe is like a guitar of 12 strings (dimensions), and every string has 12 overtones (rooms).

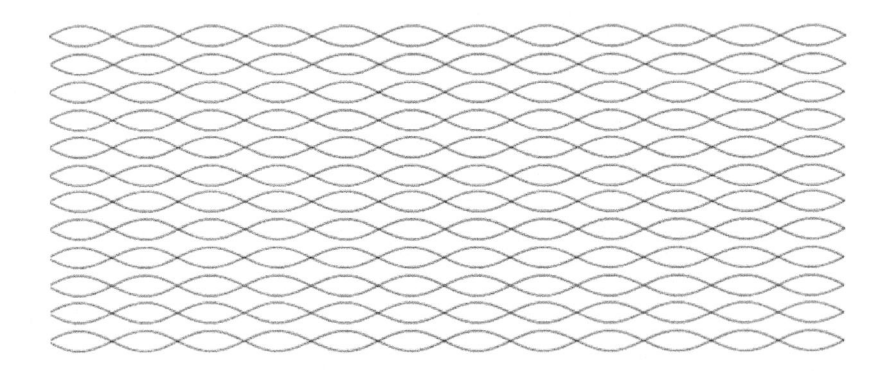

In music, the first frequency is not considered an overtone. So when we are talking about dimensions some people can count the dimensions in a different way. Some people may say that we live in the 4th dimension and when we die we go to the 5th dimension. This can be confusing. To avoid confusion, I will always refer to the 3rd dimension as the place where we live now and the 4th dimension as the place where we go when we die.

This is funny because something similar happens in Europe.

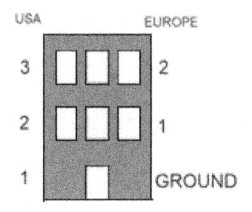

In the USA and many countries around the world, the main floor of a building (with the main door) is considered the 1st floor. But in Europe, the main floor of a building (with the main door) is called the ground floor, and the floor above that one is called the 1st floor.

Chapter 18 – The Forms

I continued traveling to reach my goal of 100 countries, but everything was different. I still wanted to visit 100 countries but I was more interested in understanding the world we live in. I continued traveling, like before, but this time I was able to communicate with my guides and this would change everything.

I used to believe that I liked to travel, but I realized that I liked to be in new places. When I was in a new place, especially when I was alone, I felt excited and full of joy. I felt like I was myself.

When I came back from any trip, I usually already had another trip prepared. This was keeping me motivated all the time. I was excited just by knowing that I was going to another place soon. Sometimes, once I was already in that place, I was not as excited as I was before the trip. I realized that I was more excited about the idea of a new trip than the trip itself. In other words, I was more excited about thinking of going for a trip than being on the trip. I was aware of this. I don't know why it was happening like this, but it was happening and I accepted it as it was.

Since I knew this, I wanted to play with my mind so I always prepared several trips in advance. Whenever I was coming back home from one trip, I always had a second trip waiting for me. The idea of going to a new place was an excuse for me to feel excitement.

I started to analyze what else in my life was similar to this. I realized that there were many things. So I started to play with them. One simple example is that sometimes it was hard for me to wake up in the morning but breakfast was my motivation. I love breakfast. I was having breakfast at home but I decided to start having breakfast at the office. Maybe this way I would feel more excited about going to the office. It worked. Every morning I woke up thinking about breakfast and I started to relate the office to breakfast. I even started to love the office. Then, after breakfast, I had to have something else prepared as motivation. Maybe that could be lunch.

I started to play with these mental images. I knew that I was using them to motivate myself. I changed my routine to the point that I ended up loving every part of the day. It didn't matter what I was doing, I had my motivation waiting for me soon. I didn't know what to call these mental images. I started to call them forms.

Basically, a form is an excuse that you give yourself to allow yourself to experience something. It is all in the mind. I called it "form" because it could take any form. It could be something physical or just an idea. I wanted happiness during the day. My happiness could take the form of breakfast, lunch or anything else.

Our mind is so limited. We don't allow ourselves to do things just because we believe that it shouldn't be like that or because we believe that we don't deserve it. I started to use forms to break the limitations. The forms could be fake, just an idea in my mind, but the limitation was also fake. The limitation was a form as well, but a limitation form.

We use forms all the time. For example, when we feel sad we talk to a friend about our problem. We expect our friend to say that we are doing the right thing. Once our friend says that, we feel better. We use the words of our friend as a form to allow ourselves to believe that we are doing the right thing.

A form is a mental image. We all have them. I didn't see any difference between an image or something physical. Both are made of energy. Everything is made of energy. It is like water - sometimes it's frozen and sometimes it's steam. Or as Albert Einstein said, "matter is just frozen light".

When somebody tells you something very nice, you are very happy about it. Later, if they tell you that it's actually not true, you would probably stop being happy. Whatever they told you, it was your form for you to experience happiness, even if it was just for a while.

Ideas in our mind can become a limitation. Even simple things like the ideas we have about friendship. Every person has a different idea about what friendship means. For some people, friendship might mean someone who talks to you often and listens to your stories. For other people, friendship could mean someone who thinks about you often but not necessarily someone you meet often. Something similar happens in a romantic relationship. All relationships are labels. Sometimes we expect something from a friendship or a relationship. If what we expect doesn't happen, we believe it is not working. But maybe we just have different ideas of what a friendship or a relationship should be.

Forms work only for yourself because the world around you is experienced only by you. Another person doesn't see the world the same way you do even if they are very similar to you. If there is another person involved, you would have to find out about their limitations and their forms. This will improve any friendship or relationship.

I was still working in an office but I didn't have much work to do. I don't know why but I started to be worried. I started to feel that I should be doing something otherwise I would get fired. Even though I didn't care about the world of business, I wanted to earn money so I could keep traveling. I decided to play with forms at work.

I was scared of being fired. If that happened, I would just find another job. When I was traveling, I always had a second trip prepared so maybe I should do the same with my job. I started to apply for jobs, even though I already had one job where I was getting paid for researching my personal things.

I had several offers, including some very good offers. I didn't take any of them. I was aware that this was not the most ethical thing to do, but since I knew that the world was not what I always thought, I really didn't care. If I was doing something unethical, it was nothing compared to what has been done to humanity since we came to the 3rd dimension. This was my form for feeling comfortable about doing unethical things. Don't get me wrong, I had values. I knew how far I could go.

Just by knowing that there were other options for me, I felt better. It was just a mental exercise for me. My happiness was more important than my job, so I was able to do this. I was using the other job offers as a form for me to feel good in the office where I was working.

I went to Latin America. I wanted to spend time alone so I didn't interact so much with people. I think this was because I was still absorbing all the information I received and understood. Basically, my whole life was a lie. But I was so happy and thankful for waking up from the manipulation. I felt like I spent my life hypnotized and suddenly I had woken up.

When somebody is hypnotized and the hypnotist tells the hypnotized person to believe that some objects in the room are not there, the hypnotized person believes it, and actually this person can see through the objects. This really happens. I felt like I was waking up after many years of being hypnotized.

Some friends living in Europe told me something interesting about TV in the USA. Many friends from Europe, when they go to the USA for holidays or work, watch TV. They can see that there is manipulated or distracting information in the media. Many people in the USA are aware of it but many others are not. They have probably seen it for the whole of their lives and so they know no different. This doesn't mean that manipulation doesn't happen in Europe. It happens in almost every country of the world.

In Mexico, several researchers have found information that the ex-president of Mexico, Miguel de la Madrid, was manipulating people. He used several techniques in media to manipulate the way people think, and eventually to influence people during the elections. Many political parties around the world do this to influence the elections. For me, it was funny that these people know that they can manipulate the way people think, but they usually don't think that they have been manipulated their whole lives.

I heard unusual stories also in Latin America but I was not surprised anymore. My understanding of the world was already different.

One of the unusual things I heard in Latin America was that some people in Argentina believe that Hitler moved there after World War II. They also believe that the reason why many Argentinians have white skin is because many people with dark skin were put in the front lines of the wars, so they would get killed first.

At that moment I felt like I had enough of dark information. I was not comfortable with any of that anymore. I wanted to know about the dark history of some places around the world, but I didn't want to put my energy there. It was low vibrational energy. I thought about the message I got in Nepal, "Focus on love." I felt like it was time to focus on love.

One of the beautiful things about Latin America is the people. I grew up there. And after many years of living abroad, I almost forgot the feeling of being around these people.

In Colombia, there is a group of indigenous people called Kogi. They are doing amazing things for the planet and not many people know about them. They are in direct contact with Mother Earth. They talk to the planet and the planet talks to them. They have their own techniques. Unfortunately, there isn't much information about them. They try to live away from other people. They believe that most humans have forgotten their connection with Mother Earth. They even have a name for people outside their tribe. The translation from their language would be "brothers who don't understand Mother Earth".

The Kogi people are able to communicate telepathically. We can also do it. We just need to practice a lot. You really have to feel love in order to do it. You may find it easier to communicate telepathically with someone you love. Or you may notice that when you are in love, you know or feel what the other person is feeling. This is because when you are in love, your body is tuned-in to communicate telepathically.

You can communicate telepathically with everything, even with your own body. Your body is made mainly of water, and you can communicate with your body. Many people put labels with beautiful messages on their water cups. This improves the quality of the water. Also, the way the water moves through the pipes is important. If you can create geometrical shapes with the pipes, this will improve the quality of the water. Even the way we plant trees is important. If we plant trees using geometrical shapes, they will grow faster. The Aztecs used geometrical shapes in their pipes to improve their water. The Kogi people also know this. They are in constant communication with nature, and they can predict the weather much better than any modern meteorologist. Many ancient civilizations communicated with nature. Usually, they waited for something to appear three times, like three birds appearing, or three clouds together, or three animals close to them.

Something similar happens in the universe. Big galactic events like eclipses or positions of the planets have meanings and affect life in the whole universe. The Moon changes the water levels in oceans, but it also changes behavior in humans. For example, when there is a full moon, you will notice that there is more violence. Many police departments around the world know it. The Moon and other planets affect life on Earth.

Something known about the Kogi is that they can reach a very high state of consciousness and it is visible in their physical bodies. When they are in caves, in complete darkness, their bodies glow. They can also levitate around one meter (3 feet) from the ground. Some people in Asia do exactly the same thing. Some magicians have met with Tibetans monks to understand how they levitate, but then they realize that they are not using any tricks. They really levitate. It's created with the electromagnetism around the body.

You can always check the electromagnetism of a place with dowsing rods.

They are objects made of a material that is attracted or repulsed by magnetic forces. Many people use them to find changes in the electromagnetism of a place. In the past, dowsing rods were used to find water underground because the water creates a change in the electromagnetism.

In the 17th century, the church decided dowsing rods were moved by the devil, and many people still believe it. I noticed that every time there is something that can help us to understand non-physical phenomena, the church wants people to fear it. These tools could be used for healing. Pendulums can also be used for healing in a similar way.

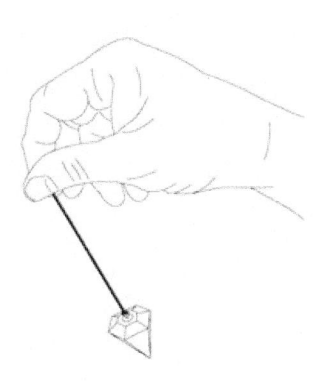

In some parts of Latin America, talking about alternative healing methods is not considered weird. Many people believe in alternative medicine. But they don't talk too much about it because they are afraid of being called crazy.

When I was in Chile, I saw flights from Santiago to Easter Island, an island in the middle of the Pacific Ocean. Almost the only way to get there was from Santiago, the capital of Chile. I took a flight to Easter Island. This island was famous for the big statues called Moai.

This place has a lot of history. Several local people told me that this island used to be part of a bigger continent. I knew this, but I didn't know the name of the continent. They told me that it was called Lemuria.

They told me that these statues were built by the ancient people who survived on the island after a big catastrophe. The people living on this island were not alone. They had help from non-human beings. These non-human beings helped them build the statues. These statues are half underground but if you uncover the whole body, you could find symbolism that is similar to other cultures around the world.

Eventually, the people of the island started to have problems with their food supply. They were very far from other places. They ate everything they could on the island. That is why there are no trees on the island today. After not having enough to eat, these people started to die. The survivors started to eat the people who were dying. This caused a very bad energy on the island. This energy was repaired around 1970. I previously knew many things about this island, but this time I was getting more details.

The Inca people in Peru had a different story, they were also related to the catastrophe that happened on the continent that used to be in the Pacific Ocean. The Incas and the people from Easter Island used to live on the lost continent in the Pacific Ocean. But the Inca people moved to the area that is now Peru because there was a special energy in the region. The Inca people believed in life after death and they mummified bodies like Egyptians.

America was not discovered by Christopher Columbus. Many people from Asia and even ancient Greece were in America before. And the name America doesn't come from the explorer Amerigo Vespucci. It relates to a mythical creature with the shape of a dragon called Amaru.

Every time I listened to a story, I asked my guides if that story was real or not. I knew most of this information because I got it with the download in Nepal. But it was great to hear it from other people.

Chapter 19 – The Movements

Since I still wanted to reach the 100 countries, I was traveling non-stop. I began to travel around Asia. I started in China. I was advised to be careful of scams in China but I felt confident that I would be able to see when someone was lying to me. Since I was able to sense vibrations of people, I could figure out if they had good intentions or not. We all do this. Some people just develop it more than others. I didn't speak any Chinese and it was hard to find people speaking English. While walking around tourist areas in Beijing, I met several people who spoke English. They looked very friendly so it was great to spend time with them. But I could feel these people. They behaved nicely to me but I could feel that they had different intentions. I wanted to discover if what I was feeling was correct.

These people invited me to eat with them. They told me that it was a Chinese tradition. They insisted that they wanted to pay for everything. I didn't want it that way, but they insisted so much so I accepted. When we arrived at a restaurant, they started to speak Chinese to the people working there. Somehow I knew that something was not okay. I played along and waited. I just wanted to confirm that I could trust what I was feeling from them. The menu didn't have prices. It was weird but I played along. After eating, it was time to pay. I checked the bill and the amount was huge. These people took money from their pockets and paid half of the bill. They asked me to pay the other half. I reminded them that they said they would pay for the lunch. Now they are asking me to pay half and the price was very high. This was clearly a scam. They were still smiling and nice to me but I could feel something else. I was so happy at that moment. I knew what was happening and I always knew. I was able to recognize the intentions of people, regardless of what they pretended to be. This was an exciting moment for me. I was able to sense when someone had good intentions or not. I talked to them. I told them that I knew what was happening. I was so happy that I didn't care about paying a big amount. I paid and I thanked them. I guess they didn't understand me, but they helped me so much.

Other people tried to scam me but since I was aware of their intentions it didn't happen again. People could lie but energy doesn't lie. You cannot fake energy.

In China, several people talked to me about Falun Dafa (also called Falun Gong). This is a meditation that consists of some simple movements of the body. This method has a lot of health benefits and many people use it to keep themselves healthy and heal many types of illnesses. Some people who practice it say they feel a special energy around their body.

Falun Dafa was very well accepted in China, it became very popular, but suddenly, from one day to another it became illegal. They also have been trying to forbid it in other places around the world. I thought, "the government against meditation?" I couldn't believe it, but I saw it. Policemen tried to stop people from practicing it. Even some policemen who have practiced it in the past believe it can really heal. The government didn't want people to believe that they can heal themselves. Falun Dafa is illegal in China, and the practitioners are given extreme punishments. Knowing that a meditation was illegal motivated me to start practicing the meditation, but of course I was not able to do it in China. At that moment I just thought, if they were trying to forbid something, it is probably good for people.

I had a clear idea. If something is easily available, it's probably because it's not good for our bodies or because it will keep us away from remembering who we are. Big chain restaurants with junk food, so much sugar in their products, and a lot of processed food are easily attainable. Addictive products like coffee, alcohol, cigarettes and pornography are all easily attainable. What I am saying is that pornography is usually used in a materialistic way - not using our energy properly. This is not natural for us. Emotions have to be involved - high vibrational emotions.

There are some substances, many of them illegal, that could help us to reach other vibrations. In part that is why they are illegal. But I don't recommend using them. They may help us get to other dimensions quickly, but they damage the body. Also, you can become addicted and that will make it difficult for you to connect to other dimensions in a natural way.

Natural products and natural medicines were used in the 4th dimension. Some old civilizations also used them. Now they are called alternative, and some of them are ridiculed or illegal. Unfortunately, we have been manipulated with the information regarding our food. For example, meat is not natural for us. The stomach has to use extra effort to digest it. Some bacteria present in the meat and some milk products can cause cancer.

Some doctors are aware of some of these things. They know about the benefits of meditation or alternative medicine, but since it's been ridiculed many doctors don't even believe that it could help. Many people believe that meditation is just for relaxation, but it can be used for so many things, including contacting other dimensions. Another practice that is not taken seriously is *reiki*. *Reiki* is an energy healing practice that is usually done by placing the hands around the body and allowing the flow of energy in the chakras. Some doctors already know the benefits of *reiki*, but they do not talk openly about it for fear of losing credibility.

Something I found interesting about Falun Dafa was the symbol.

The symbol is similar to the Nazi symbol but inverted. The Nazi symbol is called Swastika, and it has been used in ancient civilizations, mainly in Asia as a symbol of peace. But now most people know it as the Nazi symbol.

There are movements in Falun Dafa that are clockwise. When I see people practicing alternative medicine, their movements are usually clockwise.

You can find people practicing Falun Dafa in many places around the world. I practiced it and it made me feel very good - like having a coffee but for the whole body. Many people around the world are protesting the persecution of Falun Dafa taking place in China. Falun Dafa heals people without the need of medicines. Qigong is basically energy exercises for healing, and this is the most powerful healing technique for many people. We can say that Falun Dafa is a Qigong technique, therefore it is powerful.

In many places around Asia, you can find the symbolism of the dragons, the lions and many more. This is related mainly to old civilizations, and does not necessarily mean that they are working with the same beings as the people in Europe or America. There are many beings working with different governments, or some areas of some governments. Usually they exchange technology. There is so much advanced technology, incredible technology in the hands of governments right now, but this information is not public. Some beings working with some governments have plans that are sometimes different than other governments. These beings have their own plans. Some of them are helping humanity, some others are not helping so much. These differences have caused tensions between countries sometimes. In many cases, they use excuses to create wars and invade other countries, so they can install their own leaders and ideology.

In Asia, there are many hidden pyramids. China and Mongolia probably have more pyramids than any other area in the world. In China, the most well-known pyramids are probably the ones close to the city of Xianyang. They are close to the famous sculptures called the Terracotta Warriors. But the pyramids are not recognized by the government so not many people know about them.

I went to South Korea. When I arrived in Seoul, I was supposed to stay with a person I met through the internet. But at the last minute she told me that she was not able to host me that day. She gave me the name and address of a place where I could sleep. When I arrived at this place, it didn't look like a hotel or anything similar. It was a spa. I wanted to ask for a hotel at the same address, but nobody spoke English. I was not able to understand any Korean and I didn't understand the culture. The only words I heard and understood on the street came from a couple speaking English. They were saying that in South Korea they have a different way of measuring age. It took me a while to understand that in South Korea they start counting their age at conception. So if you are 25 years old, in South Korea you would be 26 years old.

I really wanted to find the hotel because my friend told me that it was a very good place. After a while, I called my friend and asked her about the hotel. She said that she sent me to a spa. She said that many people sleep there because it's open 24 hours and they provide all the services. It's also much cheaper than a hotel.

I couldn't believe it. I never thought about it, but it was actually a great idea. My mind automatically thought about a hotel because I related sleeping with hotel. In the beginning it was hard for me to be comfortable, especially because I was in a place that I was not familiar with. But I knew that it was just a form. I had to convince myself that it was okay to sleep there. I just needed to sleep, but my mind was uncomfortable because I was not in a hotel.

The mind is full of limitations. Many times we don't do things just because we believe we don't deserve it. Sometimes we don't do things because we believe that we have to do something in order to be able to do another thing. For example, sometimes when I am traveling and there is someone with me, we need a bathroom. Sometimes the only place available is a restaurant. In some cases, you are not allowed to use the bathroom unless you are a customer. Usually, my friends do not want to consume anything so they prefer to keep walking until they find another bathroom. Usually I tell them that I will order a bottle of water and in the meantime they can go to the bathroom. They go to the bathroom and when they come back, they realize that I didn't buy anything. When they ask about the water, I tell them that it was a trick. But this way they would feel okay going to the bathroom. In this case, I was using the water as a form so my friends could allow themselves to believe that it is okay to do certain things. I don't like the word "excuse" so I use the word "form".

I used to be afraid to talk to people - especially people I would consider special or important. Every time something like this happened, I knew that I needed a form to allow myself to believe that it was okay. Since I knew many things about the nature of humans, I was using this as a form to convince myself that the person was not more important than me. We are all the same energy and the same consciousness. I knew it, so just by thinking of it, I was automatically letting go of any fear. In fact, this helped me to talk to any person more confidently than ever. It also helped me to be a better listener. I paid attention to what they said and felt. This combination would allow me to help people because I could feel when they were experiencing fear or any low vibrational feeling.

In Europe, when I was walking on the street, sometimes I could see that people were looking at me. In my head, I was thinking that it was probably because I look different, because I have a darker skin color, and most people are white. Everything was fine, these people were not doing anything to me. But me, in my head sometimes I was having negative ideas about the people looking at me. I was the one creating these ideas in my mind, and I was the one who had to change them. It would be easier for me to change these ideas in my mind with a form. Since I was creating this idea in my mind because people looked at me, I could look at people and get a positive idea in my mind about why they were looking at me. I started to look at the people, I looked at them several times until I got a positive or neutral thought. By changing the thought in my mind, I was changing my idea about these people, and therefore, my experience.

Another limitation I had was with money. Since I was always saving money for more trips, sometimes I believed that I didn't deserve certain quality things like sleeping in nice places or having quality food. When I realized that I had a mental block with money, I started to find a form to unblock that. I didn't know what form I could use to delete that part of my brain that was telling me that I don't deserve quality things. I asked my guides for help. They told me that I could use any idea as a form. I just need to deeply believe it. The first thing that came to my mind was visualizing myself as a rich person. But I really couldn't visualize it, probably because deep inside I don't care about being rich. My beliefs were not strong enough to use it as a form. I had to find another form.

I was not able to visualize myself as a rich person, but I was able to visualize myself as someone who helps others with the information I had and therefore, get quality services in exchange. I could feel people so I could tell when they didn't feel comfortable talking about certain things, even if they were not aware of it. Many people didn't realize that they were hurting themselves with their own thoughts. I could help them.

I didn't know where to find people who would understand me but I wanted to meet them. I started to use this form. I visualize this idea of being someone who could help others to understand themselves better. I could easily visualize it. Many amazing things happened after this.

When we are with people, we behave in a certain way. When we are alone, we are different. This is a huge limitation. We are not ourselves in front of other people. It could be for fear of being judged, or because we try to keep an image. Regardless of the reason, it doesn't matter how cool you try to be. Someone will think that you are ridiculous.

Sometimes my guides make fun of me in a nice way. Sometimes, when I am in a meeting in the office, my guides tell me, "Here you go. You are going to put a mask on." When I am not myself, I have more difficulties hearing my guides so before any meeting they tell me, "Okay, see you later." One of my guides is from the 7th dimension. When I asked her if they have jokes there, she said that they don't tell jokes to each other. They just talk about humans and our funny limitations. I can hear my guides better after few hours of not consuming any food. I asked my guides how to hear them the easiest. They told me, "If you want to communicate fast, then fast," meaning that I should stop eating for a few hours so I could hear them better.

I have to be honest. I hesitated many times about writing so many details in this book. I was scared of being ridiculed. But what I have experienced has been impossible to deny. My guides motivated me to talk openly about all of this. I used to be afraid of being ridiculed, but I am not anymore. I realized that this is real, more real than anything else. I used to feel bad when someone called me crazy but now I can just feel sorry for these people. They probably decided to have this lifetime this way.

When I was traveling around Asia, I was able to communicate with my guides but I was not able to communicate with other beings. This would come later and it would be amazing.

I traveled to almost every country in Asia. There are many things I could say about the cultures in Asia but I will focus only on stories that helped me with my personal growth. I hope you can benefit from this as well.

In the Philippines, I was hosted by a family. They were very nice to me. The father of the family was a very open-minded person. We had some very nice conversations. They knew many things about the human body, and somehow, they knew that I knew those things as well. They were not using the same words that I was using but we were talking about the same things. I really had a good time with them. They took me to the room I was supposed to sleep in. It was a huge and comfortable room. I didn't really care about the luxury but it was important for me to understand that just by changing my thoughts many things started to change around me. In the morning, I realized that they had a chef so I had to choose what I wanted for breakfast. Having a chef was not something that was adding value to my experience but my guides told me that I was attracting this type of people. This was just after I started to unblock my ideas about having quality in my life. This could have been only a coincidence, but it happened many times after this.

In Cambodia, there is a famous temple complex called Angkor Wat.

Europeans discovered it in 1860. Then they said that the temple complex was built by the Khmer Empire, an empire that used to exist in that area. Before the Europeans discovered it, local people believed that the temple was built by gods and giants. Some people believe it even now.

There were giant humans on Earth. This was because the beings who created humanity (*Elohim*) were taller than humans. After many years of evolution, some of them started to mix with humans. The result was giant humans.

The Christian Bible and many ancient books talk about giants. Some ancient places around the world are huge, like they were made for big people.

Some archeologists have found bones from these giants, although many of them don't know what they really are. Some bodies of these giants are well preserved until today. They are in Iran and Syria, where ancient civilizations used to exist. They are in special chambers to preserve them.

Problematic beings have tried to destroy this evidence but they are not in control of Iran or Syria. They are trying to invade these countries and destroy evidence. They already destroyed some evidence in Iraq and neighboring countries. They did it by creating the group known as ISIS.

In the Middle East, I met several people who talked to me about these groups like ISIS. They told me that these groups were financed by governments or organizations to create chaos. This way they had an excuse to intervene and occupy the region. This happens in politics around the world. They create a problem, offer the solution, and try to look like the heroes. Also, whenever there is a new scientific discovery, there is a chance that this is propaganda for the benefit of certain governments or organizations. They pay or convince scientists to publish information that will benefit them and the information or the scientific conclusion is not always real. Whenever you see something big happening in the news, they are probably trying to divert your attention from something else.

Every time I traveled, I met people with many stories to tell. It was getting more and more interesting.

In Indonesia, I drove a motorcycle. When I arrived at my destination, I was trying to park the motorcycle in the only place available. Suddenly somebody else with a motorcycle came quickly and took the spot. The first thing I noticed was that there was a Flower of Life sticker on this woman's helmet. I was so happy about it, I didn't care about the parking spot. I asked her if I could see the helmet. She said yes, then she took this picture.

I talked to this woman and I asked her if she knew the meaning of the Flower of Life. She said yes. After a few minutes of talking, we realized that we were aware of the same things. I asked her how she knew about them. And she told me her story.

She said that she was watching an American TV show called The View. President Obama was there as a guest. He talked about general things, but then he mentioned something about having a reptilian side. She wanted to understand this reference so she researched. She found it interesting that many researchers believe that some American presidents are related to each other. And that almost all of them are related to kings in the United Kingdom. Many leaders around the world are also related in one way or another to the same people in the United Kingdom.

Some Indonesians believe that President Barak Obama was born there, and that his American birth certificate is fake. Some people even say that his real name is Barry Soetoro. So, this woman realized many things about leaders in the western world. She didn't like to spend her energy on these types of topics because they have low vibrational energy so she started to focus on something with higher vibration. And she found the higher vibration with several people. That is why she had the Flower of Life on her helmet.

We had different paths, but we ended up with a similar goal. We can call it spirituality, alternative beliefs, or we can use any other name - history, politics, science, religion, or many more. We just put them in different boxes with different names but everything is related.

I asked her why she didn't talk about it in public. She said that she tried but nobody believed her. So, I understood her. I was in the exact same situation.

From Indonesia, I went to Perth, Australia. I wanted to see kangaroos but I was in the city. I had to go to the wild. But my guides told me that I would see them in the city so I trusted them.

When humans were living in the 4th dimension, there were big concentrations of humans mainly in two areas. One of these areas was Atlantis, a continent in the Atlantic Ocean, but this continent doesn't exist anymore. It is now underwater. Another continent was called Lemuria, or some people call it Mu. This continent used to be in the Pacific Ocean. Some islands in the Pacific Ocean are remnants of this continent. It was also destroyed during the war in the 4th dimension. This is how I visualize it.

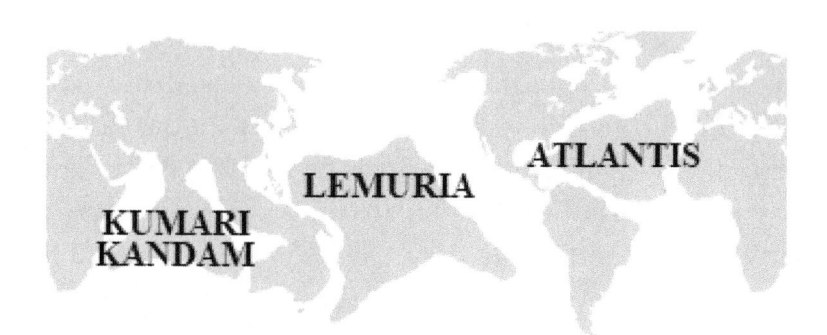

ATLANTIS
LEMURIA
KUMARI KANDAM

There was another big piece of land that doesn't exist anymore. It was in the Indian Ocean. It was connecting what is today India and Madagascar. Some people call this area Lemuria, but some others call it Kumari Kandam. The animals called lemurs exist in Madagascar. Some scientists have found fossils of these animals in India. They don't know how these fossils got there, because they are not aware of Kumari Kandam (or Lemuria). To avoid misunderstanding, I will refer to Lemuria as the land in the Pacific Ocean and to Kumari Kandam as the land in the Indian Ocean.

Some Scientists believe that kangaroos and koalas have roots in South America. They are not sure about how this is possible. This is because they are not aware of the existence of Lemuria.

In Australia, I wanted to see the kangaroos, but I didn't know where to find them in the city. I didn't want to go to a zoo. I prefer to see animals in the wild. After several hours of walking around the city, I walked on a bridge and my guides told me that I would find the kangaroos there. I was in the middle of a bridge so I didn't understand. There were no people around. I kept walking until I found a sign saying "Heirisson Island" with pictures of kangaroos.

I didn't know that I was on an island. I tried to find the kangaroos but I couldn't find them. I checked the whole island and I couldn't see them. I asked my guides but they were not telling me anything. I was confused. I didn't know if my guides didn't want to talk to me anymore, or maybe I didn't understand what they said. I walked around the island several times and I didn't see any kangaroos. I saw some people and asked them about the kangaroos, but they didn't see anything either. I believed my guides, but after few hours of walking, I wasn't sure if I would actually see the kangaroos. So, for the first time, I doubted if I was really understanding correctly what my guides said.

When my guides told me that I was supposed to see the kangaroos there, I thought that it would be immediately. But after a few hours, I didn't see any kangaroos and I was a bit desperate. I think my ego started to be involved with my thoughts. I had expectations. Something that my guides always told me was not to expect, just to trust. I was doing exactly the opposite. Many times I had the information but I didn't know how to apply it in my daily life. Knowing something is easier than doing it.

I sat down on the ground and I tried to relax. I didn't know how to meditate, but I tried to relax my thoughts with an improvised meditation. This was the first time I tried to meditate. I just wanted to stop expecting.

During my improvised meditation, I started to think that probably one of the reasons I wanted to see kangaroos was because I wanted a picture with them. This was pure ego. I had to be honest with myself. This was probably the reason, good or bad. I had to create an idea in my mind to convince myself that I already have a picture with kangaroos, so the need for having a new picture would disappear.

I thought that maybe I could take a picture of kangaroos from the internet and with photoshop I could put myself there. This idea would be my form. I never used photoshop for my pictures. I just had to convince myself that I was able to do it, at least for few minutes. It was not easy because you really have to believe it but I did it. I totally convinced myself that once I got home, I would photoshop a picture of myself with a kangaroo.

After using this form in my mind, I was happy to go without seeing kangaroos. I really didn't want to photoshop any picture but at that moment I needed to keep those thoughts. I knew that once I went back home, I would probably use another form to convince myself to never photoshop pictures. I was just playing with my mind, using forms.

I was about to leave the island when I saw all the kangaroos there. They were next to the entrance. I was thinking that all the forms I used to convince myself of several things were for nothing. But they helped me so much to control my ego, and to stop expecting. I felt like it was a lesson. I got some pictures with the kangaroos, and I never photoshopped a picture.

I was alone there, so I had to put the camera somewhere to take the picture with a kangaroo. I pretended to have ego for this picture, in honor of the lesson I just learned.

In Australia, on the streets, I saw people who called themselves Aboriginal Australians - the original people of Australia before the British colonization. I knew many things about them but these people on the streets didn't look like them. They told me that they were not real Aboriginal Australians. They were mixed with Europeans.

The real Aboriginal Australians are very different. The way they experience reality is different than the rest of humanity. They don't experience ego the same way we do. And they don't experience the same separation we experience. They are more aware that we are all the same consciousness experiencing individual lives. If you ask them who they are, they say that they are you, the tree, the river, and they are part of everything. They really don't experience reality the same way.

There were Pygmies in Australia similar to the ones in Africa. But most of the information about them has been destroyed.

Every human experiences reality in a different way. Even if you have a very similar lives, the way you experience reality will be different. This is because we interpret every object or idea. So, if I want to say something beautiful, I will use words that I consider beautiful. That doesn't mean that the other person will understand it as beautiful. It doesn't matter what I say. My words will be interpreted by the other person according to the interpretation they give to the words I am saying. One of the best ways to have a proper conversation is to understand the other person and how they see their reality. Then use words that they will understand, even if these words are not words that you would usually use. When you are talking to a lot of people, this becomes very hard. Every person has a different belief system, therefore there will be at least one who will not understand what you say the way you said it. Therefore, they may disagree, or not understand the message you want to deliver.

Everyone on the planet is literally connected with each other. There is a net of energy around the planet that is connecting us all. There are many scientific studies about this. When a person has an idea in one part of the world, suddenly another person somewhere else in the world has a similar idea. They may think that they are stealing ideas, but this is because we are all connected. When a person thinks or does something, this energy goes to the collective net of energy. Everyone else on the planet automatically has access to it. This is why it's important to work on yourself. If you work on yourself, you are automatically helping the collective net of energy (also known as collective consciousness), and everyone on the planet.

You may notice that more and more people are waking up on the planet. This is in part because, since around 1970, many souls have come to Earth to have a human experience. Just by being here, they are helping the collective net of energy. They were not allowed to help externally, but they are doing it internally.

When we lived in the 4th dimension, we had 3 nets around the planet and 3 types of humans. The first one was the Aboriginal Australians, Waitaha (New Zealand), Kogi (Colombia), and Arhuaco (Colombia). The second one is currently used by most humans on Earth. There used to be a third one, but we destroyed it during the war in the 4th dimension. When we came to the 3rd dimension, we had to rebuild this third net of energy. This usually takes millions of years but since we had it before, we were allowed to create it artificially. We had to create it before the end of the cycle. The end of the cycle was in 2012. The third net was activated around 1970. That is why we are alive right now.

Some amazing humans activated it. There are spiritual people around the planet who keep the knowledge about our real nature and history. They are normal people like you and me who are living consciously. Before activating the third net, they had to fix some problems with the energy around the planet. For example, they had to fix the problems on Easter Island where people ate human meat to survive. This created a very bad energy in the region, but they fixed it with special ceremonies.

The pyramids were built to create this third net artificially. That is why there are so many hidden pyramids around the world. There are also other sacred places on Earth. Everything is based in geometry and connected in a mathematical proportion. It's called geomancy.

The third net of energy used to be called *Christ Consciousness Grid*. Many ancient books, including the Bible, talk about it. Many people understood that Jesus was the Christ, therefore Jesus would come back someday. But many believe it referred to the Christ Consciousness Grid. It has been active since around 1970 but not all humans are connected to it.

There are also pyramids in Australia. Some of them are not hidden. The ancient Egyptians knew about the Aboriginal Australians. Scientists have found Egyptian hieroglyphs in Australia and boomerangs in Egypt.

This is because ancient Egyptians knew that the Aboriginal Australians didn't experience ego as other humans. They went there to learn from them. They exchanged gifts, including boomerangs. The Egyptians traveled in boats. They were guided by advanced beings. Some tools in Egypt were used to increase the vibrations in the body. Even in the modern world, some people use similar objects to increase the vibrations in the human body.

After Australia, I went to Central Asia. I reached the goal of 100 countries in Kazakhstan, but at this moment I didn't really care so much. I was aware that it was just a number in my mind. I was more interested in consciousness. Traveling was just a form to realize what was happening in the world.

After Kazakhstan, I traveled to Kyrgyzstan and I met very nice people. I met most of them in unusual but magical ways. I was used to experiencing unusual things. They became part of my daily life. One of the people I met in Kyrgyzstan told me about *manaschy*, people in Kyrgyzstan who tell long stories or poems. These stories are about a hero known as Manas. The stories are usually very long and contain beautiful metaphors about life. When they start telling the stories, they change. Sometimes their voice also changes. The messages are very beautiful and helpful to people. Some people believe that someone else is talking through their bodies. The messages tell about the history of Kyrgyzstan and their people in a very beautiful way. I didn't understand the language, but just listening to it made me feel good.

Usually only adults tell Manas, but there are also children telling them. The most amazing part is that these children grew up without access to books or the internet and they don't even know how to read. But they tell these beautiful long metaphors about life.

Sometimes these stories last many hours. I knew that beings from other dimensions could speak through the body of a human but this was the first time I saw it. This happened to a friend that I met at the university. Beings from other dimensions, or other rooms, can come here and communicate with us. Since they don't have a body here, they cannot interact with us so much. They are full of love and knowledge about the universe. Some people can allow them to talk through their body. It's just like having a normal conversation with another person. You can even feel their energy when they are in the body. Many people call it "channeling". A lot of information in this book is coming from these beings.

When these beings talk through the body of a person, the person doesn't always remember what happened. This is exactly what happened to my friend at the university. These beings are really amazing. They come from all over the universe and their messages are so helpful. It's not so important for us to try to understand who they are. It is more important for us to focus on their messages. We can learn so much from them.

Many people feel uncomfortable knowing that there is a being talking through the body of another person but this happens all the time. Unfortunately, many people don't know, but when someone is drunk sometimes they are actually channeling another being. The alcohol produces a very low vibration, so they are channeling beings who are not very advanced. These beings don't understand love. That is why people can become violent, and that is why they don't remember what happened. They were channeling lower beings. The alcohol goes into the blood and it alters the cells. It limits the connection between the person and their own body. They are separating themselves from their own body by their own will. By doing this, they allow other types of energy to take over the body.

I never drank alcohol so I don't understand what it feels like to be drunk. I don't want to know. I didn't know but my whole life was preparing me for something bigger. That is why I was the way I was.

I wanted to learn how to channel but I didn't know anyone who could do it. I knew there were videos on the internet of some people channeling. The information coming from these beings is amazing. They understand humans, they understand that we are learning a lesson and they know that we don't remember who we are. They are trying to help us by telling us the information that we can understand.

I asked my guides if they could teach me how to channel. They never gave me an answer. I didn't know why.

A few months later, my guides told me that I had to go for a long trip. Usually, I traveled for a few days or a few weeks but I never traveled for more than five weeks. My guides told me that I should go for a long trip outside Europe. I didn't know where to go or how to do it.

Then a good friend came to visit me. She was a very experienced traveler and she also travels alone. When we met, we were talking about our experiences around the world. We realized that we both had learned how to travel in a very cheap way.

We started to have ideas about traveling the world together in a very cheap way. Since we were very experienced, we could do it together. We were talking about it as a joke but then we started to talk about it more seriously. I talked to her about my guides. I thought that she would think I was crazy but she really listened to me and believed me. I felt very comfortable with this, so I started to think more seriously about traveling together.

She loved Latin America and everything related to that part of the world. We talked about leaving our jobs and everything we had in Europe and starting a trip around Latin America, from Mexico to Argentina. After some time, we decided to really do it.

I asked my guides if that was okay and they told me that the trip was a great idea. They told me that during that trip I would meet someone who would help me a lot.

We started to plan the trip. During the planning, we decided to change a few things. We decided to start in Alaska and travel to Argentina, and if possible, to Antarctica. We would not travel cheaply. We would do it without using any money - no money involved in the whole trip from Alaska to Antarctica. We would film everything during the trip and we would make a documentary about it.

Chapter 20 – The Money

It was official. We were doing it. We would travel from Alaska to Antarctica without money. Maybe this was too crazy for many people but we really believed it. We would travel without money and we would make a movie about the experience. This was our original plan.

For accommodations, we could use Couchsurfing. For transportation, we could hitchhike. For food, we didn't know. My friend told me something I never tried before. She told me about "dumpster diving". Basically, it means that you go to supermarket dumpsters and take the products that they throw out. I was surprised when I saw all the food they didn't sell and throw into the dumpster. In the beginning, I felt very uncomfortable with the idea but I tried. It changed my image of food forever.

I realized that food is thrown into the dumpsters for many reasons. One of the reasons is because they expire. I learned that the expiration date is something required for any product by governments, but it does not necessarily mean that the product is not in good condition and edible. Many fruits and vegetables are thrown away because they are "ugly" and nobody wants them. I found many fruits and vegetables in perfect shape and completely edible. In some cases, it was necessary to cut off some parts, and the rest was completely fine. I also found many products that were not expired yet. I learned that many supermarkets fill their displays with products so it looks more attractive to the customers and they always keep them full. When they don't have a good amount of a product to display, they remove it and throw it away because only a few products are not attractive to the customer. In some supermarkets where they have their own bakery, some burn the bread after few days because they want to sell only fresh products. They burn it so nobody can take it from the dumpster.

They do this because supermarkets have had problems in the past. The supermarket throws away bread or any other product. Then somebody takes it from the dumpster and claims that they bought the product but it was not in perfect shape, expired, or ugly. We met other dumpster divers. They knew everything about it and they shared the same information I am sharing here. They also advised us to be careful with meat in the dumpster because it's usually very bad. But since we were vegetarian, we didn't worry about the meat.

Almost 50 % of the food in Europe is wasted, not only because it's thrown away but also because many people buy things they don't use. The food stays in the refrigerator for weeks until it becomes expired and they throw it away.

We got the flight tickets to Alaska. We paid for the flight tickets but we would not use money after that.

Before Alaska, we wanted to practice in Europe. My friend and I hitchhiked around Finland, Sweden and Norway for 3 weeks. We didn't spend money. We realized that it was possible and much easier than we thought.

We were ready for our trip. We were flying from Helsinki to Alaska, but first we had to make a stop in London. At the airport in London, we started to be hungry. We were not supposed to use money even though we were not in Alaska yet. We knew how to dumpster dive, but it was not possible to do at the airport. We didn't see any dumpsters available.

We decided to go to a restaurant and tell them our story. We told them we were traveling without any money and we usually got food from the dumpster. Since we didn't see any dumpsters, we didn't know what to do. We had money on our debit cards but we would use it only in case of an emergency.

The people in the restaurant loved what we were doing. They even felt inspired. They offered us a meal. They told us that they knew about food waste and it cost nothing for them to give us food. But since they didn't want to lose customers, we should wait until they closed the restaurant.

The manager explained to us that they throw away all the food that is not sold at the end of the day because they have regulations and they have to follow them. We were so thankful for the food but he was also thankful. He said that he always wanted to help people but he never saw the opportunity to do it. It was amazing. We were getting food, we were inspiring people and we didn't have to check the dumpsters.

We were not really sure how everything would work later. We just wanted to try everything and get as far as we could.

On the flight from London to Alaska, we were curious about food waste on planes. We talked to the flight attendants. They told us that there is a lot of food waste on planes. They heard our story, and they were also inspired. My friend and I realized that many people were inspired by this idea, so from that moment we decided to share our project with everyone we met on the road.

We arrived in Anchorage, Alaska. We started hitchhiking all the way to Prudhoe Bay (the north of Alaska). The plan was working much better than we thought. We met a lot of people and we were listening to so many stories. This trip was not possible without the help of people. There was no money involved but we were having a good time. This was like our payment.

After telling the same story to many people, we started to get bored. We didn't have the same emotion while telling the story and people could feel it. This was a big lesson for us. We realized that to impact people we had to be motivated. So every time we talked to people about our experience, we added something else. This way we always had something new to talk about but more importantly, we told the stories with a lot of emotion.

My friend and I realized that the energy we used while telling our story was directly affecting the people. It didn't matter what we were saying. The energy was felt by the people. We could see the changes immediately. We learned how important it is to put authentic emotion and energy in our words. We couldn't fake it.

Something we learned was to be open to anything and accept everything. We learned how to stop expecting.

We had another big lesson. For me, this was probably one of the best lessons I ever learned. When we need something, we automatically think about how to get it. We think about buying it. We usually think about working, getting money and buying the product. When I was traveling without money, we couldn't think about that. In fact, our language changed. We were not saying, "I need to buy something." We were saying, "I need to get something." We stopped thinking about how to get things.

I stopped saying, "I will try." Instead I was saying, "I will do it." This helped me visualize something better and believe it. The language we use can affect our perception of things. You can get to know someone just by observing how they speak, the words they use and the intention behind the word.

We were able to travel and have food, somewhere to stay and transportation without having to use money. Also, we were able to enter all the national parks and many other places without money. We were hitchhiking, and the entrance fee for the national parks is per car, not per person. We could get many things without money, but we didn't know what to do if we needed new shoes or clothes. This is when the magic started.

After few weeks of traveling around Alaska, we went to Canada. We were very active every day and we loved it. Sometimes we had to take a break and stay in one place for a few days so we could think about all the places we had visited and the people we had met. Every day there was something new. After walking so much in all kinds of places, my shoes started to be damaged. I had no idea how to get new shoes without buying them.

I really didn't know how to get new shoes. I really needed them. In my mind, I was not thinking about how to get them. I just knew that I needed them. I asked my guides if I could manifest shoes out of nowhere, similar to what I did when I was a child and manifested the money. They said, "Yes, you can. But is your belief strong enough?"

I was good at observing my own thoughts. I had to be realistic. Even though I knew many things about the universe, my belief was not strong enough to truly believe that I could manifest shoes out of nowhere. But I knew that I could use forms to play with my mind and make the belief stronger.

I have big feet and I always had problems finding my shoe size. My size is 48 in Europe (around size 14 in the USA). I knew the problem. The problem was my belief about finding my size. I needed a form to change that belief. I could use any form but I wasn't sure what.

My shoes were so damaged that they had holes. I was even able to poke my toes out of one of them. I started to wonder why I was ashamed to have a hole in my shoe. Maybe it was because society would judge me and I was afraid of that. But who said how shoes should be? There are people who have holes in their jeans. They wear them because they believe that it is nice. It is all about belief. I noticed that I was looking for a form to change my thoughts. But the form didn't have to be something physical. It could be an idea. My form could be my own thoughts about what was acceptable in society.

I had the form. It would be my own thoughts about what society thinks about holes in a shoe. I tried watching people but they didn't have holes in their shoes. I needed something different. I thought about people with holes in their jeans. If they could believe that it looks good I could do it as well. But I had to be honest, I never liked holes in the pants so it would be harder for me to change that thought. It would be easier if I changed my thoughts about what society thinks about the holes in shoes.

Then I saw a homeless man. He had holes in his shoes but in my mind, the idea of a homeless person was not good so it wouldn't work. But then I realized that actually, I was homeless. I didn't have a home. I was sleeping in a different place almost every day, so I was homeless too. I may not the same type of homeless, but I was homeless.

My friend and I were very clean all the time. We were very careful with the way we looked because we knew that it was important when we were hitchhiking. People would stop their cars if they saw us clean.

Many people, including myself (at that time), think of a homeless person as dirty. This may not sound nice but we have to be honest with ourselves. Otherwise, we would be lying to ourselves and the forms will not work. We really have to analyze our thoughts as they are, not as they should be. And it's very important to accept the way you think. It doesn't matter what it is or what other people think about it.

When we met people, my friend and I started to say that we were actually homeless. Many people laughed when we said this but it was important for me to believe it. So telling people that we were homeless would help me to believe that it was okay to be homeless. Since I was homeless, I would believe that it's more acceptable to have holes in my shoes or even the wrong size.

I understand this sounds crazy but it works. We are just a bunch of ideas in our minds. We are who we think we are, just because we believe it. For example, when actors and actresses are filming a movie, they have to play a role. Some actors decide to stay in their role during the whole time they are filming. This could be several months. This means that the personality of the actor disappears. They are basically someone else. Or the idea of who they think they are has changed. When the filming is over, and they want to go back to "normal", some actors may have difficulty because they realize they can be anyone they want. Basically, we are just a bunch of ideas about who we think we are.

My guides told me this and I can see it clearly. My guides told me that when we go to the 4th dimension we don't have a body. When we decide to come back to the 3rd dimension to have another life experience, we usually choose a similar body as previous lives. This is because the body we choose is an idea of who we think we are.

Something similar happens in our reality. The world around us is an image of all of us. This may be hard to imagine, but the stars, the planets and everything around us really doesn't exist. It is a projection of our thoughts.

The world we see right now is not real. It is an illusion - a hologram. Let's say that the real world is only geometrical shapes with many colors. These geometrical shapes and the colors would be like the code of our holographic world. Plato was talking about these geometrical shapes in ancient Greece. Everything has a geometrical shape - even our thoughts and feelings.

This holographic world is related to our thoughts. We can literally change our reality with our thoughts. Our thoughts have geometrical shapes and these shapes are the code of our reality. So by changing the code, we will change our reality. For example, if you have a thought about having a new job, and you focus on having a positive job, your thought will create an energy. This energy is not visible but it creates a geometric shape. If you put more intention to this shape, eventually it will become more visible in the physical world until eventually, in your physical world, in one way or another, you will have a positive job. On the other hand, if you focus on how much you hate your current job, the energy of hate will create a different shape. This shape will be focused on the lack of a positive job. Therefore, this shape will eventually make a stronger reality where you don't have a positive job.

When you use a computer, you only see the screen. Behind the screen, there is a code running so you can see only the screen. The shapes are like the code in the computer and the reality that you see is the screen. The same way you can modify the code in a computer, you can change the code in your reality. You do it with your thoughts.

There are many comets passing close to the planet. There have been many that most people are not aware of. The media doesn't talk about them and sometimes we are not able to see them because of the hologram around the planet. It would not show the comet approaching the planet. It will show nothing happening.

Around 1970, the Sun started expanding. The Sun started to grow and it covered several planets, including Earth. This is hard to imagine but we are actually inside the Sun right now. The reason why we don't see it is because of the hologram around Earth. Also, there are cycles on the planet that cause the changes in the weather that we are experiencing now. Human activities have an impact on the weather, but it's not as severe as reported by mainstream media. The *Problematic beings* are using the changes in the weather as an excuse to create fear in people. They present the climate change as a problem, they offer a solution, and they look like the heroes. But the "solution" is an excuse to get humans' approval to implement their control on Earth. They have been doing it this way for many years. The *Problematic beings* want to create a new global organization by the year 2030 that controls activities related to the weather and environment. They don't really care about the world. They are using the excuse of global warming to implement this new organization and have more control, and they will do anything to achieve it. They will create propaganda or any other method to make it happen. They need the approval of people, so if we don't believe them anymore, it will not happen.

The hologram that is preventing us from seeing the real heat of the Sun will be turned off someday, and we will have to deal with the heat. Many ancient civilizations knew about this.

Our reality is as if we were inside a video game. Our thoughts are related to the code of the video game. We can actually communicate with the person controlling our character. This would be like another version of ourselves. Many people call it our *higher self*.

Most of the time our *higher selves* and guides are just observing because we are supposed to learn by ourselves. However, we can communicate with our *higher self* and find out more about why we are here at this time. Every time we come to the 3rd dimension we come with a mission, or several missions. Once you find out about them your whole life starts to be focused on that.

Our guides would be like someone sitting next to our *higher self*. They are also just observing. They have to let us grow on our own but they are there in case they are needed for help.

Our guides can communicate with us in many ways. They can talk directly to us, but most of the time we don't hear them because our minds are always busy thinking about something. That is why it's important to stop thinking when we don't need to. Meditation is one of the best ways, probably the best way, to stop thinking. It is also easier for us to hear their messages if we spend time in nature.

We have been disconnected from nature in many ways. If you live in a city, you may not have much access to nature. Our houses have a big layer on the floor that keeps us isolated from Earth. Also, we spend most of the time wearing shoes. It will be very helpful to spend time in nature without shoes like many of the indigenous peoples.

Also, we can hear them better if we don't eat processed food or meat. Probably the best time to hear them is after not eating for several hours because our body will not be busy digesting the food. They also talk to us in our dreams. Sometimes they talk to us through a person. When we need to hear or feel a message, sometimes a random person or even a friend will tell us something that will help us understand the message. Another way our guides communicate is through numbers.

Whenever you see repetitive numbers, for example, 111 or 333, it's a message for you. The more numbers you see, the bigger the confirmation. You don't have to search for these numbers. You will see them randomly in one way or another. It could be on the page of a book, the clock, the license plate of a car or anywhere. You have to be honest with yourself and let the numbers come to you. It is the same with your thoughts. If your thoughts are leading you to another thought, it is you creating that thought. But if a thought comes to you without any connection to previous thoughts, that was probably a message for you.

The message is related to your thoughts at that moment. If you are thinking about something and suddenly you see a number, this number is a message for you related to your thought. That is why is important to be aware of your own thoughts.

For example:

111 means energy flow. Whenever you see these numbers, the message is to let things flow. Allow things to happen the way they are.

222 means that a new cycle in your life is about to start.

333 means that you have to make a decision. When you see these numbers, you have to decide what to do about whatever you are thinking at that moment. After you make the decision, there are two options. You may see 999 which means that you have chosen the right thing or 666 means that you made the decision that is not the best for you at that moment.

444 is related to your higher purpose in life. When you see these numbers, it means that you are more aware of your purpose in this life. You are interacting with something important for you in this lifetime.

555 is an important number. It is related to the numbers 444. It means that whatever was happening with 444 is completed. These numbers are like a confirmation for you that the cycle of the 444 has been closed.

666 is related to the material world. Whatever you are thinking when you see these numbers is not the best for you at that moment. It is related to the material world, which is not helping you in your development. The material world is related to carbon. Our physical body is made of carbon. Carbon has 6 electrons, 6 protons, and 6 neutrons. This means that we are getting away from our purpose in life and focusing on our material world, which is not real.

777 is related to 444. When you see 444, it means that you are getting close to one of your purposes in life. 777 means that you are already practicing what you have learned with 444. Then, 555 would be the completion. It would mean that you have mastered it.

888 is also related to 444. In other words, 444 would mean that whatever you are thinking, is something important for you in this lifetime. 777 would mean that you already started to practice it. 888 would mean that you completed a lesson related to 444. And 555 would mean that it is closed.

999 means that you have completed the 333. It means that the cycle you started with 333 has been completed.

000 means nothing.

The more numbers you see, for example, 11111, or 3333, is a bigger confirmation.

Letters could also be translated into numbers. A=1, B=2, C=3, D=4, etc.

This is probably hard to understand and it takes practice to start noticing. But it works. We can play with the reality we observe. Communication is happening often. We just don't see it. Also, if you don't get the messages in the beginning, don't think too much about it. Thinking too much about the meaning could result in us understanding it differently. If you don't get it the first time, let it go. It will come later.

Chapter 21 – The Decision

There is another way that my guides communicate with me but I haven't heard of any other person having the same kind of communication. I like to learn languages. In my room, I have many papers on the wall with words in different languages. This way I see the words often until I learn how to speak in other languages. Sometimes, when I am in my room, my attention goes to a specific word on the wall. There are so many words, but my attention goes to one word in particular. That word is like a message for me. The word on the wall may be in German, French, or any other language, and I may not know the word in that language. But I understand that word is a message for me.

While writing this book I heard my guides telling me several things or putting images in my brain so I could write it down. Sometimes I don't hear the messages clearly, and suddenly my attention goes to a word on the wall. For example, the word can be something like *"rester"*. In French it means "stay". But when I read the word in my head, I understood "rest" like in English. So I understood that they were telling me to take a rest. So this book is not written only by me. My guides have been helping me the whole time.

Our world is alive. It is conscious. It knows about its own existence. The whole universe is a conscious being. Everything in our universe is created by us. All beings living here, including us, are creating this world. We can also have our own personal experience but this is up to each individual. Whatever we do will affect the whole universe.

The ego lives in the mind. If you are aware of your own ego and minimalize it, you can start experiencing your reality from the heart (connected to the brain). The heart doesn't have ego. Once you start experiencing reality from the heart, you can create anything you want in your life much faster. You can play with forms anytime. You may not even need forms.

The problem with the brain is that it contains ego and ego creates separation. For anything good, there is something bad. That is why the brain is divided into two. There is no good or bad. This is an illusion from the brain.

The whole universe is united. It is a conscious being. We are all part of the universe. The universe would not be the universe without us. We are the electricity (the energy) running through the battery (our bodies). And the electricity runs very fast through every battery. It is everywhere at the same time. The idea of separation is just an illusion, an illusion from the mind.

Here in the 3rd dimension, room number 4, we are experiencing a reality that we all create collectively with our thoughts and ego. We create this world with our brain (thoughts) and our hearts (no ego) connected, although most people live only in the brain.

Please try to visualize it in your own way; it will help you so much to understand your own life.

When you wish for something from the brain (with ego), eventually, you will get it, but also the opposite. For example, if you ask for a new house and you do it from the brain, you will get the new house. But then you may feel like the new house is not fulfilling what you expected when you thought about the house. In other words, the house was probably intended for the possession of the house, but not to fulfill the need of being at home. It was created from the brain which contains ego (separation). This is how we have been living since we came to the 3rd dimension. When you connect to your heart, your life will improve dramatically. Then, all life on Earth, the universe, and other dimensions will also improve.

When a person has negative thoughts, it is a reflection of the world they see. You can understand the way somebody experiences this reality just by the way they talk about everything. The world can be beautiful if you decide to look at it this way. When someone talks about "reality", it is just the reality this person is experiencing. Every person can have an opinion about anything but it's just the reality they have created for themselves. If you watch the news and you see "bad" things happening all the time, it doesn't totally mean that the world is bad. It is the reality they want you to see.

The *Problematic beings* don't understand this. They believe that they can exist without being part of the universe even though they live here. This is just not possible. They can also create a world for themselves but it's an illusion. In this illusion, they have decided to create a world where they don't belong to the rest. This is pure ego. They don't use the heart. So they don't understand us. That is why they tried to force us to live their way. Unfortunately, they will not make it to the next level. They didn't pass their own test. But somebody will take care of them when the time arrives. All beings in the universe are immortal. When the body dies, they are just relocated to a place where they can keep learning. Dinosaurs didn't die. They are on another planet. All extinct animals on Earth are somewhere else learning in their own way.

The same way every being is at the right place for their evolution, in your life you can get everything you need whenever it's needed. You can create day by day. This may sound like just a good philosophy but it's how reality works.

During the trip, we were somewhere in Canada, walking in a park. The park was empty and we were a little bit tired after many hours of walking around the city. We were walking and filming ourselves saying that we were very tired. Suddenly, we saw something black on the road. It was a pair of completely new shoes. Somebody probably didn't like them and threw them there. This could have been a huge coincidence but as my guides say, there are never coincidences.

Everything is a message. Even if something looks very bad, it's just a message. You decide how to take it. Even when we have an accident, this is probably a message for us. The result of the accident would change the direction of our lives. It may look bad, but it's the only way you could turn your life to the direction you are supposed to.

When I found the shoes in the park, I was walking and filming. When I saw the shoes, as I joke I said, "Ooh, look, I just found my new shoes." I tried them on and they were exactly my size. I know this story sounds hard to believe for some people but this is how it happened. It happens to everyone.

After traveling around Canada, my friend and I decided to enter the United States. We changed our original plan. We realized that it was much harder to hitchhike in the United States than in Canada. We noticed that people were more hesitant to pick up hitchhikers. We had to wait much longer than in Canada but we had to keep going. We were in the state of Washington. We decided to skip Seattle because it's hard to hitchhike inside cities.

We were on our way to Spokane when weird things started to happen. We were picked up by a woman. She was very nice. We talked about our project and she liked it. This woman was so excited about the project that she insisted on taking us to a restaurant. We told her that we appreciated her offer but we really wanted to continue that day. She insisted that she really wanted to take us to a restaurant. In the end, we gratefully accepted. The woman took us to her favorite restaurant. It was in the east part of Seattle. She told us that after the restaurant she would take us to any entrance on the highway where we could start hitchhiking again.

We were having a good time with the woman. There was Wi-Fi at the restaurant so we decided to check our emails and messages. My friend got a message from a friend who lives in Seattle. She knew about the project and wanted to meet us. We told her the name of the restaurant and she came right away.

We were all at the restaurant having a good time. We decided to stay with my friend's friend in Seattle. She took us to her house and showed us the city. Then she introduced us to her neighbor. Her neighbor heard about our project and she wanted to hear how we asked for food at restaurants. She didn't believe we could eat for free from a restaurant so we showed her. We knew everything about it. It was normal food. We just had to ask specifically for food that we knew they would not be able to sell and would be thrown away anyway.

Usually, we went to several restaurants. We would talk to the manager and explain our project. Some people really liked the idea. Some others just ignored us, but we always got food. Sometimes they offered us a normal meal from the menu. It really depended on the manager. We got used to doing this and we were not ashamed. We knew that everything was in our mind. This experience was helping us to understand our own thoughts.

Our new friend took us for a hike in the forest. When we arrived at the place, there was another person, a friend of our friend. This new person didn't talk much. She just said, "Hello, my name is Christina Hill," and she didn't say anything else after that.

I don't know why, but I started to talk a lot. I was talking non-stop. I even started to talk about my guides. Usually, I never talk about my guides to people I just met but this day I talked about my guides openly. After a while, Christina stopped walking. She said that she wanted to be alone but she had a message for me. She said I should call her once I am ready. I really didn't know what she was talking about so I ignored her.

We continued traveling around the United States. We visited almost every national park. The project was working better than we thought. The documentary was working perfectly. We had very good material. We even got a ride from an expert on documentaries who promised to work on our film once we finished our trip.

We traveled around for several months. We saw almost every state in the United States. Many things happened during this trip. Almost everything we wanted came to us. We knew it was important to keep our energy up and not to expect anything. There was one thing we started to expect. We really wanted to see bears. We expected it so much but it didn't happen. After a while, we realized that we were having expectations. When we realized that, we saw a bear. But it was not how we imagined. One night, we were biking.

I don't even remember how we got the bikes. A bear ran in front of me. We were not scared, but immediately we realized that the bear appeared because we stopped expecting. Even if we did expect it, we would never imagine that we would see it this way.

Winter was coming and we started to feel it. We were thinking about spending time on the beach but we were very far from the oceans. We were moving on average 100 km (62 miles) per day so it would take us more than a week to get to any beach. A few days after having these thoughts, we got a ride with a person who was going to Miami. We didn't think twice, and asked him to take us to Miami.

We had a friend living in Miami. We decided to stop traveling for a few weeks and take a rest there. Also, we would have time to check all the material for the documentary. I wanted to know more about the person I met in Seattle, Christina Hill. She was very mysterious. Maybe there was a message for me. I checked on the internet and realized she was a channeler. There was a being from another dimension who talked through her body. I remembered what she told me. She said that I should call her once I am ready. I found her telephone number on the internet and I called her. I told her that I knew who she was. I told her that I understood what she did. And I told her that I was ready. Whatever it was, I was ready.

She asked me to move to Seattle so we could work together. I told her that I would not leave the project. It was very important to me. But also I wanted to learn how to channel. The trip was planned to take two or three years. Somehow, I knew that I had to make a decision, now or never. I just knew it.

When my guides told me that I would meet someone who would help me, I thought they meant someone in South America. But I never imagined that it would be in the United States.

It was a very hard decision for me. The project of traveling without money was awesome and it was going perfectly fine. But moving to Seattle would mean a big opportunity for me. Inside, I was totally divided. I didn't know what to do. I asked my guides for help. They told me to do what I really wanted. What I really wanted was to learn how to channel but I also liked the trip. I talked to my friend. She knew that both things were important to me. She didn't want me to cancel the project but at the same time, she knew that it was a big opportunity for me.

I really didn't know what to do. In that moment I knew that with any decision I made, my life would change. I just had to decide which road I wanted to take. It was a very hard decision but I decided to move to Seattle.

Chapter 22 – The Channel

When I arrived in Seattle, Christina told me she had a free room available in her apartment. We could share the apartment so we could get to know each other better and work closely. To be honest, I didn't know exactly why I was there. I didn't know what she meant by "work". I couldn't believe that I was there. The only thing I knew was that I would learn new things and I really wanted that.

Christina told me that there was one being talking through her body. The name of the being was Athella, a female from the 12th dimension, the highest dimension in the universe. Christina told me that Athella wanted to talk to me. She was able to hear Athella all the time. I asked Christina how this happened and she told me her story.

Christina had a difficult life since she was born. Her parents died when she was only a few days old. She was adopted by a very religious family when she was six weeks old. During her childhood, Christina started to realize that she had psychic powers. She could talk to beings but her family was not able to see anything. The family denied anything that Christina said about talking to beings. She had many problems with her family because of this.

She got in trouble at school for telling the teachers that there were beings talking to her. Only Christina could see them. Many people started to convince her that these beings were not real. When she was a teenager and after many years hiding her psychic powers, she decided to shut it off. She ignored these beings until eventually she was no longer talking to them. She started to have a "normal life".

The family that adopted her was abusing her physically, psychologically and sexually. She didn't have a place to go and she was surrounded by abuse at home. Her family forgot about her many times. They left her alone in supermarkets and other places. She had a very difficult childhood.

When she was 18 years old, she left the house. She didn't know where to go so she ended up homeless. She even went to Mexico for a while. Then she went to Seattle where she ended up living on the streets.

While living on the streets, she started to have all kinds of addictions - alcohol, drugs, and sex addiction which led to prostitution. All of the people around her were trying to hurt her. This created a lot of trauma for her. She lived like this for many years. Christina told me that she felt like she was dying.

Suddenly, Christina started to be interested in hypnosis. It was something that came naturally to her since childhood. She had access to a library so she decided to study hypnosis by herself. A few years later, she wanted to learn much more about hypnosis so she started to contact people working in this field. She started to learn about all kinds of hypnosis.

In 2015, she was still having problems with addictions. She started to have a lot of health problems. She was looking for help. She tried many things but her health didn't improve. Then she started to have big pain in her throat. She saw several doctors but they couldn't help her. She started to try different things. She tried a kind of hypnosis called "past life regression". She contacted a person who does past life regressions. She tried it and then something happened.

During the session, her consciousness went somewhere else. And then she saw someone like an angelic being. She was a tall woman with long blond hair and blue eyes. This being talked to her and said, "You are suffering. You are dying. I came to help you. A long time ago, before you were born, we agreed to have this meeting. You can call me Athella."

Athella told Christina that even though they had an agreement a long time ago, she had to ask again. The agreement was that Christina would work with Athella to help other people. At the same time, Christina would be healed. Christina accepted and everything in her life changed.

Later, Athella told Christina that she appeared as a blond woman with blue eyes because the only person who loved Christina was a neighbor she had during her childhood. This person had these characteristics. Unfortunately, her neighbor died when Christina was still a child.

Athella also told Christina that she would bring people and form a team. That is why I ended up in Seattle. I became part of the Athella team.

Christina asked me not to tell anyone about her past and not to talk too much about her to other people. She was still recovering from all of the trauma. I told my family and friends that I moved to Seattle. It was not exactly in Seattle, but close to it. I mentioned Seattle because it's the biggest city close to where Christina lived. She was actually living next to a forest.

My family and friends wanted to know why I moved to Seattle. At that time, many people around me didn't know that I was going through something huge in my life. I didn't know how to explain it. At the same time, I wanted to keep Christina's life as private as possible.

Christina is much older than me, but she looks very young. We decided to tell everyone that we were a couple. This would be easier for my family and friends to understand. In reality we were doing special work that is much bigger than that. We were telling people about their real nature. Christina didn't have family or friends so she didn't have to explain anything to anyone.

Christina and I became very good friends. I respected her decision to keep her past private. The only reason I am sharing this information right now is because a few years later Christina decided to talk openly about it. There is even a movie about her life before she met Athella. The movie is called Everyone Can Change.

Christina goes into a deep state of meditation and allows Athella to talk through her body. While this is happening, Christina is unconscious and unaware of the passing of time. After Athella leaves and Christina comes back, Christina doesn't know how long she was there because she had no experience of time where she was.

There are several types of channeling. You can communicate with other beings with intuition. Some people can see and talk to these beings. Some people can allow the beings to talk through their bodies. Some people do it laying down, some people sitting, some people standing or even walking. Usually, it's done with the eyes closed but some people do it with their eyes open.

When we think all day, our brain waves are in the state known as beta brain waves with a frequency between 12 to 30 Hz. Our brain is in this state when we need to do activities such as driving or working in an office.

GAMMA	〰〰〰
BETA	〰〰〰
ALPHA	〰〰〰
THETA	〰〰〰
DELTA	〰〰〰

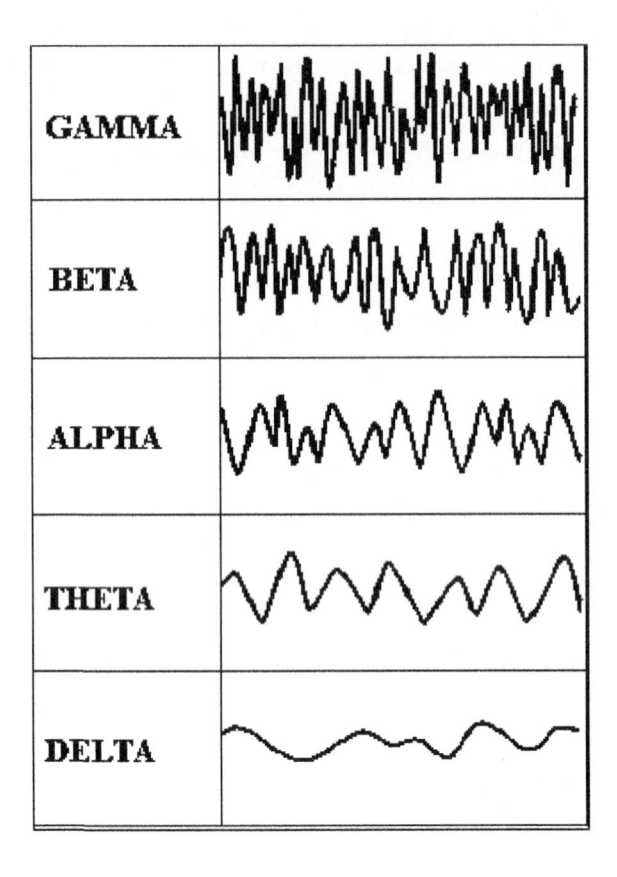

A lower level is the alpha brain waves with a frequency between 7.5 to 12 Hz. The brain is in this state when we are in meditation or deep relaxation. This state is when we are more creative. I wanted to train my brain to keep this state even when working in an office. It is possible and it helps to react more consciously about any circumstance.

The next level is the theta brain waves with a frequency between 4 to 7.5 Hz. We reach this state when we are in deep meditation or light sleeping. We experience something called Rapid Eye Movement during this stage. This happens to humans and many animals. The eyes move rapidly in different directions. It happens around 90 minutes after falling asleep.

The lowest level is when our brain is in Delta brain waves with a frequency up to 4 Hz. This happens when we are unconscious or in deep sleep. In this state, we don't have dreams.

There is another level that is higher than beta brain waves. It's called gamma brain waves with a frequency between 30 to 100 Hz. Reaching this level is very unusual. Only monks and experienced meditators can reach this level.

When Christina starts to channel Athella her eyes start to move very quickly, like with theta brain waves. When she is unconscious she reaches gamma brain waves. Athella told me that when she is in Christina's body, she slows down her heart rate and stops the functionality of all organs except the heart and the brain. This makes sense because when Athella is present, Christina's body doesn't show any sign of activity like the stomach digesting and she never coughs or sneezes.

Athella talks through Christina's body while she is sitting, standing or walking. Sometimes with eyes open, but most of the time with eyes closed.

When I talked to Athella the first time, the first thing she said was, "You are not here by coincidence. You are supposed to be here."

Then Athella told me that we already had an agreement a long time ago, before I was born, but she wanted to ask me again. The agreement was that I would work with Christina and Athella as a team. We would help people to remember who they are and show them the real nature of humanity. At the same time, Athella would train me to learn more about myself and the universe, including learning how to channel. She also said, "If you accept, you have to help

Christina heal completely from the trauma of her past and you should not leave Christina no matter what."

I couldn't believe that I was talking directly to a being from the 12th dimension. And she was asking me to work with her. This was a huge moment in my life. I accepted.

Athella is, more precisely, from room number 5 in the 12th dimension. She has never been human. She came here to help humanity. We can learn from her and she is learning about humans, although she already knows many things. She is from the star called Sirius B. The star Sirius A is the brightest star in the sky but Sirius B is not visible. Even if we could go there, we would not see Athella. She is in the 12th dimension. Athella decided to come to Earth to help humans during this time of change. Athella talks through Christina's body but it doesn't mean that Athella is here just for Christina. She is here for everyone.

I talked to Athella every day. She was giving us instructions about what to do but we also had to take responsibility for any action we decided to take. Athella knew that I was not eating meat and Christina was vegan.

Athella asked me to become vegan. Basically, I was already vegan. I just was not paying complete attention to all the ingredients in my food. I became vegan to be able to connect to Mother Earth more quickly during meditation. Having the intention of loving all life forms was my way of telling Mother Earth that I love her. The connection with her was faster and natural. Before trying to connect with higher beings, you really have to connect with Mother Earth first.

Another thing that Athella told me was that the human body doesn't require animal protein. I asked several friends who are doctors and they told me that protein can be obtained from many types of food. The only thing I had to be careful of when being vegan was to take in enough iron and vitamin B12. I was used to eating lentils or beans every three or four days and they contain iron so I didn't have to worry about that. I never paid attention to the vitamin B12. I met several vegan people who told me that they obtain the vitamin B12 through meditation. Maybe I was getting the vitamin B12 the same way and I didn't know. But now I am more careful and I eat food fortified with vitamin B12.

Another good way to get the vitamins and minerals is with supplements. I always wanted to get the minerals naturally, but my guides told me something interesting. The planet provides all the needed vitamins and minerals through the fruits and vegetables. When an ice age occurs, the planet takes all the minerals and places them in the right place so all life on the planet can obtain these minerals. But it has been several thousands of years since the last ice age, so the minerals in fruits and vegetables are not the same as in the past, therefore some vitamin and mineral supplements will help at this time.

Every time Athella said something through Christina's body, Christina was not aware of what was happening. So after Christina came back, I had to tell her what Athella said. When Athella was in Christina's body, you could feel it. It was an amazing feeling in the whole room. It was incredible and so beautiful. I felt like I was floating in clouds and didn't have to worry about anything at all. When Christina came back, it would usually take me a few minutes to return from the clouds. Christina also experienced something similar. Every person who talked to Athella said something similar about feeling like they were in the clouds.

Athella told me that I was very good at handling thoughts but she wanted me to get even better. She showed me how to meditate. Since that day, I have been meditating every day.

Meditation is very important if you want to understand yourself better. There are many types of meditation, and I cannot tell you which meditation is the best. Every person is different, and you have to try many types of meditation until you find the right one for you. There is not a best meditation in the world. You can start with guided meditations. Try as many as you can. Keep trying and don't stop. You can meditate with crystals. They will help you. There are many types of crystals. This is like meditation. There is no perfect crystal for everyone. You have to try several crystals until you find the right one for you.

Be like a child. Imagine that you are a child playing. If you take this very seriously it will not work. You have to put all your emotions into what you do, like a child. Enjoy it and have fun. It is important that you feel it.

Many times we forget that we can have fun the same way a child does. Once we become an adult, many times we think that being responsible means being serious. But you can play like a child and still be responsible. Society has a big impact on us, therefore we behave more seriously in front of other people. There are some things that are socially acceptable. For example, it is okay to express love for dogs on the street. But in some cases, the same expression of love towards other people may not be acceptable in public. This is a limitation created by society but it's only in our minds.

I tried many meditations that didn't do anything for me. My guides told me that I should keep trying and not to expect anything from it. The first time I started to meditate was in Australia when I was trying to find kangaroos. I didn't know what I was doing. Many other times I didn't know what I was doing. I just wanted to try everything.

I learned that breathing correctly is extremely important. You have to breathe consciously. You have to be aware of your own breath, always. Even if you don't meditate, you can visualize that you are the oxygen, and the oxygen is you. You are one. This is what the angels told me.

Many people were trying to talk to Athella. I realized that many people already understand many spiritual things. I was amazed and happy at the same time. I met many people coming to talk to Athella. Many of them where doctors, psychologists, scientists, lawyers, engineers, business leaders, and even celebrities. These people understood who Athella was. They knew many things about the nature of humanity. But most of them were keeping it secret because they were afraid to be called crazy. Celebrities are normal people, with problems like anyone else. Some of them are very aware of what is really happening around the world. Some others don't know anything about it. You will notice that celebrities talk about unusual things from time to time. They are just trying to help other people.

I realized that many people know about what is happening. They just feel ashamed to talk about it. Many doctors told me that they really wanted to help people, but they didn't know how to apply this knowledge using traditional medicine. That is why they were coming to see Athella. They wanted advice. I remember that there were doctors coming to ask if vaccines cause autism in babies. It seems that this was creating a lot of discussion in the USA. From what I remember, the answer was that most medicines are fine, and most of them are not directly causing autism.

But some vaccinations have toxins that can harm people, and people with these toxins may be diagnosed with autism. Many vaccinations can harm the body, but the body can always recover, especially with meditation or healing techniques. Also, some minerals can help, like ormus (white powder gold). I also remember that many people wanted their babies to develop their own immune system without vaccines, and they wanted to know if that was possible. I remember that the answer was yes, and that would be the best option.

Also, many people working in big corporations knew about Athella and high dimensional beings. Some of them wanted to use their influence to help other people but they didn't know how. Some of them were trying to find a way to make more money. In these cases, Athella was very selective. She helped people manifest money only if they had intentions to help others. Otherwise, she would say no.

When I say manifesting, it means that suddenly something appears in your physical world. For example, people who wanted to manifest money could work on manifesting it until eventually, it appears. It came in different ways. Sometimes it came to them because they got a better job or they got the money from a donation. If you want to manifest money just for the sake of having more money, ego can easily be involved. I would suggest that you focus on what you want to buy with the money and you will manifest it faster. Money is just a form to get something else. Focus on what you really want to get with that money.

In order to manifest, you really have to believe it. You have to believe that whatever you want to achieve is possible for you. You have to visualize it. Feel it with all your senses. Write it down as many times as you can until you really believe it. Write it down with your non-dominant hand. If you are used to writing with your right hand, use the left one. Use a pencil, not a pen. The natural minerals in the pencil will help to manifest things faster. Write down everything you want to manifest. Write it down as many times as you can until you believe it. Then read it many times. Record yourself reading it. Then listen to your own voice saying it until you believe it with all your senses. You can manifest anything you want. Just make sure that you are not trying to manifest anything with ego. Ego will not help you.

I saw people manifesting all kinds of things. Health, peace in the mind, money, better relationships, travel, and many other things. But most of them came to learn how to live consciously and to talk to their guides.

You are free to manifest anything in your life. You really can create anything. Some beings are so aware of this that they can even create planets and galaxies. This galaxy was created by the angel called Metatron. He is a very tall being, around 17 meters high (55 feet), and his skin is blue.

The whole universe is connected. It seems there is nothing in space, but there is something. It's just not physical. You could send a message to any part of the universe instantly. Time really doesn't exist. And since the whole universe is connected, any message can be heard in any part of the universe instantly. As long as scientists keep focusing on measuring physical objects, they will not find out about the energy in space. I used to believe that the speed of light was the fastest thing in the universe but if time doesn't exist, then the speed also doesn't exist. It's an illusion.

You can create anything in your reality. It is your reality and you can live it the way you want it. You are the creator of your own reality. Nobody can do it for you. Someone can advise you or help you with their energy but in the end, you are the one doing it. You are free to create anything you want. Some people call it "free will". But you cannot affect other people. You can create anything you want but if it involves other people, you cannot force them to do anything.

If you try to create a reality that involves other people, and you try to force it, or you don't ask for permission from the person, this will cause a big problem for you. Remember, this is a school. We come here to learn how to love everything. If you force someone, you will be changing the path of this person. This is pure ego. Trying to control other people is ego. You have to love them the way they are. If you change someone's path, you will have to come back to the 3rd dimension to learn how to love. In other words, you will have to reincarnate several times until you learn how to love others. Some people call it karma.

Some celebrities want to use their influence to help other people. But also, they don't want to be called crazy. Some of them don't care so much and they talk openly about it.

I asked Athella if she could help me to finish my trip around Latin America and Antarctica. She told me that I didn't need help. She said that I knew how to do it. She was right. I never thought about it. I could do it if I wanted. I just had to believe that I was already there. You really have to imagine that it is already there. Otherwise, if you imagine it in the future, you will be acknowledging that you don't have it. It doesn't work like that.

I started to visualize myself in Antarctica. I contacted travel agencies just to see how it was done. I wanted to visualize it so I had to know everything about it. It had to be real, something I could seriously visualize and not too far away from my imagination. After a few weeks, I already knew everything about how the travel agencies make their trips to Antarctica. I knew prices, where they go, when and how. I also knew many stories about people going there by themselves. This way was easier for me to visualize.

I wanted to go to Antarctica, but I wanted to do it without money. This was my plan before meeting Athella. But then I realized that I didn't have to do it that way. It was just a form. The idea of traveling to Latin America without money was a form for me to meet Athella. If I still wanted to go to Latin America, it didn't have to be the same way.

A few weeks later, I was talking to my guides. They told me that when I was traveling without money, I was spending a lot of time asking for food at restaurants and contacting people to see where I could sleep. At the same time, I was inspiring people. I was not using money but I was using my time. I could get the same thing in a different way, a different form.

I was doing something similar as I worked with Athella, but on a different level. I spent time preparing the events and other things. Sometimes I even cooked for people. I was doing a service for people, motivating them on a different level. And I was not using my money. I was very focused on helping people and Christina. All my energy was there, 24 hours a day. I even forgot about doing things that I love, and that is very important. You have to do what you love. I remember something that Athella said often to people, "You can have it all." You just have to really believe it.

I realized that I never stopped traveling. I was still traveling and presenting Athella. It was part of my trip. Traveling without money was a form for me to meet Athella. The idea of the 100 countries was a form for me to have my experience in Nepal.

When I met Athella, she told me that just by spending time with a channeler, I would learn how to channel. Deep inside I knew how to channel. Nobody told me how to do it. I just knew. This happens with the people around us - the more time we spend with them, the more we become like them. That is why it's important to choose wisely who you spend time with. Eventually, you will become more like them and they more like you. This is all related to the energy of the person. One good example of this is when women spend a lot of time together, eventually, their menstrual cycle will synchronize.

Men also have cycles like women do but they are very different. Their testosterone levels change daily and this affects their behavior. Symptoms may include depression, fatigue, and mood swings.

Eventually, Christina told me how she goes into a state of channeling. What she said is that you need to be in a state of total trust. There are several techniques for this. Every technique is different, and some people may feel more comfortable with one technique than another. It's like meditation. Some people will feel attracted to a specific meditation; other people may not like the same meditation. Many channelers have different techniques to enter into the state of channeling. But usually, they mention that you enter into a state of total trust.

I met many channelers and many beings from many dimensions. I also traveled to almost every country in the world. But visiting the countries was not my goal. The goal was helping people. But in between, I did many things I never imagined. Sometimes we focus on the goal but the goal is usually a form.

I had the money and I had the time. I could do it. So I did it. I went to Latin America and Antarctica.

The hardest part about going to Antarctica was passing the Drake Passage by ship.

ARGENTINA

DRAKE PASSAGE

ANTARCTICA

The waves in the Drake Passage are big and the ship moves in all directions during the two days. Passing the Drake Passage was hard, but I have to admit, going to Antarctica was one of the most amazing trips I've had. I had the chance to see many whales and dolphins, and of course, thousands of penguins.

When I met Athella, she told me that I should present her as an angel because many people didn't understand who she really was. The word "angel" was easier for people to understand. If you see videos of Athella, you will see that some people still refer to her as an angel. Angels are from the 4th dimension. Athella is from the 12th dimension.

The word "ascended master" usually refers to humans who find a way to take their bodies to the 4th dimension. Many people refer to Athella as an ascended master. This is because some people think that she was human. But Athella has never been a human. She is from Sirius B, from the 12th dimension.

When I went to Latin America alone, it felt like old times but it was different. I was so used to talking to Athella every day. I saw the world differently. Many times I would talk out loud. Many people thought that I was crazy but I knew that Athella was listening. Even if Christina wasn't in the same country, I knew that Athella would answer my questions once I talked to her through Christina's body. And yes, she always answered my questions. So, in other words, she was always listening to me, even when I was very far from Christina.

When I was getting ready to go to Antarctica, Christina told me that she wanted to go with me, so we went together. Once in Antarctica, Athella asked me to organize a presentation where she could talk to the people, so I prepared it at the last minute. We went there on a ship so the presentation was for the people on the ship.

While we were in Antarctica, we were contacted by a film director. He wanted to make a movie about channeling. He already contacted several channelers. These channelers were channeling beings from other dimensions. The director understood this as aliens but he also wanted angels in the movie, so he wanted to have Athella there.

We went to California to film the movie. The director had many questions about channeling. Since I knew many things about it, we discussed how it works. I told him everything I knew. The director asked the cameramen to film me talking about channeling. We had a good relationship. I even helped him to create the website and the trailer for the movie. I decided to create the trailer as if an alien was coming to Earth because people believe that aliens come from outside of the planet. But, in fact, many of them are here. They are just in a different room and we cannot see them. The name of the movie is *Tuning In: Angels & Aliens.*

All channelers in the world are helping humanity. They channel beings from higher dimensions. They provide a lot of wisdom. You can learn so much from them. I have a special connection with Athella. For me, she is like a friend from the 12th dimension. Athella can heal people directly. I haven't seen this with other channelers. Most channelers provide beautiful and very useful information. Athella provides information but her focus is on healing.

Athella is able to heal as long as it doesn't affect your development on Earth. For example, if you came to Earth to experience certain things like sickness, even if you are not aware of it, the higher dimensional beings are not supposed to help you. If they intervene, they may change your development. In those cases, Athella was not able to help. But if healing something doesn't change your path, then she will do it or she will help you so you can do it yourself.

In many cases, when someone is born with problems in the body it is because the soul decided to experience a lifetime this way. We may not be aware of it consciously, but the *higher self* knows and decides to experience life that way. In some cases, it is also to help a family member. For example, if you have a child with certain difficulties, it can be because some members of the family could learn compassion, love, or anything else. The child and the family volunteered for that. Everything is done under agreement with everyone involved. We may not remember the agreement, but for sure it was made.

Athella was always advising us about what to do. Many times, we didn't know why we were doing things. We just trusted Athella. Usually, it would take several months to realize why she asked us to do something.

We were also donating money to several organizations. Athella told us which ones and when to donate.

When I met Christina, she had a business for people to be able to talk to Athella. But she was doing everything by herself, without any help. We started to spread the word. We started to create videos and more material so more people would know about Athella. We called it *Athella.org* because that was the name of the website.

We started to have public sessions for presenting Athella. It was funny that during the presentations I recorded everything that happened with cameras. But many times, there were problems with electronics during the sessions. Athella told me that this will always happen because the electromagnetism in the room is different with the presence of high dimensional beings. You could actually feel it.

In the beginning we had presentations for free so more people could enjoy the energy and wisdom of Athella without restrictions. But then I realized something. When things are free, people usually don't appreciate it. I even remember people coming to talk to Athella. She told them that they could ask any question. Sometimes the questions were pure ego. Athella always answered in a very beautiful way. She always tried to help people be aware of their ego as well. But many people didn't appreciate it. After several months of doing many things for free, we decided to charge for the services. People appreciated it much more.

Many people demanded these things for free. Christina has a lot of books and many other things for free. I always thought that people working in the fields harvesting fruits and vegetables are doing the job of providing food for people, but they are not supposed to provide their service for free. There has to be an exchange, but not necessarily money. Money is just a form. The fruits and vegetables are there and available for everyone. The information and energy are also there available for everyone. But we were doing the service of bringing it to them.

I wanted to provide this book for free, but I am not alone. There is a company printing the book. If you know someone who wants to get this book and they don't have the money for it, please tell them that they can do community service. It could be anything - cleaning a place in nature, helping other people, or any service with truly good intentions. Make a short video about it or take pictures and send it to me. You will know how to find me. I will make sure that they get a copy of the book. What really matters is the intention.

Sometimes people tried to talk to Athella, but they wanted to talk to her just to see if this was real. Whenever people like this came, Athella told me in advance so I always knew when people were coming to test Athella. Sometimes Athella allowed them to talk to her but sometimes it was just not worth it to spend time with these people. I understand that some people have doubts about this being real. I used to be like that before my experience in Nepal. But trust me,

I tried everything to see if this is real and it is. I wouldn't be talking about it if this wasn't.

When Athella is talking, Christina's voice changes. Athella could also speak several languages but most of the time she chose to speak English. She said many times that she was not here to entertain people. The most amazing thing is the energy in the room when Athella is there. Athella knew everything about me. She knew about many things that happened to me that I never talked about. But the most amazing thing about Athella was that she was able to directly heal people. Many times while living in Seattle I went to play football. Sometimes I got injured. When I asked Athella for help, she helped me. I was healed in few seconds.

Many people are ashamed to ask for help. I used to be like this. Athella taught me that it is very important to ask. You have to ask. Your guides and many beings from other dimensions are not supposed to do anything if you don't ask for it. They never do anything without permission. You really have to ask.

Everything we do on Earth is done with permission. If you want to do something big on Earth, something that will change the path of many people, you will have to have permission from Mother Earth and all the people involved. The people and you may not know if the permission was granted or not, but if you do something it is because the permission was granted from everyone. Otherwise it would never happen. You are alive right now because Mother Earth gave you permission. You may not remember, but for sure you asked for it. Otherwise, you wouldn't be here.

When Athella is talking to someone, she is already in communication with that person's guides. The guides and

Athella decide what to share with the person. They are not here to tell us everything. We have to find some things out by ourselves. They just help us as much as they can. Also, sometimes they don't share information because the person is not ready to receive it. This happens with everything, even with this book. If you read this book again from the beginning, you will understand new things that you didn't understand the first time. This is because you were probably not ready the first time. When Athella talked to me, I recorded everything and checked it again a few days later. I always understood better after some time. Even right now, Athella told me many things that I am just understanding now while I am writing it in this book.

I was so thankful for the opportunity to talk to Athella every day. Little by little, Athella and I started to become friends. She even told me jokes sometimes but not normal jokes. They were full of wisdom and funny at the same time. Christina also knew many things. I was learning so much from them both.

Chapter 23 – The Predictions

After a few months, I became used to talking to Christina and Athella using the same body but I was not able to talk to many people about it because they didn't understand. After my experience with Athella and Christina, I never saw a person the same way. I became aware that every person is an energy experiencing this reality in a body. This became normal for me. I was not able to have a conversation with someone who didn't understand this. I would get bored. This made me change my preferences about the people I wanted to spend time with.

Many amazing things happened every day. What many people would consider a miracle was normal for me. One day, I got a new phone with a new number. A few minutes later, a man called me and asked me if he could talk to Christina. I asked him how he got the phone number. He said that his guides gave it to him. I explained to Christina what happened and she took the phone from my hand. She didn't say anything for more than 30 minutes while she held the phone. Then, suddenly she finished the call and passed the phone back to me. I asked her what happened. She said that she didn't know, but whatever had to happen, it was done. That was all she knew.

When someone contacted us, sometimes Athella would tell me in advance. She told me what to do, so whenever someone called or sent an email, I was prepared. This became a normal thing. Sometimes before the presentations, Athella told me what kind of people would come and what questions they would have. Sometimes Athella explained things so I could explain it to the person in the presentation later.

She is able to see the future. She told me that the future is not something solid. She said that we are moving through realities depending on the energy of the person. Sometimes it is very probable that we will go through a specific reality, so that she could guess the future.

I could visualize this using the analogy of the fish in the river. If we are the fish and every drop is a reality, and we are swimming through realities. But we cannot see more than the reality we are experiencing. Athella, from where she is, she can see the drops that are coming to us. So this is how she can see our future. But the future is not solid. We can always move to a different parallel reality.

Humans can also predict the future. We can have visions of it or use tools to visualize it but I don't recommend this. Only do this if you have pure and beautiful intentions, without ego. In the past, whenever I had a vision I shared it with some people around me. I realized later that some things that I predicted did not happen. It was because of my ego. I wanted to show other people that I could do it. This was pure ego. Then I stopped telling people about my visions. I realized that this way everything that I saw happened.

Predicting the future is like seeing the drops coming to us. But if you tell many people about it, it will create a different energy. Maybe this new energy will move us to a different drop. In other words, if you have a vision of something and you tell someone, this may change the energy and therefore, everything you saw doesn't apply anymore.

Athella had a better vision of everything. The work I was doing with Athella was amazing. It was very beautiful work and I was learning so much. Unfortunately, the *Problematic beings* didn't like our work. We were helping people to remember who they were. If many people started to remember, the *Problematic beings* would not have power over people. Sometimes they came to bother us. Many times we were not able to see them. Most of the time they were in another frequency, or in another room. We couldn't see them but we could feel them.

We didn't worry about them. We had Athella. Also, we knew how to control our egos so there was not so much they could do. Athella was able to help us any time. We just had to ask for help. We were doing it by calling her name out loud and asking for help. That was all we needed. They tried to confuse us by putting thoughts full of ego in our minds but we were aware of our own thoughts so we always knew when the thoughts were ours and when the thoughts were coming from somewhere else. I just ignored them.

Many people believe that when you are into spiritual things you are always happy. This is not true. You have to experience everything and learn from your experience; it isn't about being happy all the time. It's about experiencing everything and deciding what you prefer to keep experiencing. All experiences are lessons. When the *Problematic beings* came to visit, I knew that it was a big lesson. If the lesson is easy, we would not learn anything from it. In other words, if you don't have any big challenge in your life, you may be doing something wrong.

Christina, at that time, was still recovering from the trauma of her childhood. Sometimes it was difficult for her. I had to help her to be aware of her own thoughts or just to ask Athella for help. But sometimes not even that was possible. Sometimes it was very hard. It was harder for Christina than for me. Some organs in her body function differently than most people. That is why it's harder for her. That is also why she can channel Athella.

I had to take care of Christina and sometimes it was not easy. Sometimes it was just a few hours, sometimes it was several days. It was probably the hardest test I have had.

I even tried to leave Christina. I tried several times. But every time, I thought about what Athella told me when I met her. She said that I should not leave Christina no matter what, so I always stayed.

Now Christina has recovered from her trauma. I saw her development. It was impressive. She probably had the worst trauma a person could have and she managed to overcome everything in a few months.

I talked to Athella every day, and learned as much as I could from her. Sometimes there were other beings with Athella. These beings were there to help us temporarily with some activities. Sometimes I talked to them through Christina's body. Athella was always coordinating everything. She would be talking to me through Christina's body, then mention that we had a visitor. The visitor would talk to me through Christina's body. Following that, Athella would come back to continue talking to me.

I got to know many beings from all dimensions this way. I learned so much from them. Also, when people came to meet Athella, sometimes they would want to talk to their guides. If Athella and the guides considered it appropriate, they would do it.

One day, I was talking to Athella like any other day. She said there was someone who wanted to talk to me. The room started to feel different. Then, a very different voice came from Christina's body. It was not Athella. It was a strong male voice.

I recognized the feeling. I had felt it before. It was one of my guides. He started to talk to me and said, "I don't talk very often. I will do it only when it's necessary. You are doing well. Listen to Athella. She knows what is best for you. I am with you and I have been always with you. I love you." Then he left but I was still able to feel him.

I don't know why but I never asked for a name. I asked him for his name just after he left Christina's body. He talked to me in my head and said that I could call him "Bembolio". Athella came back to Christina's body. She asked me to write it down so I did. When I was writing down the name, I didn't know how to spell it. I started writing "Ben", but then I heard a voice in my head say, "With an M." I think that was Athella. I was able to hear her in my head. So I wrote "Bembolio". Then my guide told me in my head, "Yes. That is correct." That day I realized that I was able to hear Athella and my guides, like having a normal conversation. And I was able to recognize who was talking to me. This was something amazing for me.

There was a second time I talked to the same guide. The second time was different. He talked to me and told me that he would talk to me only in important moments. The first time was to introduce himself and the second time he wanted to do something special for me. He said, "I am going to do something for you and once it's done there is no way back." He asked me if I wanted it. I said yes.

Then Athella came back and asked me to close my eyes and allow her to enter my body so I did. Suddenly I started to feel a very beautiful feeling in my body. I noticed that my spine went straight. I started to feel something in my forehead. It was not something physical. The only way I can describe it is like feeling light. I felt light in my forehead. I could see the light. I even felt as if something inside my head was opening. I was not scared. I knew it was fine. After a few seconds the light disappeared. Athella told me, "It is done and there is no way back." She didn't say what exactly happened. She just said that I would feel tired for a few days.

During the following week I was very tired. I slept more than usual. I didn't feel good but somehow I knew that it was fine and it had to be like this. After a week I started to feel much better. I noticed that I was able to feel much more than before. I could sense what was happening without asking. I was more sensitive and I was able to sense my guides around. Usually, I identified them as colors. I could see four colors all the time. The colors were red, purple, sky blue and blue. I knew that Bembolio was the red one, I asked Athella and she confirmed it. I asked about the other colors. She said that she (Athella) was the blue one, and the other two were my other guides. Most of the time I talked to the purple light and somehow I knew she was a female. But I never talked to her through Christina's body.

Another thing that I noticed was that I started to be very sensitive to Wi-Fi. Whenever I had a phone or computer connected to Wi-Fi close to me, I started to have a weird and not very nice feeling in my heart. I realized later that my heart was sensing the Wi-Fi. I was not able to have a phone or laptop (connected to Wi-Fi) close to my heart because I could feel it, and it's not a good feeling.

Sometimes I felt the phones even when they were not connected to Wi-Fi. I believe that the feeling I was getting was from the cellular network. Every time new technologies are created we usually don't see the consequences to the human body, especially because we are misinformed about how the human body functions. Every time there is a new cellular network, it is more advanced. These waves affect people. It affects some people more than others because some people have bodies that can handle many things. Any kind of wave affects the human body in one way or another. This happens with all electronics. We are affected by everything. Most people are not able to feel them but it doesn't mean that they aren't affected. We are just not paying attention to the vibrations because our minds are very busy thinking.

The cellular network called 5G will be implemented. It will affect some people but it will take probably 20 years to see any symptoms. Some people will have headaches or migraines. Some people will develop heart problems. There will be more people who will need devices to control their heart rhythm. Some people may become less social because of these effects. Some people will not be able to see colors - their vision will change. It will also cause problems in some animals. This will not affect every person but the best way to avoid it will be to live somewhere in nature away from big cities. There will be studies about 5G, but they will say that it's safe. Don't believe the studies. It's not healthy. These waves pass through your body and it affects your blood. These waves can hurt you but you can hurt yourself more just by having fear. If you decide to live in a city, do not live with fear and you will be okay. Fear can be more destructive than anything else. These new technologies will come and there will be more and more in the future.

We are all affected by the waves from microwaves, Wi-Fi, Bluetooth, etc. In the beginning, I thought that being sensitive to these waves was not a good thing because I wasn't feeling good. Later I realized that the waves affect every person. I have a similar feeling when I am walking around high voltage electrical cables. When I am close to a microwave warming up food I can feel it. The microwaves are not good for the food. It will affect your body in the long term. It took me a while to realize this because I don't use microwaves. I started to notice when I was at friend's house and the microwave was on.

I noticed that I can also feel electric blankets (used to keep people warm), and waterbeds (with an electric heater). The feeling coming out of these items was not good. The electricity produced by these items can be felt even if you are in a different room. It's similar to Wi-Fi - you can still feel it even if there is a wall separating you from the device.

More and more people are deciding to move out of cities. Some people may not know why but they are following their intuition. This intuition, in many cases, is their guides talking to them.

There is radiation in several places around the world. We just don't know it. The radiation can be caused by various things. It affects some people more than others. There is radiation in the city where I was born, Ciudad Juárez, Mexico. Many people don't know it but there was an accident several years ago just a few months before I was born. Some people in a hospital wanted to throw away old equipment. They sent many parts of the old equipment to companies where they could recycle the metallic components. They didn't know, but amongst the equipment for recycling, there was a machine used for therapy. This machine contained radioactive material. The metallic components were taken to a recycling company and eventually it was used to create new material for construction. Many buildings were created with this contaminated material in Mexico and the USA.

Unfortunately, we also have other problems that the *Problematic beings* are causing. Whenever they sense that a certain population is becoming more aware of who they really are, especially in big cities, they spread chemicals in the environment there. This affects some organs of the human body and limits its connection with higher consciousness.

Also, the *Problematic beings* have been sending waves of energy that affect human behavior. These waves come from the Moon, more precisely, from the dark side of the Moon. Little by little, these waves have been deactivated by the friendly beings. By 2024, these waves coming from the Moon will stop completely, thanks to some friendly beings. Something interesting about the Moon is that in 1969, the first Moon landing was shown on TV. But they didn't arrive on the Moon that day. They did it before, but they were taken there by the *Problematic beings* in their ships. The video shown on TV was not real. It was a film created by the director Stanley Kubrick.

The *Problematic beings* are in part responsible for some changes in our reality. They don't want us to move to the 4th dimension. They have been trying to change our reality to a reality where we don't move to the 4th dimension. They created CERN, a nuclear organization in Switzerland to alter our reality. The changes in reality that we know as the Mandela effect, in part, are created by CERN.

The Moon doesn't exist in the 4th dimension. Because it doesn't belong to this solar system. It was put there as an artificial satellite but it was not there originally. The Moon is not a natural object; it is artificial. It was put there by some advanced beings. The planet Mercury was a natural moon moving around Earth, around 13,000 years ago. This explains why Mercury is not as hot as Venus. And this explains why Venus is the hottest planet in the solar system. The planet Saturn was a star. In other words, the planet Saturn was the sun of our solar system at some point, but this was a really long time ago, many thousands of years ago. The rings around Saturn are artificial; they are not natural.

Ever since I was a kid, I've always wanted to know why the days of the week are related to planets, the Moon, and the Sun. For example, Monday is named for the Moon. Tuesday for Mars. Wednesday for Mercury. Thursday for Jupiter. Friday for Venus. Saturday for Saturn. And Sunday for the Sun. I always had the idea that Saturday had to be named for the Sun because we did not have school on Saturdays and Sundays. So, maybe this thought came from memories from another lifetime.

Saturn was used as a portal to bring energies from many places around the universe. Everything related to Saturn used to be positive and the soul of Saturn is still positive. But it was corrupted by the *Problematic beings*. Now the energy of Saturn is used for negative purposes, and it affects the whole solar system. The rings of Saturn, the hexagon shape on the north pole, and the axial tilt appeared after the corruption.

The rings in Saturn have been used by the *Problematic beings* to send waves of energy around the solar system. These waves of energy have been affecting humans for a very long time. The *Problematic beings* used to live on Mars, but they destroyed the atmosphere. It used to be a beautiful planet, similar to Earth.

Christmas is a celebration for Saturn. The real name for Christmas is Saturnalia. It comes from the Romans. They exchanged gifts and there was a sacrifice. This is similar to what happens now. There is a lot of symbolism happening when decorating the Christmas tree. They even used a hat like the one from Santa Claus. It was called pileus.

The *Problematic beings* also have colonies in other stars. Orion's Belt is one of them.

Aldebaran

Betelgeuse

Orion's Belt

Rigel

Sirius

These three stars form a triangle. We cannot see it from our position, but from a different angle you would see a triangle. That is why the *Problematic beings* use a lot of triangles in their symbolism. This doesn't mean that Orion's Belt is bad. In fact, this constellation is very important in our universe, and many friendly beings live there. My guides talked to me about Saturn a long time ago, but I didn't understand correctly because they said that Saturn used to be a star, but I thought that they were talking about a star from another solar system. Many beings told me the same thing, but they said clearly that it was the Sun of this solar system.

I met my purple and sky blue guides later. They also gave me their names but I prefer to keep them private. The purple one talks to me often. We choose our guides for every lifetime. It's related to our personalities. I chose them and they chose me. The red one, Bembolio, is related to my passion for sports. The purple one is related to wisdom and spirituality. In fact, I have been writing this book with her. She is putting images in my mind all the time so she deserves credit for this book. The sky blue one is more connected with me when I am traveling. She is more about adventures.

You also have a guide for every part of your personality. Try to communicate with them. They can help you so much. You have at least two guides. Some people have more than two. The number is not really important. Having many guides isn't necessarily better. It's just the amount of guides who are with you right now. If you haven't talked to them yet, try to imagine that they are next to you. You will start to communicate with them faster by doing this.

Sometimes when I am talking to someone, especially if the person has a specific question, I can hear one of my guides (the purple one) telling me, "Let me handle this." So I start talking, but the ideas in my head are not coming from me. This is a type of channeling. Everyone can do it. The type of channeling that Christina does, trans channeling, is different. That type of channeling is something you usually choose before being born.

The name of my other guide (the sky blue one) was not given to me by Athella. It was given to me by Sarita Otero and Alaniso. Athella asked me to meet more channelers. I checked on the internet and a famous channeler in Mexico caught my attention, especially because it was the first time I found a Spanish speaking channeler.

Sarita Otero has been channeling for over 40 years and she has been on national TV in many countries. She channels a being called Alaniso. When Alaniso talks through the body of Sarita Otero, her voice doesn't change like it does with Christina and Athella. The voice remains the same. The only way you can hear a different voice is when the voice is recorded with an old voice recorder. You can hear a male voice.

I heard many stories of people who were healed by Sarita Otero and Alaniso. The most amazing story I heard was that Alaniso helped a woman to restore her brain. Basically, she got a new brain while talking to Alaniso. I had to meet Sarita Otero and Alaniso.

I went to Tepoztlan, Mexico, where Sarita Otero lives. This place is famous for UFO sightings. Alaniso asked Sarita to move to this specific place because of the energy. Alaniso gave instructions to Sarita about where to build her house. Sarita built her house in the specific location. Athella confirmed for Sarita that the place was correct. Christina and I talked to Alaniso. He knew about us. He knew what we were doing. He congratulated us for doing this job. He talked to us about the pyramids. He knew that we were going to visit some pyramids after the visit with Sarita.

Alaniso told me that many of his friends have been preventing nuclear disasters. He said that they have been in several nuclear plants controlling the radiation. They have been destroying bombs and missiles all over the world. He said that some people have made videos of them. So I checked on the internet. I found several videos of lights floating around several nuclear plants around the world and videos of lights destroying missiles flying in the air. He said that these lights were his friends.

Alaniso also said that many beings around the universe started to pay attention to Earth after the atomic bombs hit Hiroshima and Nagasaki. These bombs affected the energy of the whole universe so they started to check more deeply into the activities of humans.

Since I was in Mexico, many memories from my childhood started to come up. When I was a child I had to learn about the history of Mexico, including old civilizations. But what many people are taught in school is that old civilizations didn't know anything about the world. They were just primitive people without real knowledge of the world. Also, I had to learn about ex-presidents, I remember one day when my teacher in primary school was talking about one ex-president of Mexico named Francisco I. Madero. My teacher told us that Francisco I. Madero publicly said that he was getting instructions from spirits. The information was about how to manage the country. Many people considered Francisco I. Madero one of the best presidents in the history of Mexico. Unfortunately, many presidents and leaders in Mexico (and around the world) have been trained and put in those positions by humans working with the *Problematic beings*. In many cases, the leaders are not aware of the real nature of what they are doing.

When we returned to Seattle, my life was very different. I really wanted to share it with more people but most people thought that I was crazy. Athella advised me to work on myself. She said that the best way to share something with someone is by being an example. This way I wouldn't even have to say anything. People would see how I lived. They would feel it and they may want to copy it. So I did it. I worked on myself as much as I could. I followed all of Athella's instructions. I meditated every day. I did not eat for several hours before meditations so it would be stronger. I was very careful with food. I tried to avoid processed food. And I ate less. Athella told me that we (humans) eat much more than we need. Exercise was also part of the training. I worked with my thoughts. I learned to feel my energy and other people's energy. I also learned many techniques for changing my reality. These techniques were related to my thoughts.

Almost all of my training with Athella was not as much about the information, but about practicing every day. I learned how to stop thinking at any time. I never imagined this, but after some training, you can literally switch off your thoughts when you don't need to think. The results you can get with this are amazing. You need to be aware of your own thoughts. If you have some fears or traumas, first you have to take care of them with a psychologist or a specialist. Then train your mind to be aware of your own thoughts. Eventually, you will be able to know your own thoughts. When the time is right, you can switch them off. Playing with forms is much easier once you are aware of your thoughts, and when you connect your brain with your heart, you are unstoppable. You can create any reality you want. The brain doesn't have intelligence. It just decodes information. We can put any information there that we want.

Athella spoke to me in English most of the time but I knew she could speak other languages. One day she told me that she could speak all the languages in existence. This makes sense because many beings have been in contact with humans all over the world and they always communicate in the local language.

One day, I asked Athella if she would speak to me in a different language. She didn't say anything. A few seconds later, my body started to be totally straight. I felt as if someone was stretching my back. Then I could hear Athella but it was not in English. It was not a sound. It was totally different. It was something similar to telepathy but different. I knew that it was her and I knew what she was saying. She was saying something like, "If you want we can speak like this." I could feel it all over the body but mainly inside my head. I just knew what was happening. When she talked to me this way, I tried to tell her that it was amazing.

Before meeting Athella, I knew many things about our real human nature but she gave me more details and different perspectives on everything. Sometimes it was something very simple. What I remember the most was a very simple example she gave me. She asked me to imagine that there was a chalkboard like the ones we used to use in schools. Then I had to imagine that I was scratching it with my fingernails. She asked me what I felt. I said, "I feel an uncomfortable sensation." She said, "You see? You were thinking about nails scratching the chalkboard. This thought created a feeling in your body and your reality changed. At that moment, your reality was uncomfortable and you reacted according to the needs you have in your reality." I liked the way Athella could explain things in a simple way.

I also remember when somebody asked Athella why some animals kill other animals. Why do they have to suffer? Athella said, "How do you know they suffer? If a lion kills a zebra, the human suffers because the human thinks that the zebra is suffering. But the zebra may not be suffering. Animals volunteer to experience certain things in life and they also volunteer to die. This may look bad, but they wanted to have this experience. Also, humans volunteer to experience things that may look bad. They may not be aware of it, or they may not remember, but humans volunteer to do things that some people may consider bad."

I always liked how Athella reminded humans that everything we experience is created by our thoughts. Basically, it doesn't matter what happens in front of you. Your reaction is what matters. But we forget. We forget many things all the time. Sometimes Athella asked me to write things down because we tend to forget. She knew it. On many occasions she had to remind me of things several times. Beings in other dimensions don't forget like we do.

I asked Athella how many lifetimes I have had on Earth. She didn't want to tell me because she said that too much information is not helpful for humans. Too much information can become entertainment and she was not here to entertain people, and I agree. We can know a lot of information, but if we don't know how to use it, it's not so useful. She told me because I was part of the team. I came from Sirius and I have been on Earth 562 times, including some lives in Atlantis.

Chapter 24 – The Smoke

We had presentations with Athella around the United States and Mexico. I talked to Athella before every presentation. She told me details about the people coming to the event. She knew before it happened but I was not able to share this with the people at the presentation.

In some cases, certain people would need a particular kind of help, like reading a specific book or listening to a meditation. So I took a copy of the book with me or we recorded a meditation in advance so we would have it ready to give it to the person.

In Mexico, I had to translate into Spanish during the presentations. Sometimes Athella told me the questions and answers before people asked. She told me so I would be ready to translate properly.

One day in Seattle, before getting ready for a presentation, I was talking to Athella about the details of the presentation. Suddenly the apartment started to smell like someone was smoking. The smell was so strong that I checked every room. There was nothing unusual.

I went outside and checked everything around but there were no people. The smell was only inside the house. I don't like the smell of cigarettes. I didn't know what to do. It was too much.

After few minutes, I realized that it was getting late for the presentation so I tried to ignore the smell. Christina allowed Athella to talk through her body. I was ready to take notes related to the presentation. Then Athella told me, "There is someone who wants to talk to you, Warrior." Athella calls me Warrior because she says I am very strong physically and spiritually. I also used to be a warrior in previous lives. As usual, I was recording the conversation with Athella. When I record video or sound with Athella, there are always problems with the electronics. This time I was recording with three cameras.

I asked, "Who wants to talk to me?" Athella said, "I will bring him forward." A few seconds later, Christina's body started to look a bit different and the feeling in the room was different. I was very used to talking to Athella. I could feel her energy but this time the energy was different. The smell of smoke in the house got stronger.

Then, there it was. Someone started talking to me through Christina's body. The voice was a male with a very strong southern American accent. Athella talks to me in English but she doesn't have an American accent.

I remember that moment perfectly, especially because it took me a few seconds to understand what was happening. The man told me, "Stop recording. Athella says that I am not ready to talk to humans in front of a camera." So I stopped filming, and I asked, "Who are you?" He said, "Hi, my name is Josef. I'm really sorry for the smell. It is me. I'm here to tell you a few things. I asked Athella for permission and she agreed."

I was very surprised. I had talked to other beings before but this time he was speaking very fast and with a very strong southern American accent. I asked him, "Where are you and how did you end up there?" He explained to me what was happening. Josef told me that he committed suicide, and then he didn't understand where he was or what was happening. Athella helped him.

Then he wanted to thank Athella for helping him but he saw me. And he wanted to talk to me and congratulate me for the job we were doing. I was very surprised. There was a human somewhere in another dimension telling me that I was doing an amazing job.

Josef told me so many things. He was not like the beings from other dimensions. He was a human. I felt like I was talking to a guy in the gas station.

I talked to Josef again the next day. I asked Josef so many questions. He told me everything without hesitation. It was different. It was not like talking to Athella.

Athella is very smart and full of love. She always told me things that I needed to hear at that moment but nothing else. If I asked something that I didn't need at that moment, she would tell me that it was not the right time.

Josef was different, he told me everything without hesitation. I remember asking Josef what Athella looked like. He said, "Ooh man, she's so beautiful and smart. She's awesome. She loves everyone."

I also asked him about life in that place. He tried to describe it but he couldn't find the right words. He basically told me that the laws of physics are not the same. What I understand is that when he died, he didn't go to the 4th dimension. He stayed in the 3rd dimension but without a body.

I felt so confident in talking to Josef. I even told him that I felt like I was talking to a guy in the gas station smoking cigarettes. He said, "Ooh man, I regret not trying to stop smoking when I was on the other side. Many people think that when you die you forget about everything, but it's not like that. I feel like I want to smoke here but there aren't cigarettes." He said that once you are there you keep the image that you have about yourself.

When Josef was talking, I turned off the cameras. But one day I forgot. I didn't realize that I was filming him until we stopped talking and I saw that the cameras were recording. I checked the video but his voice was not recorded on any camera.

I went to the internet to see if there were other people channeling humans who stayed in the 3rd dimension. During my research, I found the story of a doctor from Texas called Elisa Medhus. Elisa had a son called Erik. Erik committed suicide when he was young. A few days after his death, he started to appear in the house and the family could see him. Elisa was a very respected doctor who didn't believe in ghosts but she couldn't deny that she saw her dead son in the house. She started to contact psychics to see if she could get answers. Some physics told her that Erik decided to stay in the 3rd dimension and he was trying to communicate with his family. In the beginning Elisa didn't believe it. She talked to many psychics until she understood what was happening.

Now, Elisa contacts several psychics who can talk to Erik. The psychics are the translators between Elisa and Erik. Elisa asks Erik all kinds of questions. All the sessions are recorded on video and Elisa shares everything on the internet. The information that Erik provides is pretty much the same as you have been reading in this book. I contacted Elisa and I must say, she is an amazing woman. She stopped working as a doctor and now she is helping people as much as she can. You can find all her material on the internet. She calls it "Channeling Erik". You can even hear Erik's voice in some videos.

I found out about Elisa and Erik during the night, a few hours before I went to sleep. That night, I had a dream. In my dream, I was walking somewhere in nature. Then, a guy stopped me and said, "Hey, let's do something funny." I said, "Something funny like what?" He told me that I was working too much and I should rest a little bit more. In my dream, I realized that he was Erik. I told him, "I know who you are. You're Erik." He said, "Yes. Don't take me wrong but you really have to rest." Then he left.

In the morning, I woke up very late. I had something important to do in the morning and I almost missed it. For the first time ever, the alarm clock didn't work. The first thing that came to my mind was Erik. I knew he did it. I don't know how but I knew. In the end, everything was fine with my appointment. Actually, I slept better that night. I wrote to Elisa explaining to her what happened but then I realized that this is a normal thing. Erik loves pranks and he pranks people all the time. He likes to prank people who watch the videos on the internet. Many people who watch the videos say that they have seen Erik in their house, or that something was moved in their house, and they knew that Erik did it. Somehow he always lets them know that it was him. He is a funny and nice guy. He never hurts people, he just plays a small prank. He reminds me a lot of Josef, but without the smell and with a different accent. Erik explained that he has to prepare the energy and after a while, the energy becomes matter. And this is how he moves things.

During Athella's presentations, I recorded from several angles. In many presentations, you can see orbs moving around the room. These orbs are spirits who decided to stay in this dimension. Some of them could be people with a physical body but in deep meditation. The physical body can become light and the meditator can explore any part of the world this way.

One day, in Hawaii, after a presentation, Christina and I went to the beach. We were just sitting on the sand. Then, Christina told me that Athella wanted to talk to me.

Christina started to be in the position for channeling. Usually, it takes few seconds for Athella to start talking. This time was almost immediately. I talked to Athella about the people in the presentation. Sometimes we wanted to contact people after the presentations to see if we could help more but I had to ask Athella if she could recommend something. After we talked about all the people, I asked Athella about Josef. I hadn't talked to him for several days.

Most of the time I was either alone or with Christina or Athella. But I liked to talk to people who know about these topics. However, most humans are interested in other things. Talking to Josef was like talking to a human who knew many things. Athella said that I could talk to Josef one more time but then he would have to go somewhere else. Then Josef appeared. I recognized him because of the smell.

I had a very nice and long conversation with Josef. I knew it was my last time with him. I didn't know where he was going after that but I guess he was going back to the 4th dimension. I could ask him pretty much anything. Josef told me that there were things that he was not supposed to tell me because some things could be just negative information that we don't need. I understood that. If we get involved in too much negative information, it will affect us. I asked Josef what exactly he was not supposed to talk about. I thought he would not tell me but he started to talk about many things. I thought that we were not supposed to talk about negative things. That was why he was not supposed to talk on camera. But he talked about them anyway.

Josef talked through Christina's body. There were no people on the beach, only Christina and me. We were sitting around 15 meters (50 feet) from the water. When Josef told me all these things, suddenly, like magic, a big wave came to us. The wave only came to the area where we were sitting. We were all wet. Christina woke up and she asked me what happened. I didn't know how to explain it. I saw the big wave coming only to us.

I believe this happened because Josef was not supposed to talk about negative things but he did it anyway. I knew what Josef talked about. Basically, he just talked about the *Problematic beings*. Athella doesn't want me to focus on them. They are just full of negativity and we don't need to focus on them.

I still remember the movement of the wave. It was incredible, like magic. A big amount of water moved directly to the area where we were sitting. In that moment, more than ever, it was very clear to me that this world is not real. It is an illusion.

Also during an event in Hawaii, Athella told me that I would see dolphins. She said that I would be standing and watching the dolphins jumping and there would be people with me. The dolphins would be jumping because they would be saying hello to us. After one week in Hawaii, I didn't see any dolphins. I was about to leave Hawaii. I thought that for the first time Athella was wrong.

I was getting ready to leave. I left the event for a few minutes to prepare my things so I could go to the airport after the event. As I was going back to see the people in the event, I walked in a place where I could see the ocean. Then I saw a dolphin jumping. I ran closer to see it and many dolphins appeared out of nowhere. The first thing that came to my mind was that Athella was right. I was alone there but I was able to see the dolphins jumping. I stayed there for a few minutes and the dolphins didn't stop jumping. Then I turned around and saw the people from the event coming to me. They were also looking at the dolphins. I didn't say anything. I just laughed. I was very happy to see that Athella was right. Everything happened exactly the way she said it would. I didn't tell anyone what Athella told me. I was very happy. After several years of experiencing many incredible things, I was still able to be surprised. This made me laugh.

Chapter 25 – The Past

If we want to understand the world now, we need to understand our past - our real past. I grew up thinking that the history of humanity and many things around the world would never have an explanation. I thought there were many mysteries in the world and they would stay mysteries but deep inside I knew that there had to be an explanation about who we are and why we are here.

There are many studies that talk about these topics and many researchers have found similar information. In some cases, the details of the findings are different but in general, they all talk about the same thing.

Many things I have shared in this book are a combination of information I got from Athella, other channelers, my guides, other higher dimensional beings, Drunvalo Melchizedek, research with the help of my guides, several ancient texts from ancient civilizations and my personal experience.

I will mention some other things from our past although we already talked about the most important parts. The most important thing to know right now is to learn how to live consciously.

The planet Earth is six billion years old but the galaxy is much older than that. Millions of years ago, the dinosaurs were brought to Earth. There were two intelligent races living among the dinosaurs. One of the races was a humanoid race. The other one was a reptilian race. These two races lived on Earth for many years. These two races had several wars that ended up destroying life on Earth. During these wars, the dinosaurs died because of some energy bombs. The souls of the dinosaurs were moved somewhere else. The planet was smaller at that time. The gravity was different. It allowed the dinosaurs to have the big size they had. Many dinosaurs had feathers on some parts of their bodies. Many of the bones found by scientists are not from dinosaurs. Some of them are from beings who used to live on Earth.

All types of life around the universe are moved from one place to another according to their needs and development.

The Earth was damaged after the wars but eventually, it changed and took a shape similar to the Earth we know now. Several different types of beings started to arrive.

Between five and six million years ago, there were giants on Earth. These beings were not human. They were beings from many places around the universe.

There were huge animals in the oceans. We know them as sea monsters. In the Jewish traditions, these beings are known as Leviathans. There were also huge dragon-like animals, these animals were the biggest animals that existed on Earth. Their fossils can be found at the bottom of the oceans, but no fossils have been found yet. Also, there were huge beings on the land. The tallest ones were up to 120 meters (394 feet).

Around 500,000 years ago, Earth was not very stable. Then, some beings came and put the Moon in place. Although Earth doesn't really need the Moon, it helped to make it stable at that time. The Moon is artificial and it is hollow. There are many beings living on the surface of the dark side of the Moon, the side we cannot see from Earth. Even some humans live on the Moon; they have been there since around 1947.

Athella talked to me about the Moon a few years after my guides told me this. Usually, she doesn't give me information about our history. She just waits for me to find out. Every time I ask her for something that I consider interesting, she says that the information will make me more curious, and I would focus my attention on the information without practicing and working on my development. Many times, I asked her things that I already knew about our past. I did it to get a confirmation but she was always aware of what I knew. Usually, her answer was, "Why do you ask if you already know the answer?" My guides share more information with me, but not always. Many times they guide me to find the information elsewhere. Josef was the one who talked to me openly.

The Moon affects life on Earth the same way as other planets do. Their electromagnetism is connected to Earth and therefore, all life on Earth.

The Reptilians were one of the first races who came to Earth. Their bodies are humanoid but their head and skin are like a green snake. There are many types of reptilians, but it's not important for us to know details about them. Only a small group of them are causing problems for humans. It is the same with humans. The majority are nice people, but some humans don't really care about others. Many Reptilians are helping humans. Some people channel Reptilians and they provide wisdom.

Most people don't recognize the Reptilians because they can manipulate people's minds and make them believe they are seeing a normal person. Some of them can also change the shape of their bodies and pretend to be humans. Many Reptilians are on the 4th dimension, and others are in this dimension. Some are in human bodies, but the soul is Reptilian.

When I was traveling without money I had to hitchhike all the time. I met several truck drivers. They told me stories about beings that were not human. They mentioned that these beings could change their bodies. Most of the truckers told me that these beings were found in Nevada, Utah, Arizona, Colorado, and New Mexico.

I heard similar stories in Mexico. In Mexico, there are people known as shamans. They are known for having a lot of knowledge about the spiritual world and they usually use their knowledge to provide healing for people. Some of them can transform their bodies into animals. This is because some shamans are aware that we live in a hologram and they know how to manipulate their bodies. Shamans are able to go to the 4th dimension for a while. That is why they can disappear from this 3rd dimension, at least for few seconds. Time is not the same in the 4th dimension. It may look like they were gone for a few seconds, or maybe a few minutes but in the 4th dimension, they experienced a much longer time. Humans are able to do this as well but it requires training and we would have to stop living like most people.

In the 4th dimension and higher, all beings can change their bodies. The 5th dimension is almost pure light with just a little bit of mass. There, we can transform our bodies into whatever we want. We can play with our bodies.

The beings mentioned by the truckers were beings who live underground, under big cities. They have tunnels to many parts of the world, especially in the Americas. One of the most well-known bases is close to a small town in New Mexico called Dulce.

There are many beings living underground. Many of them are under Antarctica. Some people call the underground world *Agartha* and believe that there is an internal sun. This is not totally true. The Earth is hollow but not completely. There is not a sun inside the Earth. There are networks of caverns of different sizes. Many of these caverns are connected by tunnels all over the world. There are main entrances in the North and South Poles, and in Asia. The caverns are underground, no longer than 40 miles (64 km) under the surface. They have artificial light, artificial weather, animals, rivers, lakes, crops, and everything they need to live.

Many beings live there. Most of these beings are very friendly to humans. But also some *Problematic beings* live there.

There are many beings on Earth, many outside our visible light. Let's say that they are in this 3rd dimension but in the rooms next to us, in rooms number 5 and 6. There are many friendly beings. They observe us and take care of us all the time. You will see beautiful lights in the sky more and more often. You may see some lights creating crop circles. They are our friends leaving us messages, usually related to geometry. If you go to these crop circles, the real crop circles created by aliens (because some of them are made by people), you will find humic and fulvic acids. These acids are very good for your health. You will also find white powder gold, the same type of gold that the *Elohim* were looking for on Earth. This white powder gold can still be found in South Africa. In fact, many buildings in South Africa are built with this white powder gold because it was mixed with the material for construction.

Another thing that a few people believe now is that the Earth is flat. I have asked many beings about this and the answer is always no. Some beings have said that they are surprised that some humans believe that.

If you see a video of an astronaut in space, you will see how objects float around. The water floating in space forms in the shape of a ball. Because of the lack of gravity, the molecules attract each other and form a drop of water. When the astronauts in space drink water or cry, or when they are in the bathroom, the water floats around and makes small drops. When the drops touch each other, they form a bigger drop. This is similar to how the planets get their shape with time. That is also why astronauts have special bathrooms.

Astronauts cannot go too far away from Earth. If they do, they may lose their memories or even die. They cannot be too far from the Earth's magnetic field. Astronauts use special devices that simulate the Earth's magnetic field. This is the only way to survive if they want to get away from the planet. Some astronauts have lost their memories, but we are unaware of it.

When I was traveling without money, hitchhiking in Arizona, United States, I got a ride with a guy who told me that he knew some hidden caves. I asked him if we could see the caves so he took me there. He had to drive through a place without a road, and he parked the car in a place that was a little bit hidden. He said that it was illegal to be there. We had to walk to the caves. When we arrived there, there were some paintings on the walls. They looked very old. One of the paintings looked like a monster. I asked him if he knew what it was. He said that his grandfather told him Native Americans used to live there. He told me that the

Native Americans were trying to hide from some beings who were half-human, half-snake. When he told me this I asked him why this information is not public. He said that many things related to the Native Americans are not very well understood and are sometimes hidden by the government. Actually, it was illegal to be in that cave because it was federal territory and nobody was allowed to be there without a permit.

Some old tablets from the Sumerians, one of the first civilizations, were found in the place now known as Iraq. The texts contain information about the creation of our solar system but it has been interpreted in many ways. These texts are called the Sumerian Tablets and they are written in Cuneiform, a Sumerian Language. These tablets talk about things I have mentioned in this book; although they have been mistranslated on purpose by some people related to the *Problematic beings*.

There are more planets in the solar system than the ones we know. At least two of these planets are huge - bigger than Jupiter. There used to be another planet between Mars and Jupiter. It was around 10 times the size of the Earth. It was destroyed during a war of the *Problematic beings*. It was destroyed completely with something that we would understand now as atomic energy, but more powerful. It was destroyed from the center. That is why there are so many small pieces now. It happened around the same time when we were having the problems in Atlantis. Now there are only pieces of rock floating in space. We know it as the asteroid belt but it used to be a planet called Maldek.

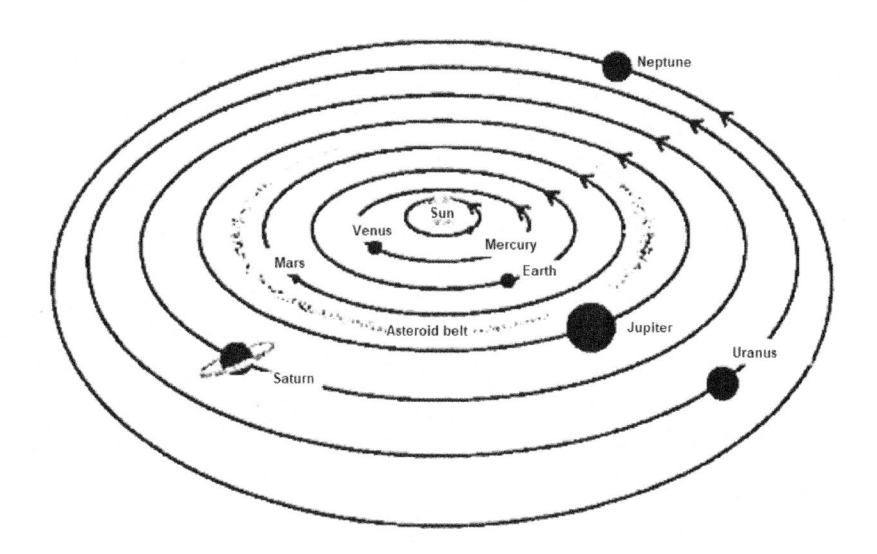

Many of the asteroids in the solar system are pieces of Maldek. There have been other planets and moons that were also destroyed during wars. The *Problematic beings* were on Maldek. They destroyed it. Then they moved to Mars. They almost destroyed it. Many structures found on Mars were created by them. At that time, Maldek and Mars were located in another position because the Sun had a different mass. Maldek and Mars were habitable, therefore the *Problematic beings* were there.

A long time ago, Earth, Mars, and Venus used to be the satellites of Maldek. The size of Maldek was huge, much bigger than Earth. It had an atmosphere, clouds, and mountains that were much higher than Mount Everest, and even higher than Olympus, the highest mountain on Mars.

Pluto is not considered a planet because it's too small. In fact, Pluto is a moon from one planet that was destroyed. There are other planets similar to Earth, but they don't have usual orbits.

There is another planet with an unusual orbit. There is information about this planet in the Sumerian Tablets. It doesn't go around the Sun the same way as the other planets. It comes to our solar system, then it leaves for a few thousand years. This planet passes between Mars and Jupiter, but in the opposite direction. All the planets orbit in the same direction as the Sun's rotation, but this planet's orbit goes in the opposite direction. Some people know this planet as Nibiru or Planet X. Some scientists had have confirmed the existence of this planet. My guides and several high dimensional beings have told me that Nibiru is not a planet. It's a star. Nibiru right now is very far from Earth, and it will not be visible for several hundred years. Scientists talk seriously about other planets and they mention that life could be possible in other planets, but usually they don't talk seriously about other beings.

The beings that are half human/half snake are mentioned in many ancient books, including the Christian Bible. They are represented as snakes. The Vatican acts as a modern Roman Empire. They have been manipulating information especially since the Vatican created the New Testament and removed 14 books of the Bible in the year 1684. When the Bible was translated from Latin to English some things were missing or mistranslated. Even the name of Jesus was translated from his original name Yeshua.

I have asked several higher dimensional beings about the existence of Jesus. They all say that he existed but his life was different from the one told in the Bible. Something they told me is that Jesus, when he was between 12 and 29 years old, he went to Tibet and India where he learned everything he taught. Also, Jesus was different because he was born in a different way. He was created in the 4th dimension. His parents didn't have sex in this dimension. That is why his mother was a virgin. When we were living in the 4th dimension, some people knew how to have sex without using the physical body. This was in Lemuria, even before Atlantis was created.

There have been several people like Jesus, even now. Jesus has had many reincarnations on Earth. Right now he is having a lifetime in India as a female spiritual leader, but not a popular one. She wants to keep it this way.

Several beings came to Earth after the Reptilians. There is also a race called the Raptors. They look very similar to a velociraptor. Now they live underground. I heard an interesting story about these beings. A few years ago, the velociraptors started to help humans. They decided to have a better relationship with humans but they didn't like ideas humans had about velociraptors. Especially because of movies like Jurassic Park, we see them as the bad guys. They are in contact with some humans. They asked humans to change the image of velociraptors. They don't want to be seen as bad. Now there are movies in which velociraptors are friends with humans.

Then the *Elohim* (the race that created humans) came to Earth. They came from a parallel reality of the constellation Cygnus. Many people believe that they came from Nibiru because it was interpreted this way from ancient texts. Several high dimensional beings have told me that the *Elohim* came from a parallel reality - not from Nibiru. They were in Nibiru before coming to Earth but they are not originally from there. The *Elohim* came to Earth looking for minerals, mainly gold, but not the typical gold we know. They were looking for white powder gold (ormus). They could also take the typical gold we know and pulverize it and create the type of gold they needed. They were looking for gold because they were having problems with the atmosphere on their planet. It would be used to bring balance to the weather.

The *Elohim* were humanoids, taller than humans. They had elongated skulls, almond eye color, blue-tinted skin, narrow waists, broad chests, thin limbs, and black hair.

Scientists have found elongated skulls in the region of Peru.

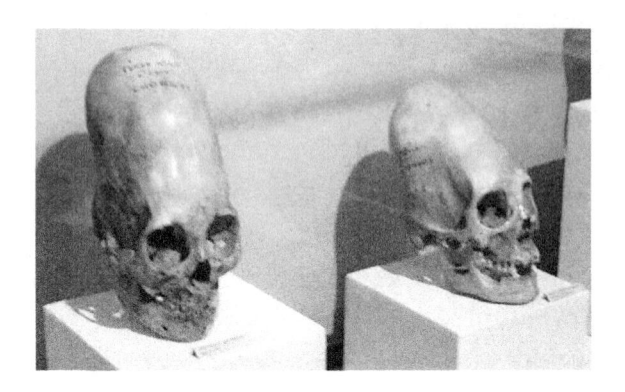

Scientists believed that ancient people in that region were using tools to modify their skulls by pressing the forehead. But then they found the skeleton of a pregnant woman, and the baby also had an elongated skull. This confirmed that these beings had elongated skulls from birth.

These beings were not humans, but they were not *Elohim*. They were a different race, similar to the *Elohim*, but not the same.

In India, many gods have blue skin. They are also not the *Elohim*.

The skin is very similar, but they are not the same race, although they were related. We can say that the Indian gods with blue skin were the cousins of the *Elohim*.

Elongated skulls have been found in several places around the world. Some of these skulls belong to the *Elohim*.

Some humans have blue skin. Their DNA is different. Probably the most famous case is the Fugate family in Kentucky, USA.

The *Elohim*, after many years of digging gold on Earth, needed help to extract more gold. They decided to create a slave race to help them. They couldn't create a new race without help. They were helped by some beings from Sirius. The *Elohim* and the beings from Sirius mixed their DNA with the DNA of several beings on Earth and created a new being. In order to create life, there has to be a male and a female. We can say the *Elohim* were the female, and the beings from Sirius were the male.

The *Elohim*, who came to Earth first were all females. They created the first humans, who were only females or were androgynous (partly male and partly female). These first humans were created through Parthenogenesis (without the need of sexual interaction). The first human beings were not slaves. Basically, they were something like an experiment. All this happened in the region now known as South Africa. There are several pyramids and stone circles (like Stonehenge) in this area. Under these structures, including Stonehenge, there are rings of energy that connect with Mother Earth, and using this energy, the portal is activated. The rings are in the 4th dimension, so they are not visible in this dimension.

Eventually humans started to mine gold in this area. Several thousand humans were working on mining gold. The *Elohim* had a laboratory where they worked on improving the DNA of humans. This laboratory was next to the river Euphrates, now known as Iraq. The Garden of Eden is referred to this area.

The reason why many humans are obsessed with gold is because human bodies have DNA of the *Elohim*, and they were obsessed with gold. The *Elohim* and many alien races don't use money as humans do. Money was created as a way of control.

The reason why humans automatically experience fear for some *Problematic beings*, especially the reptilians, is because humans are mammals and mammals usually fear reptiles. Also, human DNA was created to fear the Reptilians and stay away from them.

This was a long time ago and it happened in the 4th dimension. These humans were very different compared to humans today. The bodies of humans were created and new souls started to be born in these bodies. The souls come from the universe. The human body was created at this time but the souls already existed. The souls came from all over the universe to occupy the new human bodies. So, in other words, every human on Earth is actually an alien. The spirit is not from this planet. We all came from somewhere else in the universe.

In the universe, there is a source of all energy. New souls are created from there but it usually takes many millions of years for a soul to be able to take a body and eventually become a race. Some people refer to this source of energy as the universe, "all that is", God, or just Source.

When a spirit comes to Earth for the first time, it splits into two parts. The world contains separation and duality. This means that in this world there are two parts for everything. Let's say, if there is good, there is bad. If there is black, there is white. If there is positive, there is negative. It's just how things are in this world. That is why we have two hemispheres in the brain.

When a spirit comes to this world for the first time, the spirit splits into two and they are born as twins. When they come for the second time, they don't have to be twins but they come separately as male and female. Some people know this separation of the soul as twin flames. Many people believe that during your lifetime you have to find your twin flame so you can be completed. I asked my guides and many other beings about this. They told me that it's not like that. We came here to experience everything, all types of life, as male and female. That is why we switch from male to female during our lifetimes. When a soul decides to leave this world, the two souls have to reunite and leave this world together as one. In other words, right now there is another person somewhere in the world who is the same spirit as you but having a human experience as the opposite sex.

There is a spirit who has been with you many lifetimes. They are not necessarily your twin flame, but they are known as a soulmate. Sometimes this spirit comes as a family member, a friend, or a very close person. Usually every lifetime they switch roles. One lifetime they come as brother and sister, another as father and son, another as a couple, or just as friends.

When we were created by the *Elohim*, there were many other beings and animals on Earth. Most humans were taking gold from caves in Africa. The *Elohim* came to Earth several times and improved the physical bodies of humans.

It's funny that we call them aliens when in fact they were on Earth before humans. But for now, I will continue calling them aliens because it's the way most people would visualize them. There is no exact vocabulary to describe many of these things because many of these concepts don't exist in our language. I am using many words that other people use so if you want to research more about it, it would be easy for you to find. I just want to advise you, if you decide to research more, please focus on love. Don't listen too much to people presenting fear-based information. This information may affect you negatively. Sometimes they want to create controversy or cause confusion. If you don't feel good about something, just forget about it. It will drain your energy. It is helpful to be aware of the existence of the *Problematic beings* but we don't have to focus our energy on that. Many conspiracy theories are real but we don't have to put our energy on that. It will affect you in a negative way.

I asked several higher dimensional beings why many people on Earth believe that God is an external being who judges people. They told me that what we call God is everything in existence and not external to us. It is everything, physical and non-physical.

My guides told me that I can visualize it as if "God" or *"All That Is"* is a big cake. The cake represents *"All That Is"* and every person or any being is like a very small piece of the cake having an individual experience. But we all come from the same source. Even though we see ourselves as separate from each other, the cake is not the cake without us and we cannot exist if the cake doesn't exist.

When we talk to another person, we believe that we are talking to someone different than us, or someone not part of us. But we are all the same, literally. Even the high dimensional beings are the same energy. In other words, there is no difference between you and me or any other being in the universe. We are having individual experiences but we are the same consciousness.

The high dimensional beings and advanced humans understand this perfectly. *Problematic beings* don't see it this way because they decided to experience reality as separation. They are also part of the same consciousness but they have decided to separate themselves from the rest.

As long as we are in the 3rd dimension, we will experience separation. This is part of the 3rd and 4th dimensions. The 5th and upper dimensions are different. We don't experience separation there.

My guides told me that the human mind cannot understand what exactly comprises *"All That Is"*. The closest thing we can understand to it is the feeling of unconditional love.

A very interesting thing that my guides told me is, "If you want to create a new animal starting from zero, first you have to create a universe because the universe will be running through the body of the animal."

Eventually, The *Elohim* mixed their DNA with the DNA of the beings we know as Homo erectus. The Homo erectus beings that were not altered by the *Elohim* have evolved. They exist in a different dimension but they come here from time to time. Some of them are underground. Some people have seen them on the surface. These are the beings we know as Sasquatch or Bigfoot.

They don't interact with humans because it is not allowed. We have been in a test period and we are not supposed to be contacted. That is why aliens don't show up just like that. They are always observing but outside our visible light. That is why we cannot see them. Using infrared cameras, you could see UFOs that are invisible to our eyes. The Mexican government made public videos of UFOs that can be seen only with infrared cameras. This is because they are in a different room of this 3rd dimension. The UFOs in the sky don't disappear - they just change their frequency. Our eyes are not capable of seeing them anymore because they have left the frequency of our visible light.

In total, there were seven different beings involved in the process of creating the human race. Five of these races were hybrid races (a mix of two races). We can say that the human DNA comes from twelve different races. The *Elohim* is a hybrid race. They are half Pleiadian and half Reptilian, but not the same Reptilian race that is causing problems on Earth. The *Elohim* were much taller than average humans but started to be shorter because the gravity on Earth was different compared to their planet. They shrank to around 4 meters (13 feet).

On Earth, some beings who were *Elohim* started to mix with the humans. They were not supposed to, but they did. This created a new race - a new type of human. They are mentioned in the Christian Bible as giants. The Bible used to have more books, but some of them were removed by the Vatican. These beings were talked about in the book of Enoch.

The Vatican has been hiding and manipulating information. Some popes have mentioned that Hell does not exist. It was an invention of the church, probably to cause fear. Hell doesn't exist, but the being called Lucifer does exist. Lucifer is a female archangel who was in the 4th dimension, she could not stay there and she was sent to the 3rd dimension. The *Problematic beings* sometimes work with her. There is really nothing to fear. I always found it funny that the Vatican decided to hide information about the giants but not about Lucifer. They probably just wanted to cause fear.

The giants mentioned in ancient texts were beings from other planets and dimensions. There were many giants from Maldek, the planet that used to be between Mars and Jupiter. Some animals (insects, unicorns, aquatic animals, and others) also came from Maldek. These giants from Maldek were in direct contact with Celtic people in Europe. That is why you find giants and unicorns in Celtic symbolism. The giants from Maldek came to Earth as refugees because Maldek was destroyed. It took them some time to adapt to the gravity on Earth because it's three times heavier than on Maldek. This caused health problems in the giants, and their lifespan became shorter. Some of these giants became aggressive and started to have problems with humans. Many humans started to see the giants as a threat, and eventually a big conflict started. Humans started to haunt the giants. The giants were very strong but there were many more humans than giants, so eventually almost all of the giants got killed. At that time, the humans who were killing giants were seen as respected people. Now, we have stories about humans vs giants (like David and Goliath). These stories come from the times when the giants of Maldek were on Earth. Some of these giants now live underground. Other giants on Earth were a mix of human DNA and *Elohim*.

The *Elohim* realized that there were giants with human DNA mixed with theirs. This was not supposed to happen but they decided to let it happen. They decided to let humans evolve by themselves. At that time, humans lived around 200 years or more. Many ancient books, including the Christian Bible, talk about humans living that long.

Once they completed their mission of collecting gold, most of the *Elohim* decided to leave Earth, but some of them decided to stay.

The Pharaohs of Egypt were one of many giants that existed on Earth. They were a mix of human DNA and the *Elohim*. That is why they had elongated skulls.

The *Hathors* is another race that helped people in Egypt during many years.

Some giants were in contact with ancient civilizations. The giants helped humans to build cities and structures.

There were also Reptilians and other beings on the planet. The *Elohim* and the Reptilians didn't have a good relationship. The *Elohim* told humans not to talk to the Reptilians but humans talked to them anyway. In the Christian Bible, this is represented as the snake talking to Adam and Eve.

Adam and Eve were the first modern humans created. First Adam, then Eve. The more accurate names are Adama and Ava. Adam represents the first human form created, and Ava is an upgraded form.

Humans were originally created to be slaves. They were not supposed to know the knowledge about life, just to serve as slaves. When the *Elohim* realized that humans got the knowledge about who they were, they helped humans to grow on their own, and eventually, the *Elohim* left.

Humans at that time considered the *Elohim* to be gods, because they were creating life. This idea of God as an external being that most people on Earth believe today started here. The *Elohim* wanted to teach humans that we are all one God. But humans were not ready at that time.

When the *Elohim* left Earth, they left humans in Africa. Some other humans were in the area where the *Elohim* had their laboratories – the area we know as Iraq. But the majority of humans were moved to Lemuria (in the Pacific Ocean).

Between 250,000 and 60,000 years ago, humans were evolving very fast. Some *Elohim* were with them. Humans were in contact with other beings on Earth. In general, humans didn't have problems with the other races. Almost all beings were helping humans evolve. The humans in Lemuria started to grow much faster than the rest.

We were having a great time in Lemuria. We were evolving quickly. We had brown skin and similar bodies to the ones we have now. We learned how to use the energy in our bodies, especially sexual energy which is very powerful. We had several experiments with ourselves. We learned to leave our bodies for a while. We discovered that having sex this way (without our bodies) created a different, more advanced, type of human. Many Lemurians learned how to do this, and this improved human evolution tremendously.

Before we are born, before the embryo becomes our heart, the spirit decides to be male or female and then the body starts to develop. Something similar happens when a new race is created. Some species are male and others are female. A male species is more left-brained and advanced in physical technology. A female species is usually more spiritual and it can create the similar technology, but in a different way. Both are powerful, just different.

Some human races have more DNA from a male species and others from a female species. Therefore some humans are more rational and others more emotional.

When humans were living in Lemuria, we were a female species. We were able to create things just with our feelings, and were very intuitive. We had a better understanding of time and space than we do now, and we could see things before they happened. We could see the future, but just for a few hundred years. We were aware of the events happening all over the planet.

Some beings in Lemuria were more advanced than others. They constantly taught others so they could all grow together. The advanced beings of Lemuria prepared a plan. They went to Atlantis. The advanced beings of Lemuria went to Atlantis because there were natural vortexes of energy coming out of the planet. The advanced Lemurians moved there and started to build cities in Atlantis so other Lemurians could move there if they felt attracted by the energy.

They were preparing Atlantis. Many Lemurians were ready to move but others decided to stay. Little by little, some Lemurians started to leave the island and they moved towards America. Most of them moved to South America. Many Lemurians established a new home in the area we know as Peru, Bolivia and northern Chile. Some others moved farther north, all the way to Mexico and the United States.

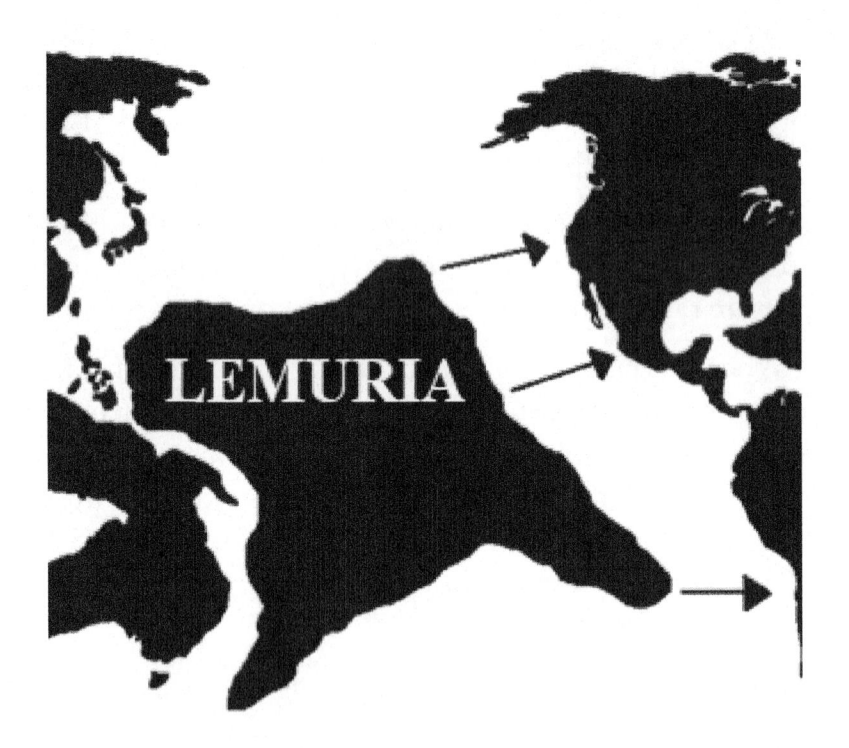

These people were the Inca, Aztec, and Native Americans. The Mayans were different. They moved to the Yucatan Peninsula later. That's why the Aztecs and Mayans are different.

There were also Lemurians who went to the west of Lemuria to the area we know as New Zealand, Australia and Indonesia. This area used to be bigger and we were in the 4th dimension, so it was not exactly as it is now in the 3rd dimension.

Once Atlantis was ready, many humans started to move from America to Atlantis but some of them stayed in America.

I had several lifetimes in Atlantis. I have some memories of how Atlantis looked although I don't have memories of how humans or other beings looked. I used to have visions of it. I was not sure if the visions I had were from Atlantis so I asked Athella and my guides. They confirmed it.

When we lived in Atlantis, we ate mainly plant foods. We did not eat meat as many people do today. Some Atlanteans didn't have the need for food. The land was very fertile and since we were able to communicate with Mother Earth we knew what to do all the time.

There were many coral reefs. There were very advanced cities with pyramids. There were also active volcanos but since we were in communication with Mother Earth we knew how to handle any weather. We were connected to Mother Earth and all the universe. We were able to manipulate the weather with our thoughts. We were in contact with alien species and we shared information. We were good friends with many races but we never went outside the planet. We didn't have jobs like we do today and there were not laws like we have now. We had the freedom and time to decide what we wanted to do. Nobody took advantage of others. Usually, we ended up doing something we loved that suited our personality.

Whatever you decided to do, it was welcome in Atlantis. After all, we were all working for Atlantis. There were leaders but we were very independent. At the same time, we depended on each other.

Crime was very rare. We didn't experience fear and ego as we do today. Crime requires ego because it's basically a desire to control others. We were very good at handling energy in our bodies and around us. We were able to communicate with plants and animals.

We were able to capture energy with crystals and use it whenever possible. It was a very different than what we use today. Sickness was very rare. We understood that illness was directly related to an emotion. A sick person would be advised to focus on a specific emotion in order to heal.

We used free energy, mainly from the Sun and quartz crystals. We had special days, like the holidays we have now, but during these days we had ceremonies. We celebrated unity and love towards each other and Mother Earth. We were especially connected to Mother Earth when the Sun and Earth were in a special position. We could communicate with her all the time.

We used only natural materials and we did not use anything we didn't need. We recycled what we used. We had a better understanding of our bodies and we knew the importance of the heart. We created from the heart.

Some parts of Atlantis had red soil because of the minerals, especially iron and copper. This created special vortexes of energy that helped the Atlanteans. It was pure energy from Mother Earth. We also had orichalcum, a metal used mainly to create buildings and artifacts.

There were humans in Atlantis, Lemuria, America, Africa, Iraq, and other places around the world but the humans in Atlantis and Lemuria were developing faster. We were in communication with the rest of the humans through crystals. You can store and send information through crystals. Crystals are alive and very advanced.

We were able to create anything we want. Our emotions were not crazy like they are now. We were aware of our thoughts and emotions. We could choose what to feel and experience anytime. Whenever we were experiencing something we didn't choose, we understood that as something that had to happen in order for us to learn something new and keep growing.

One alien race from the future came. Usually, one race cannot interfere with the development of another race unless they have permission to do it. Permission from who? From the Galactic Federation, a group of very advanced races who take care of the balance in the universe. There are many names for this group but to keep it simple I will call it the "Galactic Federation".

There was another race who came but this one didn't have permission. They affected our evolution. This race is known as the Tall Whites. They are humanoid and some people confuse them with Nordics or Pleiadians because they have similar bodies. But they are not the same. Nordics and Pleiadians are friends. The Tall Whites are *Problematic beings*.

Before I continue, I want to remind you that if you are feeling uncomfortable with this part, take a break. Some people feel uncomfortable with anything related to the *Problematic beings*. Our human history has a very beautiful end.

The *Problematic beings* came to Earth and tried to take control of the planet but the advanced beings of Lemuria and Atlantis didn't allow it. We were very powerful and we had more people than them. We were able to stop them anytime. The Tall Whites were a male species. We were a female species. There were many misunderstandings because of the way we see reality.

The Reptilians, who have been on Earth since before humans, don't have emotions like humans do. Therefore, they never understood humans. They are much more rational than humans. The Tall Whites and Reptilians understood each other more than they understood humans.

There were misunderstandings between humans and Tall Whites, mainly because of the different ways of understanding reality. Humans experienced reality with emotions. For example, when we were walking from one place to another, we just visualized ourselves already in the second place. Since we were living in a higher dimension, whatever we thought of manifested almost instantly. So we stopped being in one place and we appeared in the other, like teleportation. This was the way we understood things. We were not logical. We did not visualize what happened in between. We did not think about the how.

In this 3rd dimension, we can manifest faster this way because it's natural for us. Whenever we want something and we really wish for it - without ego - we will get it. It may not come the way we expect it but certainly, in one way or another, it will manifest. It is important to visualize everything with details and without ego.

Many beings told me that teleportation is possible but I have never seen it. It requires working with the vibrations in the body. Another thing that is possible is passing through walls or passing objects through a wall. They do it by changing their vibrations until their vibration is different than the physical mass in the wall.

In Indonesia, there is a person known for doing this, although it is not easy to find him. His name is John Chang.

He is able to send objects through other physical objects. He has learned this from higher dimensional beings. After many years of meditation and training with higher dimensional beings, he has good control of his vibrations. He moves objects through other objects as if they were not solid. He can also modify reality around him and create things like fire and electricity. Using his root chakra (first chakra) as a negative pole and his solar plexus chakra (third chakra) as a positive pole, he can produce electricity in his body. He can also change the vibrations in his hands and stop bullets shot by a gun. He also practices telekinesis. But he focuses his work mainly on healing people with his vibrations

The *Problematic beings* are more logical. Their reality is different than humans. If they want to move from one place to another, there has to be something in between. You can walk or somehow move from between these two places. Most humans now see reality this way. This is because we have been influenced by the *Problematic beings* since we came to the 3rd dimension. But we used to think differently.

The *Problematic beings* are good with technology but they don't have emotions and they don't understand how powerful emotions can be. They were disconnected from Earth and the universe. They care only about themselves. They tried to have control over humans but we were very powerful and they couldn't do much against us. They had to learn how to deal with humans to be among us.

Whenever we had discussions with the *Problematic beings*, we had to agree on something. There were always misunderstandings. Every time something happened, we saw it differently compared to them. We welcomed any new experiences, whether they looked good or bad, because that experience would teach us something and this is how we grow. They just wanted to take control over everything.

Around 26,000 years ago, the most advanced humans lived in Atlantis and Lemuria. There was a comet coming to Earth. There was a big discussion about how to handle the situation. Humans believed that it should hit Earth because it was supposed to be like that. The *Problematic beings* wanted to destroy it. In the end it was decided that they would allow the comet to hit Earth. When it hit, it destroyed several of the *Problematic beings'* settlements and some of them got killed. They got very angry and the relationship with them became very bad.

Problematic beings started to manipulate the leaders of Atlantis. They were trying to implement ego into the minds of the leaders. The leaders of Atlantis were women. Eventually, they did it. They manipulated the leaders of Atlantis and they started to change things for the people. The leaders of Atlantis started to argue with the leaders of Lemuria about how the rest of humanity should be ruled. The main problem was related to wealth. The leaders of Atlantis wanted to have more.

The rulers of Atlantis wanted to rule the other humans around the planet. The Lemurians wanted to leave them alone and allow them to develop by themselves. The situation in Atlantis and Lemuria got worse with time. Some Atlanteans started to move to the Yucatan Peninsula in Mexico. Some Lemurians started to move to the higher parts of the island and some others went underground. They got permission from the beings living there as long as they behave peacefully. This happened around 13,000 years ago.

Every 13,000 years, there are changes on Earth. It is related to some of Earth's movements.

The Earth rotates around the Sun, but the axis has a tilt of around 23 degrees. That is why we have seasons on Earth.

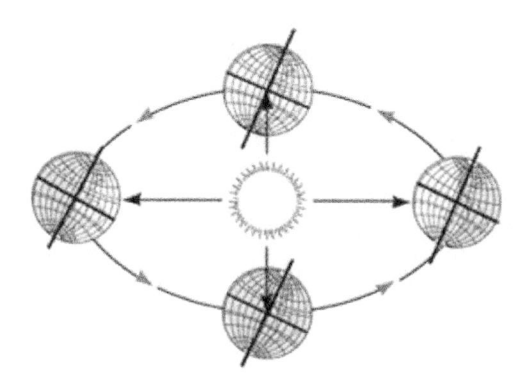

The axis of Earth moves. It takes around 26,000 years to make a complete round.

Every 13,000 years, when the axis is halfway around, there are changes on Earth.

In the year 2012, we were exactly at the end of a cycle. This means changes. The changes are happening now. That is why we are seeing an increase in technology. Thousands of years without so much improvement and suddenly exponential growth. This is in big part because of the changes on Earth. But the main changes are related to the consciousness of the planet.

When there are changes in consciousness, they eventually manifest in physical reality. Another change happening during this time is that Earth is going through several physical changes. The electromagnetism on Earth is changing. The poles are changing and all beings on Earth are affected by it. 26,000 years ago, we knew how to handle these changes, especially because we were able to see the future. But 13,000 years ago, the leaders of Atlantis were manipulated and there was a lot of tension between humans in Lemuria and Atlantis.

Planets have male and female energies just like humans. Mother Earth changed a few years ago. For the last several thousand years, the energy of the Earth was male. That is why some religious leaders misunderstood that being a man was more important than being a woman. That is also why many spiritual leaders in the last thousand years were men - Jesus, Muhammad, Krishna and many more.

A few years ago, the energy of the Earth became female. This doesn't mean that women will be more important than men but women will be the dominant sex. These changes are happening now. There will be more and more female leaders in the world.

When we come to Earth, we choose our gender. In some cases, we are still attached to previous lifetimes when we had an experience as the opposite sex. Let's say you were a man and now you are a woman. In this lifetime (as a woman), you might still be attached to a previous lifetime (as a man). This causes you to keep some aspects of the previous lifetimes as the opposite sex. That is why some women feel like they are men, and vice versa.

Around 13,000 years ago, we had a lot of problems in Atlantis and Lemuria. Some leaders of Atlantis wanted to have more and more wealth and they didn't care about humans in other parts of the world. Something similar is happening today in the USA. The leaders of Atlantis didn't realize that by doing this, they would accumulate a lot of karma.

The leaders and some humans in Atlantis, under the influence of the *Problematic beings*, started a war between Atlanteans and Lemurians. Atlanteans started to use their weapons against Lemurians. Many Lemurians escaped to the region of Australia and Indonesia.

Eventually, the Atlanteans destroyed Lemuria. The whole continent was damaged. The only remaining part of Lemuria is Easter Island, Hawaii, New Zealand and the islands in the South Pacific.

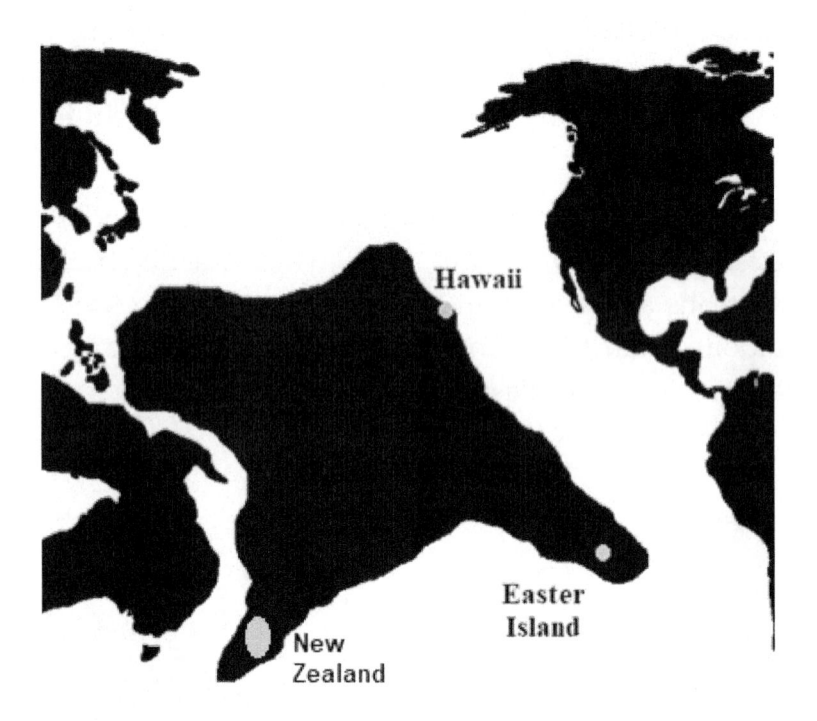

Then Atlantis was also destroyed. The only remaining parts of Atlantis are the island of Azores in Portugal and the Caribbean.

What happened in Atlantis was something that had never happened on Earth. These problems caused the destruction of many vortexes of energy- specifically, one part on the west side of Atlantis, now known as the Bermuda Triangle.

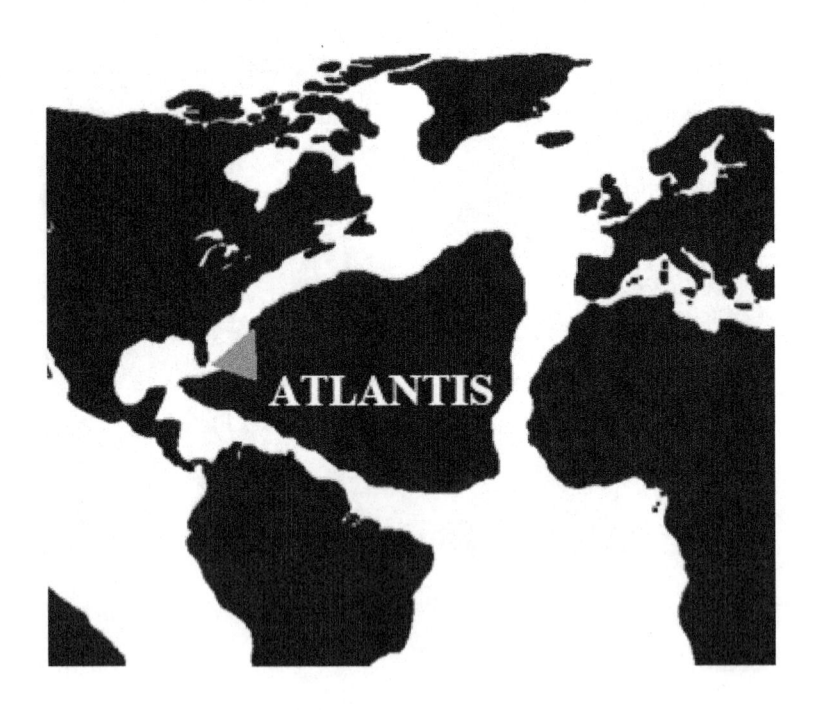

Many planes and ships disappear in this region. In part, Atlantis was established there because of this vortex of energy. They used it for its healing energy. After the changes on Earth caused by the bombs of energy, this vortex started to pull energy. Therefore, there is a distortion of energy in that region. There are more vortexes of energy like this one in other parts of the world.

Because of the problem with electromagnetism in the Bermuda Triangle, planes and ships are moved to other frequencies (rooms). The people who went through this process of changing frequencies in the Bermuda Triangle are now somewhere else and have been taken care of. There are other places in the world similar to the Bermuda Triangle. These places are usually in nature.

In Mexico, there is an area called *"zona del silencio"* with unusual electromagnetism. Many people compare it with the Bermuda Triangle.

In Slovakia, there is a mountain called Tribeč, famous for mysterious disappearances of people. There are natural portals in this place. Some places in nature have natural portals. When people go through these portals they go to other frequencies. These portals are usually deep into the nature, and are activated naturally only during the night. These natural portals are usually between two big trees, or a natural circle on the ground. This is why many people have disappeared in national parks. The location of the portals can be checked with dowsing rods.

The weapons used in Atlantis were very advanced in technology. Crystals were used as weapons. The *Elohim* were able to see the future and they could see that the destruction of Atlantis was coming. They tried to stop the Atlanteans, but the Atlanteans didn't care. In fact, the Atlanteans wanted to destroy also the *Elohim*.

At that time, there were beings on Earth that were half-human, half-animal. These animals are mentioned in the Greek mythology and other ancient cultures. The Atlanteans were using some of these beings as soldiers.

Atlantis was destroyed when the Atlanteans tried to use a powerful weapon against the *Elohim*. The weapon didn't work as they expected and it destroyed Atlantis. The bomb created a huge wave of dust and water around other continents. Some parts of Africa and America were covered by several kilometers of mud.

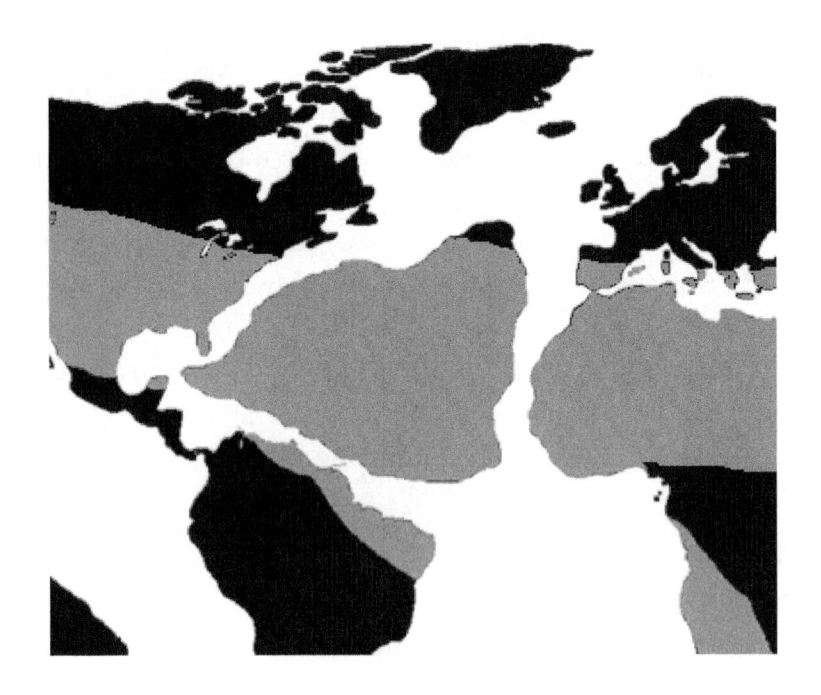

Eventually the mud dried and became sand, this is how some deserts around the world were formed.

Atlantis was not destroyed completely. One part of Atlantis remained in the Atlantic Ocean for a while, and started to move south, until it eventually became Antarctica. In other words, Antarctica used to be part of Atlantis. Many beings live underground in Antarctica. Antarctica doesn't belong to any country because they don't allow it. Hitler tried to create settlements in Antarctica but it was not allowed. The United States tried to do something similar but they were also not allowed.

Egypt and other parts of Africa used to be full of vegetation, but after the bomb of Atlantis it became the Sahara Desert.

The destruction of Atlantis happened during the time of year that we would consider to be November 1st. Many people around the world celebrate this day as All Saints' Day, or All Hallows Eve, or Halloween. This is also around the time when elections are taking place in the USA. This country is like the representation of Atlantis. Their leaders want to take control over the rest of the world. This is not a coincidence. It is how things are. But this time, everything will be very different in a positive way.

Higher dimensional beings saw what was happening in Atlantis and Lemuria. There is a universal law – one race cannot interfere directly with the development of another race. We caused the problems for ourselves so we had to fix them. The advanced beings of Atlantis didn't know what to do. They had to ask for help from beings in higher dimensions.

The higher dimensional beings came. They knew that there was only one way to solve this because it had happened in other parts of the universe. The same solution should work here as well but it was the first time something like this happened on Earth.

The high dimensional beings gave instructions to the advanced beings of Atlantis about what to do. They told them that humans on Earth would have to move to the 3rd dimension and we would have to learn our lesson. We would lose our memories from the 4th dimension and we would have to start over. This was the only solution.

The lesson would have to be learned before the end of the next cycle which was in 2012 - December 21, 2012 to be more precise.

When we were living in Atlantis and Lemuria, before we had the problems, there was a net of energy around the planet that connected all humans on Earth. This was a real net of energy that went all over the planet. It was located around 100 kilometers (62 miles) above the Earth. This net of energy had a special geometry that made the connection between all humans possible. In fact, there were three nets of energy. During the war in the 4th dimension, we lost one of them. We would have to recover this third net of energy before 2012.

We were moved to this 3rd dimension. We were not used to this heavy and dense reality. Earth was different - more physical. Our bodies were different - heavier. The advanced beings of Atlantis were able to stay in the 4th dimension. They are now known as Ascended Masters.

If falling into this 3rd dimension wasn't hard enough, something else was also happening. Do you remember that every 13,000 years, there are changes? Well, those changes were about to happen and we were not ready. There were changes in the electromagnetism on Earth and this caused humans to forget everything. We lost our memories so we don't remember the events on Atlantis and Lemuria.

We started to lose our senses. We used to have more than the five we now have. We were able to sense the energy of others and we could sense electricity like sharks do.

The same beings from Sirius who created the first humans saw this. They knew that it would be very hard to survive in this 3rd dimension. They gave us a gift, a very beautiful gift, so we could understand this 3rd dimension better.

They changed our reality. They created something like a screen in front of us so we could understand the world were experiencing better. This screen they made for us is the reality you see right now. Everything you see and touch is the reality they created for us. Everything around you - your house, your neighborhood, the sky, this book, even your body - is an illusion. It looks and feels real but it is not. It is an illusion - a hologram. Many scientists around the world are aware of it now. They know that the world we see is a simulation like a very real dream.

This hologram doesn't exist in other planets. It is happening only on Earth. Earth was a planet created specifically for insects, which is why there are so many here. Also, some beings that look like humanoid insects live all over the solar system. Humans were invited to be here but this was not our original planet. The soul of many humans used to live in the constellation Lyra. Eventually, the place was no longer habitable and many humans had to move to other planets until eventually we were allowed to live on Earth.

In the 3rd dimension, for the last 13,000 years, most humans have been connected to one of the two nets of energy available. That is why we are all connected. That is why when something happens in one part of the planet, people on the other side of the planet can feel it.

Since we fell to the 3rd dimension, we had to create the third net of energy again (Christ Consciousness Grid) and connect to it. Usually creating a new layer takes many years of evolution and 13,000 years would not be enough time. Our case was different. We had achieved this level before so we just had to activate and connect to it again. We had permission to do it artificially because we had done it in the past naturally. Otherwise, it would not have been accepted.

Most humans are connected to the second layer but there are very few who are connected to the first one. They are the indigenous people from Australia, New Zealand, Colombia, and the United States. The people who moved from Lemuria to Australia and America.

Before we fell to the 3rd dimension, when the high dimensional beings talked to the advanced humans of Atlantis, they also told them how to create an artificial layer around the planet. The advanced humans of Atlantis started to prepare for the creation of the artificial layer. In order to do this, they had to create many structures around the planet in a precise order and location so this energy could work.

There is a Chinese technique called Feng Shui where people organize objects in their house in order to have positive energies. This is similar to what they were doing. It is called *geomancy*. It is like Feng Shui for the planet.

First, they created the Great Pyramid of Giza. It was not created by slaves as we are told. The pyramids were created there because of the energy coming out of the planet in that area. The energy is not exactly located where the pyramid is but it's very close to it. The Great Pyramid was created before we came to the 3rd dimension. It was built in the 4th dimension and eventually manifested in the 3rd dimension. What we see is like a shadow of the 4th dimension. Actually, everything we see in this dimension is like a shadow of higher dimensions. Another interesting thing about the Great Pyramid is that it was built from top to bottom.

The Great Pyramid of Giza is like a north pole of energy running through the whole planet. The south pole is in the Pacific Ocean, in an island called Moorea.

In Mexico, many people believe that the pyramid of Chichen Itza is the main point of energy of the planet. The people of Bosnia believe the same about their pyramid. I asked several beings why people believe this. The answer is always the same - ego. Many people, including spiritual people, experience ego. In some cases, they believe that because they are spiritual they don't experience ego. So every time I went to a certain place in the world, there were people saying that the pyramid close to them was the main pyramid running the energy around the world.

After creating the Great Pyramid of Giza, the advanced humans of Atlantis created more monuments around the world. These monuments were created with exact mathematical precision in specific locations around the world.

Some of these monuments were pyramids. There are pyramids all around the world. Many of them are covered by grass, like the pyramids in Bosnia, in Rudňany, Slovakia, in Puebla, Mexico, in Xi'an, China, Mount Padang, Indonesia, and many more.

Other pyramids are underwater. Some are found in western Cuba and in the islands of Azores, Portugal - more precisely between the islands of Terceira Island and São Miguel Island. Many others exist in locations around the world.

Some other pyramids, like the ones in Alaska and Antarctica, are under snow. Other monuments were temples, and others were natural places like lakes or mountains. There were many monuments created in order to activate the third layer.

The third layer was activated around the year 1970. That was before 2012 so we made it. We passed our test.

We created the Christ Consciousness Grid, but the problem is that most humans are still not connected to it. Changes are coming soon but I don't know when. Only Mother Earth knows.

Who activated the third layer? The advanced humans from Atlantis and a group of humans collaborated. Who are these humans? Spiritual people around the world. People with a big heart who love humanity, have had a hard time since we fell to the 3rd dimension, because most humans lost their memories, and were manipulated by the *Problematic beings*. Some humans have recovered some memories during their life, or sometimes they are contacted by higher dimensional beings in one way or another. These humans have been having a hard time with other humans who don't have any knowledge of any of this. We are alive thanks to these spiritual humans, and the advanced humans from Atlantis. Without them, the human race would not exist right now.

The third layer is called Christ. Many Christians are waiting for the return of Jesus. But Jesus will not come and say hello to people. She is a woman in India right now, and she doesn't want to be a public person. The Christ Consciousness Grid is here available for everyone. We just need to connect to it. Jesus was experiencing a reality as if he was connected to this layer.

The survivors of Atlantis moved to Egypt, and some leaders of Atlantis moved to Sumer, between the Tigris and Euphrates rivers.

Because of the changes on the planet, the poles started to move. This caused an ice age on the planet. This is the last known ice age that occurred around 11,400 years ago.

Some parts of the world were covered by ice. Humans at this time were living in caves and we didn't have memories from our past. Even though we were in contact with the advanced beings from Atlantis, they could not do much to help us at that time. They had to wait a little while until we adapted to the 3rd dimension and developed ourselves a little bit more.

Then eventually, the ice started to melt and caused water levels to rise. It created a big flood. This flood is referred to in Bible as the story of Noah's Ark. The flood happened only in few parts of the world. Noah was not a human and he was not using an ark as we think of one, it was a UFO.

The advanced humans from Atlantis stayed in the 4th dimension but they came to the 3rd dimension to visit us often. The only problem was that we were not capable of understanding their teachings.

During this time, the advanced humans were working on preparing the monuments around the planet for the activation of the Christ Consciousness Grid. They worked very hard to create these monuments around the world.

During the time we were living in caves, several beings came and modify our DNA. That is why there are different races now.

Chapter 26 – The Modern

The human races around the world are the result of the manipulation of DNA made by several alien races. In total, humans now have the DNA of 22 races.

In the north of Spain, there is a group of people called Basques. They have different DNA. Most of them have blood type O negative. In fact, the negative blood type originated there. Their DNA was altered by beings from Sirius. Their language is even different. It's the only language in the region that isn't Latin-based. Many scientists haven't been able to explain where the Basque people came from.

In North Africa, there is a similar story about a group called the Berbers. They have their own language and different DNA. They look different than the rest of the people in the area.

In Mexico, scientists found a human skeleton that is at least 12,000 years old. They don't know how this skeleton got there. Scientists believe that all humans emigrated from Africa millions of years ago so they have been creating theories about how this skeleton ended up there. They even have a name for the skeleton - *Naia*. The skeleton was found in a cenote in the Yucatan Peninsula. Cenotes are underground caves found all over the Yucatan Peninsula in Mexico. There is water in these caves so they have become underwater lakes that are a big attraction for tourists. These cenotes used to be caves used by the Mayan people who moved to the Yucatan Peninsula after the destruction of Atlantis.

Around 6,500 years ago, in Mesopotamia and Egypt, people learned how to write and use tools. They knew many things about the world and the universe. They didn't learn by themselves. It usually takes millions of years of evolution to grow to that extent. The humans in Mesopotamia and Egypt evolved very quickly because the *Elohim* improved and provided knowledge. Then they left and that was the last time humans were in contact with the *Elohim*.

At that time, there were humans all over the world. There were humans in Mesopotamia, Egypt, in the region known as Mongolia. In the American continent, there were Native Americans, Aztecs, Mayans (who moved to Mexico after the problems in Atlantis), and the Incas in Peru. There were humans in Africa, Central Europe, India, Australia, and some islands in the Pacific Ocean.

The Aztecs talked about a very special place where humans used to live. It was called Aztlan. This is the Aztec name for Atlantis. The Aztecs even mentioned that people had to leave Aztlan because there were problems related to snakes.

Once Mesopotamia and Egypt were established, the advanced beings of Atlantis taught us how to work with our bodies in the best possible way so we could return to the 4th dimension as soon as possible. There are several ways to do it.

You can just simply die and your spirit will go to the 4th dimension (room number 10). But you will have to come back to the 3rd dimension to be born again as a baby with a new body.

You can take your body with you to the 4th dimension. This is called ascension. If you do this, you will end up in the room number 12 of the 4th dimension. Usually, very advanced humans like teachers and very conscious people do this. They take their bodies with them to the 4th dimension. They just disappear from here. There may be a little flash of light when this happens. You can also ascend if you are a conscious person - loving and aware that you are light and infinite.

Another way is called resurrection. You die, leave your body and go to the 4th dimension. Then you come back to the 3rd dimension without a body and take your body to the 4th dimension. You have a maximum of 4 days to take your body with you. If you do this, you will end up in room number 11 of the 4th dimension. It doesn't matter if your body is damaged in the 3rd dimension. Once you take it to the 4th dimension, you can reconstruct it. The body is an image of our consciousness. Once we are in the 4th dimension we will understand this and we can modify our body by changing the image we have of it. Some Christians deeply believe in resurrection, and may resurrect. They will go to the 4th dimension as spirit. If they understand that they are in the 4th dimension and they could come to take their body, they may do it.

It really doesn't matter how you move to the 4th dimension, but taking your body with you would be the best. If not, you can be born in a new body in the 4th dimension. This was previously not available but now it's available because we recovered the Christ Consciousness Grid around 1970. There will be people teaching you everything you need to know.

The Egyptians were practicing resurrection. That is why they were trying to preserve their bodies as much as possible. After they died, they could come back to the 3rd dimension and take their body to the 4th dimension. The pyramids have a special shape that creates a special energy inside and around them. Jesus also resurrected. He died and came after three days to take his body to the 4th dimension.

There are many beings living in the 4th dimension. Most of the *Problematic beings* stayed in the 4th dimension but some of them are in this 3rd dimension. *Problematic beings* wanted to take control of humans. Because we lost our memories, it was easier for them. They went to Mesopotamia and established themselves in the ancient city we know as Babylon. They presented themselves as gods and started to manipulate people and created the first empire of the world. They are the same beings that are controlling the world today. The governments and leaders we know are basically puppets - they are put there. There is a secret government. They own many big companies in the world. They manipulate anything they can to keep us from remembering our past.

They manipulated human DNA and mixed their DNA with humans. In Atlantis we used to have 12 strands of

DNA. Now we only have 2 strands, or a pair, in each chromosome. The symbol called caduceus is the symbol for medicine. This symbol has 2 strands in the form of a snake.

Friendly beings came from other planets, other dimensions and from underground. They came to help humanity all over the world. They taught us what they know. The *Elohim* were on Earth for a while, mainly in Egypt. That is why the ancient Egyptians knew so much about the universe.

The pyramids create a powerful vortex of energy that moves in a specific way, rotating clockwise. This benefits the people around the area, and the planet in general. The *Problematic beings* appeared to many ancient civilizations and demanded sacrifices on the top of the pyramids. This was done with the intention of inverting the vortex of energy around the pyramid. Instead of connecting to higher dimensions, the *Problematic beings* wanted to connect to lower dimensions. The negative energy of the sacrifices had to be maintained. Therefore, they demanded sacrifices often.

The *Problematic beings* did the same in many ancient places around the world. There are many places like

Stonehenge around the world. Some humans, mainly shamans and spiritual people realized what was happening in the ancient places, and they destroyed the structures to avoid them being used by the *Problematic beings*. This is why these places are usually destroyed. Some of these structures were made a long time ago by some friendly beings. They were made even before humans were created.

Nikola Tesla created a tower that can transmit electricity without the need of cables. With the proper adjustments this tower could be used for healing as well, simulating the effects of a pyramid.

In school, we learn that the first civilizations of humanity were in Mesopotamia. This is not true. *Problematic beings* want us to believe this because they started to manipulate humans there.

I remember asking my teacher in primary school how it was possible that Europeans discovered America if there were people living in America already. My teacher told me that we were supposed to learn history this way because Europeans wrote history.

In Egyptian symbolism we see many types of beings. In some cases, there are humanoid beings combined with other animals on their bodies. I always thought that these beings were mythological but they are real beings (these beings exist, but their real bodies don't look like that). For every animal on Earth there is an alien race with similar characteristics somewhere in the universe. Dogs, cats, snakes, spiders, birds, fish, elephants and even dinosaurs.

Dolphins and whales are basically aliens. That is why they have different tails than other aquatic animals. They are very smart and very conscious. We could learn so much from them. They are from the star Sirius. They used to live in Atlantis. There were canals connecting buildings of Atlantis with the ocean. The dolphins and whales used to interact with us every day during the times of Atlantis.

There are many beings helping humanity right now. Many of them look humanoid - very similar to humans. They might appear as someone from Northern Europe. Some other beings are not humanoid but they are helping humanity in so many ways.

There are six races causing problems for humans, but there are more than 350,000 different races helping humanity right now. There is really nothing to worry about. We have always been protected.

The six *Problematic beings* are the Reptilians (one of many reptilian races), the Tall Whites (one of many tall, white humanoid beings), the Amphibians (the frog people), the Grays (one of many types of gray alien beings), and two more races.

Many people around the world say that they have seen mysterious tall men in black suits doing unusual activities.

These beings are clones, they don't have souls. They are more like artificial intelligence.

The Grays are probably the most famous aliens because they were abducting people a few decades ago. They needed to take samples of human DNA to improve theirs. This is because they are not able to reproduce and they needed human DNA to do it. Many people remember being abducted and they started to describe the Grays (also some Reptilians and Amphibians). That is why many people know about them.

There are so many friendly beings that it is impossible to name all of them. Some of these friendly beings are in contact with humans. The most common are the Arcturians, Pleiadians, Lyrans, many beings from Sirius, the Raptors, some friendly Reptilians, some friendly Grays, the Nordics, beings from Orion, angels, archangels, many beings who are a mix between humans and the Grays, the Yahyel, the Sassani, the Avians, and many more.

The Yahyel, a race that is very similar to humans, will be the first one to have direct contact with humans in the future. Their physical appearance is very similar to that of humans, therefore they will be the first to make open contact with us.

The Pleiadians are able to turn their bodies into light because they understand that we are light. They have been trying to move to the 5th dimension. After many years trying, they just did it recently. They also helped in the creation of humanity but the main races that created humanity were the *Elohim*, as the female species, and the beings from Sirius, as the male species. The Pleiadians were in contact with the Mayans. That is why they knew so much about the universe. The Mayans and other ancient peoples had long hair because it helped them connect with higher dimensions.

Many characters in the Christian Bible were actually friendly beings. Many characters in ancient times were helped by friendly beings. Sometimes even their name was similar to their race. For example, King Arthur was an Arcturian.

There are many beings living in several dimensional levels. Many mythological beings described in ancient cultures live in other dimensions. Some mythological beings like fairies and elves live in this dimension but in a different frequency (room). But the spirit of fairies live in the 4th dimensions, room number 4. In other words, when fairies die, they go to room number 4 of the 4th dimension. This also happens with trees.

Many friendly beings have formed something like a galactic police. They make sure that everything in the universe is the way it's supposed to be. Many people call them the Galactic Federation.

Our guides are part of these friendly beings. Our guides are with us during our whole life. There are also temporary guides - beings who come to help in specific moments of our life, like when big changes happen or in difficult times. They come for a while and help with the energy that is needed in those moments of big challenges.

There are also animal guides but they are mainly for company. You may talk to these animal guides during your dreams or you may encounter certain animals several times during your lifetime.

Animal guides can be animals that you helped in previous lives and they are helping you now.

When I asked Athella about my animal guides, she didn't say anything. But suddenly I started to see pictures of wolves everywhere. I started to dream of wolves. Usually, I have dreams with dolphins and whales, but during these days I had many dreams with wolves. At the time, I was traveling around the USA and I went to Yellowstone National Park. It was winter so I was not able to drive around all the parks. Special busses with special tires are required to handle all the snow. I came earlier in the morning so I was driving in the area where I could drive with the car. Eventually, I started to hear a wolf howling. It was a very strong sound but I was not sure where it was coming from. Then I realized there was a wolf next to the car. It was a white wolf. It howled for few minutes and then went away. I took it as a sign. It was beautiful and impressive. Later on, I talked to a person working in the park. I told him what happened with the wolf and he was surprised. He told me that I was very lucky to see the white wolf because there is only one white wolf in the park and only a few people have seen it. Many times, when I ask Athella or my guides something, they don't give me a direct answer. I always find the answer by experiencing it. I believe this is the way they answer - by allowing me to experience it. That is why it's very important to ask them. They will not do anything for you unless you ask for it.

The best guide you have is your *higher self*. You can visualize your *higher self* like another version of you but in a higher dimension. There are several versions of yourself in other dimensions and you are connected to all of them, all the time. There is another version of yourself in the 4th dimension. Actually, we have a second heart on the right side of our body, but this heart is 4th dimensional. We can use it, but we have to connect to ourselves in the 4th dimension.

Through meditation, you can connect to your *higher self*. Once this is done, you can better understand why you are here on Earth. In order to connect to your *higher self*, you have to first connect to your lower self. Your lower self is the child inside you. You have to be like a child if you want to connect to your *higher self*. The way I visualize the *higher self* is by visualizing myself in a video game. I am the character on the screen and my *higher self* is the person playing the video game with the control.

The planet has a specific point of energy around the planet like the one we used to have in Atlantis, like chakras. The main point of energy running through the planet was in the mountains in Tibet. That is why many people in that region of the world became very spiritual. They could feel the energy of the planet and connect to it.

A few years ago, this energy moved to a new position. Now it is in the mountains between Peru and Bolivia. You will see how people living in this area will become more and more spiritual with time.

Many governments are now aware of beings outside ourselves and are working with several beings. Some countries work with friendly beings and others with *Problematic beings*.

The souls of some *Problematic beings* have been taking the human bodies of several leaders around the world, since Babylonian times.

The symbols of the eagle and lion comes from Babylon.

These symbols are now used by the *Problematic beings*.

A coat of arms is created to represent a person, family, organization, or corporation. The symbols are related to other groups related to them, like their supporters. These symbols are used mainly in Europe. All kings and queens have been related to the monarchy of Babylon.

The lion was used first in Europe with William the Conqueror, the first king of Normandy. Normandy comes from the word Northman. Normandy is in France. France has not been a monarchy since Napoleon III. The Normans eventually moved to England. The lion comes from the Mesopotamian goddess Ishtar, which is in reality a *Problematic being*. The celebration of Easter with eggs and bunnies is not a Christian celebration. It is related to this Mesopotamian goddess.

The eagle symbol comes from a mythological being called Anzu, in Mesopotamia. This symbol has been used in many empires around the world.

Sometimes these symbols are combined and they are represented as griffins, or other mythical creatures. Sometimes they are represented with wings.

The symbols appear in the Four Evangelists, and usually they are represented with wings. Mark the Evangelist is represented with the lion.

John the Evangelist is represented with the eagle.

There are two more Evangelists. One is Luke the Evangelist, represented by a bull. And Matthew the Evangelist is represented as a man with wings.

These fours symbols can be found in the Tetramorph, which means the union of the symbols of the Four Evangelists.

The bull is also found in some statues around the world. The most famous statue of a bull is the one in Wall Street, in New York City. This area is known as the financial center of the world.

The symbol of the bull has been used since Babylonian times.

These symbols are related to four constellations. Taurus, Leo, Scorpius, and Aquarius.

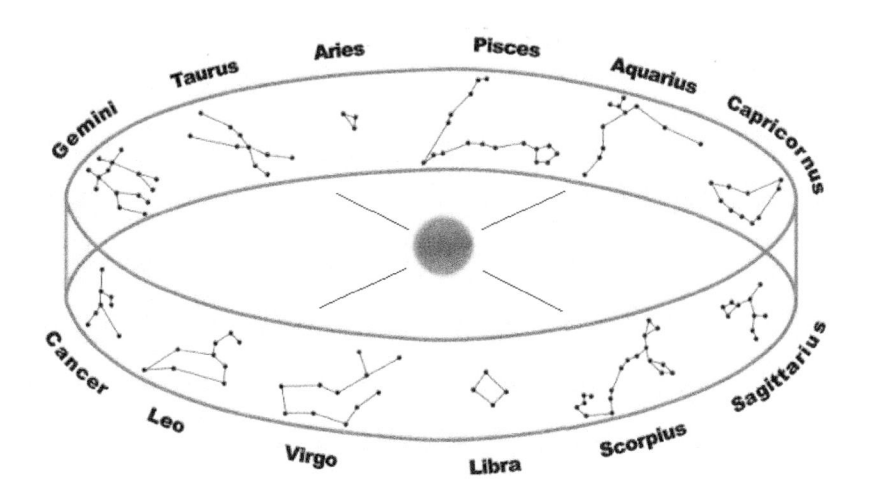

Taurus is represented with the Bull; Leo with the lion; And Scorpius with a Scorpion. The zodiac symbol of Scorpius is the only one with more than one symbol. Scorpius can be also represented with an eagle or snake. Aquarius is represented by a man.

The symbol of the fours directions in the constellations relates to the cross used in Mesopotamia, and their desire to control all corners of the universe.

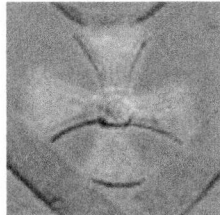

This cross has been used for the church and some governments since Mesopotamia. This symbol was also used in ancient civilizations where the *Problematic beings* wanted to be seen as gods. In Teotihuacan, the Aztec god Quetzalcoatl was represented as a serpent with feathers, and he was represented by a cross.

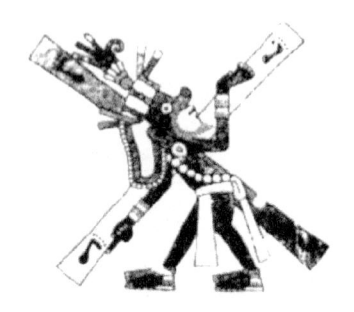

The snake and dragon are also in the Babylonian symbolism. They are often related to the god Marduk.

In Astrology, every zodiac sign is related to a planet. They are called the "planet's domicile". Taurus relates to Venus (goddess Ishtar). Leo relates to the Sun (god Utu). Scorpio relates to Mars (god Nergal). Aquarius relates to Saturn (god Ninurta). All these gods and goddesses of Babylon were *Problematic beings* who introduced themselves as gods and goddesses to be worshipped in Babylon. They are still doing it in modern times in several religions, mainly in the Western world.

Venus was also corrupted in a similar way as Saturn. Many symbols used now relate to Venus (goddess Ishtar). Venus is the only planet that rotates clockwise, and the orbit and rotation of Venus are synchronized in such a manner that Venus always presents the same face to Earth. There are also many other mathematical proportions related to Venus and other planets. The rotation of Venus in relation to the Earth creates a pentagram, that is why this symbol is often used by the *Problematic beings*.

The obelisk is another symbol that existed in Babylon. The obelisk has been moved from Egypt to Rome, then to London and Washington.

The pine cone is related to the pineal gland, the organ related to our third eye chakra.

The fleur-de-lis symbol also comes from Mesopotamia, and grew more common in Europe with the King Clovis I, the first king of the Franks who were a group of Germanic people.

Basically, the rulers of almost all empires have been related to the *Problematic beings*.

Mexico was a monarchy for a few years. Napoleon III offered to support Maximilian I as the ruler of Mexico. But then the monarchy was abolished, and Benito Juárez, a well-educated lawyer from indigenous origins became president.

When Mexico was a monarchy, a new flag was introduced by Agustín de Iturbide, an Emperor of Mexico. He was working with the *Problematic beings*. The flag is called the Flag of the Three Guarantees.

The three stars make reference to the Orion's belt, where the *Problematic beings* have colonies. Then, Maximilian I of Mexico introduced a new flag with a coat of arms. This is the coat of arms.

The *Problematic beings* were trying take over Mexico. Eventually, when the monarchy was abolished, the crown was removed, and only the eagle in the middle stayed. This doesn't mean that Mexico is not related to the *Problematic beings*. The United States has a big influence over the government in Mexico, and it controls the Mexican government in several ways. The government of Mexico sometimes forbids people from visiting the Pyramids on specific dates. These are direct orders coming from the United States. This is how the *Problematic beings* control the pyramids in Mexico.

Something similar happened in Egypt. When Egypt wanted to be independent from the United Kingdom, they accepted with the condition that the Sultan of Egypt would change his title to King and the flag would contain three stars.

Many humans around the world have kept the knowledge about our past and our real nature in one way or another. Many old civilizations kept the information in their stories. These stories have been passed from one generation to another, but some of these stories have changed after several thousand years.

Some humans used the knowledge for their own benefit. They created secret societies to keep the knowledge but they started to use it to create control over other humans and get more wealth. These people are now some of the richest people in the world.

The same problems that we had in Atlantis are happening now. *Problematic beings* don't realize that manipulating humans is not going to help them to move to the next level. Some of them already know and have been trying to "buy" a ticket to the 4th dimension. But this is not possible. They have even tried to stop us from going to the 4th dimension, but this is not possible either. We are going to the 4th dimension in one way or another and nothing can stop us.

Chapter 27 – The Pyramids

When I met Athella and agreed to work with her, she told me that there would be a time when we would have to move to another place.

Christina and I still lived close to Seattle, near a forest. Part of our training was to spend time in nature every day. One day, just like that, Athella told me that we had to find another place to live. She didn't say where. She just said that it had to be outside the United States.

She told me that the place would have to be in a warm area, in nature, away from big cities and close to the ocean. She said that we would find a house. She even gave me all the details about the house.

I didn't know where to go. My guides didn't tell me anything about it so I knew that I had to find out on my own. A few days later, a friend from Slovakia contacted me. When I left Slovakia for the trip to Alaska, I just had my backpack with me. I donated all my things except my bicycle. My friend was taking care of my bicycle. She told me that she was leaving the city and she was not able to take care of my bike. I found another friend who could take care of it. My friend sent me a picture of the bike just to tell me that he would take care of it. My friend was from Mexico but he lived in Slovakia. He told me, "This is funny - the brand name of your bike is Merida and we always talked about moving to Merida someday." Merida is a city in Mexico. When I lived in Slovakia, my Mexican friend and I always talked about moving to Merida someday. I don't know why we always talked about it, but we did it often.

I checked the map. Merida is very close to the ocean, only 30 minutes by car. It was a sign for me. I asked Athella if this was the place but she didn't confirm. I just knew that I had to learn how to trust. I had a good feeling about this so I told Christina about it. She didn't know anything about Merida but she accepted immediately. She was handling it much better than me.

We donated everything and booked a flight. We were ready to go. A few days before leaving, we had a lot of problems with some documents that had to be fixed before we left. We had only a few days. Christina needs special care because most of the time she is in communication with Athella. Sometimes she does not spend much time in the physical world so I did the physical things and she did the non-physical things. Many amazing things happened to me during the last hours before going to Mexico. I never told Christina about them. It was better for her to stay in the non-physical world so there were many things I did not tell her.

I had to go to several places around Seattle. I was supposed to meet someone to deliver some documents. I couldn't find the person so I decided to call. Suddenly my phone stopped working. I couldn't believe it. There were no people around - only a small restaurant. I went to the restaurant to ask to use their phone. Then somebody shouted my name. I turned around and saw a woman coming to me. I didn't have friends in Seattle. Most of the time I was alone. This woman came and said, "You are the guy who donated a lot of things." I didn't recognize her but she recognized me. I asked her for her phone and she gave it to me happily.

Then I had to go to another place but there was a lot of traffic and I didn't have much time. I was waiting in traffic.

In the car next to me, there was a person who used to attend Athella's presentations. I didn't know what was happening. I asked my guides why I was meeting these people. They told me that I was closing circles. I was saying goodbye to the people I helped there.

Then, I came home. Christina told me that some friends from Hawaii were in the city. We went to see them but we didn't tell them that we were leaving. These people from Hawaii went to many of Athella's presentations. It really felt like closing circles. The synchronicity of the events was amazing.

Christina and I didn't have friends. Most of the time we were with Athella or doing our training activities. We didn't have human friends so the people meeting Athella were the closest thing we had to friends. Our understanding of life and people was different so I preferred to spend time with people who understood us. Although most of the time, we were not totally in the physical world.

We arrived in Merida. We went to the beach area in the north of Merida and rented a house for few days. The first day I talked to Athella. She told me that the first thing we should do in the morning was to be on the beach and find our new house.

The next morning, I woke up and went to Christina's room but she was not there. She was on the beach. It was very hot and we were not used to that kind of weather. Seattle was always rainy and cold. We spent a few hours inside the house trying to adapt to the weather. We totally forgot what Athella said the day before.

In the evening, we realized that we ignored what Athella said. We were supposed to be searching for the house. Christina and I started to walk next to the beach trying to find the house with the specifications from Athella. We were not able to find it. We kept walking and walking, but nothing.

It was almost sunset and the sky was completely orange. This is because the sand from the Sahara Desert in Africa goes up to the sky and moves towards Mexico because of the rotation of the planet. So every day at sunset, in that part of Mexico, you can see an orange sky because of the reflection of the sand.

Right at the sunset, we saw the house. We knew it. It was our new home. The house was empty. I talked to people living next to the house, they told me that the house was not available for rent or sale. They said that the owner comes to the house only a few times per year and he just left that morning. That is why Athella asked us to go there in the morning.

I told them that I really wanted to live there and I needed to talk to the owner. They said that the owner would not allow anyone to live in the house. I was so sure that it was the house. I got a local phone and gave them my number. I told them to call me once the owner came.

Two weeks later, I got a phone call. It was the owner of the house. He told me that he was not interested in renting or selling the house but this was something special. He told me that his mother always talked about many mysteries of the world. She was able to communicate with invisible beings. Nobody understood her and nobody believed her. But before she died, she said that someday some people with a mission would come and they would explain the information better.

The owner believed that we were the people with the mission. He asked me a lot of questions. I told him what I knew. The same day he gave me the keys to the house. It was a house in front of the beach. We moved to the new house. We cleaned the house physically and energetically. This can be done by cleaning normally and at the same time having a full intention of cleaning it energetically. When you do this, you can ask your guides for help. You can also use a sage plant or parts of a tree called Palo Santo.

After we moved to our new home, Athella told us that we would begin stronger training. It would require more mental discipline, more hours of meditation and more time talking to her every day.

After a few days, I had become used to the weather. I used to spend time just watching the waves. They relaxed me and reminded me of something but I didn't know what. I had the feeling that I had been there before. I had this feeling of *Déjà vu* - when you see something and have the feeling that you've seen it before.

Déjà vu happens because we see a place or something else that reminds us of a similar thing from a previous life - not exactly the same but similar. For example, when I was on the beach in Mexico observing the waves, I had a feeling that I had done the same before, in a previous life. In this life, I have been on many beaches around the world. But this one, in particular, made me feel like I had been there before. *Déjà vu* is also seeing the future, but usually we do it only for few seconds.

Later, I was talking to Athella, and she told me that I used to live in Atlantis. Then after the problems in Atlantis, I moved to the Yucatan Peninsula in Mexico. She said that every time I see the waves, they remind me of Atlantis and also some lifetimes with the Mayans. She said that since the fall of Atlantis, every lifetime, I spend some time in the Yucatan Peninsula.

We started to have an intense training. Athella asked us to wake up at 7:00 am every day. The first few days it was hard, and many times we were not able to wake up at 7:00 am. Then, something unusual started to happen. We had a cat in the house. The cat started to come to my room every morning, and meowing in my face, exactly at 7:00 am. Then, the cat would go to Christina's room and wake her up. The cat did it every day. The cat even found the way to open doors. In the beginning, we thought that the cat was just hungry, but right after we woke up, the cat would go to sleep. I asked Athella why the cat was waking me up every day. She said that the cat agreed to help with the training.

Also, I noticed that whenever we were experiencing some weird energy around the house, the cat started to behave differently. Athella told me that animals are just behaving according to the energy they feel. They can usually feel the energy faster than humans. Many animals will know about an earthquake or storm even before it starts.

This also happens with the mosquitos. If you try to kill a mosquito, they will react before you actually hit them. Because they can feel your intention. Your intention has an energy and they can feel it. They even think that you want to play with them. That is why sometimes they come back to you. Athella told me that you can ask the insects to leave. I tried many times, and it actually worked. Not all the time, but many times.

The training we had was changing depending on our development. But there were things that never changed. We were fasting every morning. We had to have physical exercise, but Athella didn't called it exercise, she called it "moving the body with joy". She called it this because many people refer to the word exercise as something that you have to do. And the intention behind the word changes everything.

We had meditations several times during the day. We had some mental exercises to focus on our thoughts and manifest in our reality anything we wanted to experience. Something very important, every day we had to do something we love, something we are passionate about. In my case it was playing football and other sports, for Christina was singing and dancing.

When you do something you love, you are acting with excitement. This excitement creates a vibration in your body. Passion, love, and excitement, without ego, can do many things in your reality. And you can manifest anything you want, very fast. It is very important not to have negative thoughts, because you can also manifest the negative things. In higher dimensions, we can manifest much faster. So I had to be very careful with my thoughts every time I was talking to Athella. Because I could manifest anything much faster. Although, when I was with Athella, it was very hard to have negative thoughts. Her energy is so pure that you cannot even imagine negative things.

The training was focused mainly on thoughts. The problem that many people have is that we think too much, all the time. Thinking is just like an activity, whenever you need it, use it. But when you don't need it, you can stop thinking. This is hard to imagine for many people, especially because during our whole life, at school, we learned that we have to think all the time. Basically, we are programmed to believe that with thinking, we will learn more and more. There are many types of intelligence, including emotional intelligence. Unfortunately, at school, we learn mostly only about one type of intelligence, and we are measured by it. We can learn so much by not thinking. You can get information by not thinking, like a download.

Inge Bardor is able to read information about people. This information is contained in the electromagnetic field around every human body. Many people call this field the "Akashic field". We also have access to this information. This field contains information about every person, and even information about the universe. But we have to access this information using different senses, and we have to work with our thoughts and emotions.

Athella told me to get ready for visitors. I didn't know who or when. There were many rooms in the house. I started to prepare all the rooms as if we were having visitors.

A few weeks later, several people from the United States contacted us. They wanted to meet Christina and Athella. They didn't want to talk through the internet. They wanted to come and meet in person.

Eventually, more and more people from all over the world were coming to the beach house in Mexico. We started to prepare workshops and retreats for them.

During the retreats I learned so much. Most of the people coming to meet Athella were very educated people. In most cases, these people wanted to have a totally private retreat, afraid to lose credibility among their colleagues.

I was surprised. Several people know about Athella and other higher dimensional beings. They know about what is really happening in the world. They just don't talk about it in public. Many professionals were coming to Athella to ask her for advice on how to apply this knowledge in their work.

Many of these people understand that this knowledge is very important. Many of them changed their life completely so they could focus on their personal development, not only regarding this lifetime, but all their lives in general. They didn't want to live like most people on the planet live. Some of them didn't want to have a family. They wanted to focus their lives mainly on helping others, and helping themselves. They knew that they would come back again to the 3rd dimension and keep learning. They wanted to learn and improve as much as possible in this lifetime, so having a family was not their priority.

Some of them knew that having a family could cause karma, since they could be affecting the path of their partner or children without knowing it. Then, they may have come back to the 3rd dimension several times to learn how to respect other people's paths.

I was in a similar situation. I realized that helping other people is very important. So I thought about focusing my life only on that. I was not interested in having a family. Most people who are spiritual leaders don't have families. I didn't want to live like a normal person. Even if I tried, most people would not understand the way I see life. I have seen so many things, so it's hard for some others to relate to me. I was talking with many spirits through the body of one person. I did it every day. This would be too weird for many people.

I was divided, one part of me wanted to fit into society, and another part wanted to be of service to others. I decided to live 100 % in service as long as I worked with Athella.

And after my training was done, I would like to split between 60 % service and 40 % private life.

The people coming to the retreats motivated me to write this book, and to be more open by talking about these topics. I used to keep everything to myself. I used to be afraid that people might call me crazy. But little by little, I started to meet more people who really get this. I felt great. I felt more confident. These people were trying to find a path to help people in their own way. Also, many of them wanted to talk directly to their guides, through Christina's body.

Doctors were trying to find a way to heal their patients, but they couldn't talk so openly about all of this, so they were trying to do it in their own way. Scientists and celebrities were also doing it in their own way. They were speaking about what they knew, but in a way that people would be able to understand, and at the same time not sounding too crazy to lose credibility.

Several doctors told me that in Cuba, the patients are treated a little bit differently from the rest of the world. Cuba has many doctors and they are some of the best in the world. The doctors told me that they must have direct contact with the patients. Since there are many doctors in Cuba, every doctor has only a few patients so they can focus on them easily. The treatment is more personal, and the doctors visualize the patients as healthy. Visualizing is extremely important. Athella always told me that. If you want something you have to visualize it. This is exactly what these doctors from Cuba were doing.

We were having many visitors in the house, people from all over the world. At the same time, we were having a training to learn more about the real nature of humanity. After a few months of training with Athella, she started to tell me that I should play football. She knew that I really enjoyed it.

I started to play football with local people in regional tournaments. After a few days I realized that I was not enjoying football the same way I used to. I noticed that I didn't like everything about football, I didn't even like to watch it on TV. What I really liked about football was the specific moment when I am running very fast and I can pass the opponents. I didn't even like to score a goal. I play football in a very technical way, so I could do some tricks to pass the opponents. This is what I really liked, not football in general.

This happens to a lot of people. We think that we like something, but in most cases, we like one specific part of it. For example, if you like running, you may not like everything about it. Maybe you like the feeling of the wind in your face. Or maybe you like the feeling of having strong legs, or the feeling in your body after running. Once you discover what is exactly what you like, you can focus on that feeling, and you may even find the same feeling doing another activity. In other words, maybe you like to run, but you really like something you experience while you are running. So "running" is the form you use to experience what you like. But you can use other forms to get the same feeling.

Sometimes, during the football tournaments, some players are very rough. They will do anything to win, even playing unfairly or very aggressively. I didn't like this, and started to focus on friendly football matches, where people were not so aggressive. Several times I was invited to play professional football but I didn't want to. I knew that I would not enjoy it. I like to play but I don't enjoy the pressure during the football matches. I started to play indoor football where I have more opportunities to do tricks. I enjoyed it much more. Something similar happens to a lot of people. Maybe we like what we do in our job, but we don't like our boss or colleagues. This may make us think that we don't like what we do. We may love what we do, but not the people around us. Or we may like the people, but not the job we do.

I learned how to move things without touching them but it happens only when I really need something. The first time when it happened was when I was driving. I needed to park the car. There was only one place available but there was a plastic chair blocking the parking spot. I remember that I thought, "I have to move the chair." Then, just like magic, the chair started to move very fast, almost as if somebody kicked the chair, grabbed it in the air and placed it on the ground again.

When it happened, I was not thinking too much. I was just focused on parking the car. Actually, I forgot that the chair moved. That evening I talked to Athella, and she told me that she was happy to see my development. I told her I was not sure what she was talking about. Then she mentioned the chair. In that moment I realized that the chair moved in an unusual way. When the chair moved, it seemed normal. I didn't think it was something unusual until Athella mentioned it.

I have tried to move objects many times but it never happens when I want to do it consciously. It happens only when I am not thinking and when I really need it. When I try to do it consciously, my ego usually gets involved in my thoughts. It is not possible to do it with ego. Some people believe moving things is possible with your brain but it's done with your heart. There are children who are able to do it with their brain but they usually lose the ability during puberty. Some children can also move through walls and many other things that we consider magic. They do it by altering the vibrations in their bodies.

Athella often told me to make a fire on the beach. She said that we all need to have the four elements in our daily lives - water, earth, air and fire. Usually, we always have air, earth and water around us but many times we miss the fire. That is why Athella asked me to make a fire on the beach. You can have candles or anything that produces natural light, but not the artificial light from light bulbs. It's not the same. If you live in a city and don't spend much time on nature, you may be missing the earth as well.

The house on the beach was close to many pyramids. I spent a lot of time around them and other magical places. There are many pyramids in the jungle that haven't been discovered. There are also many cenotes. They are like underground lakes. The water in these places is magical. Mayan people used to live in these places. Today, some Mayans live underground in a region of Antarctica.

One day I came home and there was a dog having puppies. It was not my dog but I understood that the dog came because it felt safe there. The dog was very tired so I had to help to make sure that all the puppies were alive. I didn't know how to do it but I quickly checked on the internet. I spent the whole night with the dog until all the puppies were born. Then, in the morning, I went to sleep. While I was sleeping, I had a dream where several beings thanked me for the help. When I woke up, I observed the puppies and wondered how it's possible that a dog knows what to do when the puppies are born. They didn't learn it from anywhere. This is because there is a net of energy around the planet for dogs. There is a net of energy for every animal on Earth and they are connected to it. That is where they get their information. Dogs and cats cannot mix. They are connected to different energy layers. I grew up with dogs but I never thought about it. It was interesting that I was learning many things about life that I never previously wondered about. It was like discovering the world with eyes more open.

After two years of talking to Athella every day, I felt like I was ready for anything. I learned so much with Christina and Athella. I learned how to channel but not exactly the same way that Christina does it. Some energies in her body work differently than most humans. What she does is something you choose before being born. My mission is different and I chose not to channel like she does. I learned how to channel my guides. They can talk through me but using my brain and intuition. This means that my ego and my belief system are part of the channeling. In the case of Christina, her ego and belief system are not involved.

One day, Athella told me that I was ready to go and spread her teachings. At the same time, Christina was healed from her trauma. I was not used to being around people so I didn't know where to go.

I came back to Europe and I started to write this book. At first, it took me some time to get used to being around other people. It was difficult for me to see how many people hurt themselves with their own thoughts but they are learning in their own way. I used to be like them so I understood them. I noticed that people needed constant entertainment, and couldn't stop thinking. I was not even able to have music around me because I wouldn't be able to hear my guides. I listen to music but not very often. Being in silence allows me to hear so many things from many places. This is much better than any type of entertainment.

This book is a form for me to put all my thoughts together. It helped me so much. Now I want to use this knowledge to help others. This information is the way I understand it. It doesn't mean that it is the only way. You may get it in your own way, with your own words. As I said at the beginning, not everyone needs the information. Every person understands this reality in a different way. Some people don't know this information but they are living it. Many people know the information and they are not doing anything about it. Now you know this information. What are you going to do about it?

As I mentioned before, we passed the test. We are going back to the 4th dimension. Some people will ascend. Some people will resurrect, which means that they will die and come back for their bodies. Some people will die and be born as a baby in the 4th dimension with a new body and a new family.

We are all going back to the 4th dimension - all of us. I don't know when it's going to happen. It was supposed to happen a few years ago. It hasn't happened yet because Mother Earth is prolonging the time. She wants more people to be aware of who they are so when we move to the 4th dimension, it will be easier to understand what is happening. Changes will come and changes are happening. These are very beautiful changes. If everyone understood what is happening, we would be celebrating right now on the streets. We are living the most exciting times of humanity, ever.

This is the last time we will reincarnate in the 3rd dimension. When we die, we will go to the 4th dimension and we will stay there. We don't have to come to the 3rd dimension anymore. You may choose to come one more time before all the changes happen but that's your choice. Everyone will eventually go to the 4th dimension.

I don't know when the changes will come. Something huge will happen several times. Many people who came here to help will go back home. These people will die in this physical world and they will go home. Some of them will go to other missions on other planets. It's up to them.

Maybe there will be a global problem like an earthquake, an epidemic or something else. I don't know. This may sound bad but it is how things work. Many people will be confused - especially people living with a lot of ego.

Some governments know about this and they have created tunnels with all kind of equipment to survive. This is useless. It's not going to help them. The changes will come and there is nothing physical that can help. Everything has to do with your heart. Stay in your heart and you will be okay, and it doesn't matter what happens around you.

There is really nothing to fear. If you are connected to Mother Earth, she will protect you. It may even look like magic but she will certainly protect you.

We will be in the 4th dimension. Many of us have been there before. Some of us in Lemuria, Atlantis or other places. Once we get back, we will remember. We will be there for a while. We will wait for everyone to come back in the 4th dimension. Once we are all together, some amazing things will happen.

In the last years, I have noticed that many people manifest things very quickly. For me, sometimes it takes only a few minutes. We used to live like this in the 4th dimension. So I have a theory, and many spiritual people around the world have a similar theory. Maybe we are already in the 4th dimension. Maybe Mother Earth duplicated our world from the 3rd dimension and created a copy of it in the 4th dimension. Maybe we are already in the 4th dimension even though everything seems to be physical like in the 3rd dimension. This could be a reason why we have been manifesting much faster than usual. I really don't know. This is just a theory. Maybe we are still in the 3rd dimension but manifesting much faster.

I have asked my guides if this world is already the 4th dimension, or if I will ever experience the changes from the 3rd dimension to the 4th dimension. They only answered me once. They said that I will be 52 years old. So, maybe, around the year 2037 we will experience a big change on the planet. Some high dimensional beings have talked about the same year. It seems that there will be a 3rd dimensional Earth and a 4th dimensional Earth. There will be two planets. Earth will split into two. One day, some people will wake up in the 4th dimension, and they will not know how they got there. The friendly beings will do the transfer. This will be like ascending to the 4th dimension.

Around this time, there will be Problematic beings flying around the planet in their UFOs. They will pretend to be friendly beings helping us move into the 4th dimension. Just ignore them. They can't do anything to us unless we give them permission. So just ignore them.

The ascension to the 4th dimension will be internal. You will feel it. It will be a beautiful feeling of unconditional love. Some people will stay in the 3rd dimension, and these people will be okay. They just need more time to keep learning. The people in the 3rd dimension will experience three days of darkness. This is because of the changes in the electromagnetism on Earth. Many ancient civilizations talk about it. It has happened in the past. It happened few years after the fall of Atlantis. These three days of darkness will be like a test for the people who stay in the 3rd dimension. This is not something bad. It's an opportunity to grow. We will go to the 4th dimension anyway.

It doesn't matter what the situation is right now. We are going to be in the 4th dimension. We passed the test. The test was very hard, but we made it. It lasted around 13,000 years. It was not easy. Many people participated. Our experience on Earth has been like a motivation to other beings around the universe. We were so manipulated but we still made it to the next level. The story of humans is a legend in other places in the universe. It was not easy, but now we are an example for many beings.

Many things happened in the last 13,000 years. We have learned so much. We passed the test and we have improved the energy of the entire universe. The whole universe is going through changes, in part, because of the test humans had on Earth.

We will be in the 4th dimension; we will wait for all humans to evolve and eventually move to the 4th dimension. Following that, something huge will happen. For the first time ever, we are going to a new level. We are going to the 5th dimension.

This is something new. We have never been there. Life there is very different. Our bodies will be almost pure light. Usually, it would take us several million years to move from the 4th dimension to the 5th dimension but because of all the changes happening in the universe right now, we will have access to it.

For the first time ever, humans are going to experience the 5th dimension. This is going to happen and there is nothing that can stop it. We are just waiting for it. There is no separation in the 5th dimension. There is no ego. We understand that we are all one. We choose to experience only love.

I want to thank you for reading this book. Now, it's time to keep learning on your own. Before we were born, we agreed to meet in this dimension in this way - through a book.

We will meet in the 4th dimension. We will talk about our experiences in the 3rd dimension. Once we move to the 5th dimension, we will have fun playing with our reality. We will change it anytime we want. We will be like children playing with new toys.

Please do everything you can to live consciously in the 3rd dimension. Eventually, you will die consciously and you will be able to ascend. It will help everybody on the planet. And everything will be easier in the 4th dimension if you live consciously here.

Please meditate and eat high vibrational food. If you can, eat only vegan and unprocessed food. Spend time in nature, talk to your guides and be like a child. Drink clean water, sleep well, take care of your thoughts, take care of the animals and take care of the planet. Let's leave the planet the same way we received it. Take care of yourself, help other people, be thankful and focus on love.

We forget things. This happens to all humans. Do not forget to live consciously. Now that you are more informed, you will start noticing things that you didn't notice before. Even if you read this book again, you will read things that you didn't see before.

See you in the 4th dimension. We may meet in person in this 3rd dimension. If we meet, let's create things together in service to others. If we don't meet in the 3rd or 4th dimension, I hope we can play together in the 5th dimension. We will probably be playing with forms but the forms will be different. They will not be only ideas in our mind. They will be our reality.

Every time I talked to Athella, she told me that she was not leaving and she was always there. There is no leaving. And always, the last thing she would say was, "I love you." This is not the end of a book. This is a beginning. Let's keep creating and let's keep playing. Thank you so much, from my heart. I love you.

Bibliography

Arellano, P. (n.d.). *Pablo Arellano*. Retrieved from www.youtube.com/user/arthousemovies

Cassidy, K. (n.d.). *Project Camelot*. Retrieved from www.youtube.com/user/jagbodhi

Hill, C. (n.d.). *AthellaORG*. Retrieved from www.youtube.com/channel/UCMHJnzvSgiHjozkYeQ9QQ1A

Johnson, B. (n.d.). *Brad Johnson New Earth Teachings*. Retrieved from www.youtube.com/user/selfempowermenttv

Jordan, R. (n.d.). *Spirit Studios*. Retrieved from www.youtube.com/user/spiritsciencelive

Mace, L. (n.d.). *Lilou Mace*. Retrieved from www.youtube.com/channel/UCOpwg-UMqzuHxfcK5SSiZ2A

Medhus, E. (n.d.). *Channeling Erik*. Retrieved from www.youtube.com/c/ChannelingErik2121

Melchizedek, D. (1999). *The Ancient Secret of the Flower of Life: Volume 1.* Light Technology Publishing.

Melchizedek, D. (2000). *The Ancient Secret of the Flower of Life, Volume 2.* Light Technology Publishing.

Melchizedek, D. (2003). *Living in the Heart.* Light Technology Publishing.

Melchizedek, D. (2008). *Serpent of Light: Beyond 2012.* Weiser Books.

Melchizedek, D. (n.d.). *Drunvalo Melchizedek*. Retrieved from www.youtube.com/user/DrunvaloFlowerofLife

Rodin, M. (n.d.). *Marko Rodin*. Retrieved from www.youtube.com/user/MarkoRodin

Printed in Great Britain
by Amazon